NARRATIVE IDENTITY AND DEMENTIA

Other titles in this series, published in association with CEDR
(Series Editor: *Robin Lovelock*)

CHANGING PATTERNS OF MENTAL HEALTH CARE
A case study in the development of local services
Jackie Powell and Robin Lovelock

PARTNERSHIP IN PRACTICE The Children Act 1989
Edited by Ann Buchanan

DISABILITY: BRITAIN IN EUROPE An evaluation of UK
participation in the HELIOS programme (1988-1991)
Robin Lovelock and Jackie Powell

THE PROBATION SERVICE AND INFORMATION
TECHNOLOGY
David Colombi

VISUAL IMPAIRMENT; SOCIAL SUPPORT
Recent research in context
Robin Lovelock

WORKLOADS: MEASUREMENT AND MANAGEMENT
Joan Orme

LIVING WITH DISFIGUREMENT Psychosocial implications of
being born with a cleft lip and palate
Poppy Nash

EDUCATING FOR SOCIAL WORK: ARGUMENTS FOR
OPTIMISM
Edited by Peter Ford and Patrick Hayes

DEMENTIA CARE: KEEPING INTACT AND IN TOUCH
A search for occupational therapy interventions
M. Catherine Conroy

SUICIDAL BEHAVIOUR IN ADOLESCENTS AND ADULTS
Research, taxonomy and prevention
Christopher Bagley and Richard Ramsay

Narrative Identity and Dementia

A study of autobiographical memories and emotions

MARIE A. MILLS

Ashgate

Aldershot • Brookfield USA • Singapore • Sydney

Published by
Ashgate Publishing Ltd
Gower House
Croft Road
Aldershot
Hants GU11 3HR
England

Ashgate Publishing Company
Old Post Road
Brookfield
Vermont 05036
USA

British Library Cataloguing in Publication Data
Mills, Marie A.
  Narrative identity and dementia : a study of
  autobiographical memories and emotions
  1. Senile dementia 2. Reminiscing in old age 3. Memory in old
  age 4. Emotions in old age
  I. Title II. University of Southampton. Centre for Evaluative
  & Developmental Research
  362.1'9'897'68983

Library of Congress Catalog Card Number: 98-70989

ISBN 1 84014 175 1

Printed and bound by Athenaeum Press, Ltd.,
Gateshead, Tyne & Wear.

To my husband Ces Mills for making all things possible.

Contents

Figures

Acknowledgements

To Ed Conroy, who organised and prepared this entire text for publication - `a friend indeed´.

To Peter Coleman, the most encouraging and generous of mentors.

To my children Jem, Jon and Anne-Marie for their contributions and belief.

Abbreviations

AD	Alzheimer's Disease
BSE	Bovine Spongiform Encephalopathy
CAMDEX	Cambridge Mental Disorders of the Elderly Examination
CRBRS	Crighton Royal Behavioural Rating Scale
CT	Computer-assisted Tomography
CVA	Cerebral Vascular Accident
DAT	Dementia of the Alzheimer's Type
DIY	Do It Yourself
GP	General Practitioner
ICS	Interacting Cognitive Subsystems
JCD	Jacob-Creutzfeldt Disease
LBD	Lewy Body Disease
LTM	Long Term Memory
MEM	Multiple Entry Memory
MID	Multi-Infarct Dementia
MMSE	Mini-Mental State Examination
MSP	Malignant Social Psychology
MSQ	Mental Status Questionnaire
MTS	Mental Test Score
NATO	North Atlantic Treaty Organisation
NVQ	National Vocational Qualification
OPCS	Office of Population and Census Surveys
PD	Parkinson's Disease
POW	Prisoner of War
SDAT	Senile Dementia of the Alzheimer's Type
STM	Short Term Memory

Introduction

This is a book of many contrasts. It seeks to establish a firm theoretical base in order to sustain an argument that has frequently been anecdotal in nature. Consequently, the reader will move between the empirical world of evidence to the experiential world of the individual. It is hoped that the interplay between these two perspectives will strengthen the debate. The main discussion will focus on the characteristic features of emotional memories in a small group of older people with some form of dementia. However, the literature on the presence of emotions in dementia is relatively sparse, although several publications have appeared on the subject in recent years (Bromley, 1990; Hausman, 1992; Kitwood, 1990a; Mills and Coleman, 1994).

A small pilot study (Mills, 1991) suggested that some demented elderly people could recall past and current concerns. In this particular study, informants were seen on an individual basis over a period of three months. Counselling strategies were used during the research interviews in order to facilitate recall and disclosure. The findings implied that these informants displayed appropriate emotions associated with their memories and suggested that the relationship between memory, emotion and dementia were worthy of further exploration.

However, the questions to be asked of a future study were many. With the use of a similar approach, was it possible for older people with dementia to recall intact emotional memories associated with past and present events? Further, did these memories of a personal past contain pieces of information which formed part of their life histories or life stories? What type of emotional memories would be found amongst these older people? Would they be `good´ positive memories or might they be `sad´ and possibly negative? Finally, did

1

the aided recall of these emotional memories, over time, allow these memories to remain, or would they gradually fade into oblivion due to the progression of the illness?

Thus, the investigation was interested in the concepts of dementia, memory and emotions, and their corresponding psychological, biological and social characteristics. It was concerned with an illness without certain aetiology or proven cure, the mysterious frameworks and processes of a mental phenomenon which is poorly understood, and the significance of the emotions for which there are over a hundred known theories.

Generated theories for this study, therefore, were cumulative in nature, but Baddeley (1992) suggests that his own preference is for breadth of application, as opposed to detailed prediction. The application of `a broad sweep theory´ has great bearing on this inquiry which investigated aspects of an illness that disrupts and destroys the lives of sufferers and their families alike. Certainly, Bond et al. (1990) argue that many new referrals for long term care are due to some type of dementing illness, an illness which Kitwood (1990a, 1993, 1997a) suggests can lead to the disintegration of personhood. Tobin (1991), too, maintains this process may cause the `de-selfing´ of the person.

I have long been interested in the preservation of `uniqueness of being/personhood´ among this client group, beginning with my involvement in the residential care of older people over many years. The last eleven years have been spent as an owner/manager of a residential home, now a specialist residential home, for twenty elderly people. My own practice suggested that the use of basic counselling skills in a discussion of their past life led to an immediate reduction in negative behaviour. Some years ago I began to notice that confused residents also enjoyed a discussion of their past lives. It tended to reduce high anxiety levels, providing it was handled with empathy and skill. It was also more effective when undertaken on an individual basis. Residents looked as if they were happy when discussing their past. They smiled and laughed during this activity. Reminiscence therapy gradually became a personal interest which widened into a desire to understand more about the process. I wondered if other older people with dementia would also enjoy this activity. Was it effective in the Home because I knew these people so well? Would it be as effective with strangers? This interest formed the basis for the pilot study.

Of great importance to me was the fact that our elderly people with dementia also seemed to enjoy recalling pieces of their life story with other formal carers. The work of Adams (1984, 1986, 1994), Bender

(1994), Gibson (1994, 1997) and Goldsmith (1996) underpin these observations. These shared memories not only helped staff to see these people as they once were, they also enabled the generation of sustained staff/client relationships based on understanding, respect and affection, rather than mere protective concern. Further, Kitwood (1993, 1997a) suggests that it is this type of approach which will encourage well-being and personhood for sufferers of dementia.

This investigation, too, is concerned with professional/personal relationships as well as those which are more `scientific´ in nature. The eight older people with dementia who took part in this study became important to me and I to them. This attachment enabled them to voice their concerns and share some of their emotional personal past with another human being. As a listener, it was an exhilarating, happy, anxious and traumatic experience which was not for the fainthearted. The stories they told with humour and sadness, were of living hard lives and coping with upsetting events, of the loss engendered by their illness, but also of many positive life experiences both large and small. It is hoped that their accounts may lead to a greater understanding of dementia and of a more positive approach in our treatment of older people with this disease, through the sharing of a reality which may be different to our own.

1 Dementia and the therapeutic approach

Introduction

This chapter will focus on the background to the study and will include a discussion of the dementias, together with the increasing use of reminiscence and counselling strategies within dementia care work. This was the approach used in the pilot study and which formed a major part of this particular investigation. The literature on reminiscence and counselling, therefore, will be discussed in some detail. The chapter concludes with a review of the significant findings of the pilot study which has led to this present investigation.

Demographic changes in the elderly population

Population statistics indicate that we are part of an ageing world. Throughout this century, the proportion of people aged sixty years and over, has increased. There is a fear that an ageing population supported by a smaller working population may lead to an inability to sustain expenditure on their health and welfare. By the year 2010, one fifth of the population of Switzerland and Germany is expected to be over the age of sixty-five years. Other developed countries will rapidly follow suit after this date (The Economist, 1990). In 1985, two hundred and eighty-six million of the total world population were aged sixty-five+ years, and it is estimated that by the year 2025 this group will rise to eight hundred million. The elderly will, by this time, account for 9.7 per cent of the total world population (World Population Prospects, 1986).

In this country, there is also a significant increase in the number of older adults. Falkingham (1989) points out that in 1981, Britain had a total elderly population of 9.7 million. The numbers of young elderly, that is those aged sixty/sixty-five to seventy years, are decreasing but the numbers of those aged seventy-five+ years are increasing. It is this latter group which is expected to increase until 2030. Ineichen (1987) suggests that it is probable that seven per cent of the total population of elderly in industrialised societies will develop a dementia and, among those aged eighty+ years, this figure may be as high as twenty per cent.

In this country, OPCS (1982) estimates that by the year 2001 this age group will form a total population of 1.1 million people and, of this number, one in five will have some type of dementia. Thus many numbers of elderly people will suffer from a chronic loss of brain function, due to some type of dementia. This group will require medical and social interventions on a large scale, if their quality of life is not to be further eroded. This is not a simple matter. Research into the dementias has led to a greater understanding of the problem, but to date, has provided no proven cause or effective cure.

The dementias

The term dementia is often widely and inappropriately used to describe any syndrome that is not obviously an acquired cognitive impairment due to a delirium or psychiatric disorder. Holden (1995, p.54) argues strongly that it is not a disease but a deterioration in social behaviour and intellectual functioning. Odenheimer (1989) defines dementia as a clinical syndrome of acquired decline of cognitive functions that is characterised by impaired memory, plus deficits in higher cortical functions, such as language or visuospatial function.

Every type of dementia, therefore, has one thing in common: a loss of intellectual power (Woods, 1989, p.18). Potentially reversible dementias can originate due to a variety of causes or aetiologies such as toxic, metabolic, neoplastic (malignant or benign tumour) and infectious processes. Further, drug overload, constipation and infections in intellectually intact older people, can lead to short term confusional states. However, normal cognitive functioning usually returns after the successful treatment of the underlying cause of the illness.

The two most common forms of irreversible dementia seem to be Alzheimer's disease (AD) and Vascular Dementia. However, some researchers argue that the incidence of Lewy body disease (LBD), a cortico-sub-cortical condition, is higher than that of Vascular Dementia (Perry et al., 1989, 1990a, 1990b, 1991).

AD is thought to account for approximately fifty per cent of the dementing elderly population, although it is now recognised that AD is not a single condition but consists of sub groups, such as frontal lobe dementia, with the probability that there are many other unidentified sub groups (Holden, 1995). Certainly the term `AD´ as a diagnosis has now tended to give way to less specific descriptions such as `senile dementia of the Alzheimer's type´ (SDAT) or `dementia of the Alzheimer's type´ (DAT). The aetiology of AD/DAT is unknown, although there are fairly well established guidelines for clinical diagnosis. Various hypotheses have been postulated to explain the structural and neurochemical changes in the brain, but the trigger for this degeneration remains unclear. Odenheimer (1989) suggests that any or all of these aetiologies, such as toxic, genetic, infection and trauma theories, may play a part in determining the key cause of this type of brain degeneration. At present, it is not possible to give a definite diagnosis other than by brain biopsy.

AD is clinically defined by Schwartz (1990) as the progressive decline in two or more major areas of cognition, where this decline cannot be attributed to other known systemic diseases or brain disorders. Further, Schwartz suggests that when a diagnosis is made on clinical evidence alone, the patient can only be assumed to be suffering from possible AD or dementia of the Alzheimer's type (DAT). Other dementias of the Alzheimer's type, such as Pick's Disease or simple non specific dementia, are probably due to a primary idiopathic neuronal degeneration. This can be contrasted with strokes associated with Vascular Dementia and other toxic, metabolic and viral encephalopathies known to cause dementia. AD itself is characterised by specific changes in the brain structure, which were recognised during autopsy at the turn of the century by a German neurologist, Alois Alzheimer. These changes are plaques, found mainly in the outer layer of the brain or cortex, and tangles, which are neurofibrillary tangles present within brain cell neurones. Future research, however, will have to account for the plaques and tangles, which occur in lesser numbers in the brains of non demented elderly people. Further, research indicates that plaques and neurofibrillary tangles are clearly dissociable events (Damasio et al., 1990). Schwartz and Stark (1990, p.79) argue that these various degenerative changes may be quite selective in their sites of action, targeting the neuronal networks and neurochemical systems that form the fundamental `modules´ of the brain in relation to cognition. These neuronal networks include the hippocampal formations which are known to be closely involved in retrieval and recall. These findings relating to episodic memory will be discussed in greater detail in chapter two.

Neuronal changes, however, are not only selective in their targets, but will also indicate an individual pathology within patients. Damasio et al. (1990) argue that it is this individualised process that does not permit a standard cognitive profile, with affected cortical regions functioning defectively rather than not at all. The symptoms associated with AD tend to emerge insidiously and gradually over many years and, in some parts of the system, this damage may affect more than half of the available neurones before symptoms become manifest, although intervening factors such as depression and stroke may precipitate diagnosis (Damasio et al., 1990, pp.97-8).

Vascular dementia

The most common form of Vascular Dementia is Multi-Infarct Dementia (MID). A number of elderly people are found to have suffered infarcts or miniature strokes, leading to the death of brain tissue during old age. Stuart-Hamilton (1991) suggests that this can be seen to be symptomatic of normal ageing, with little effect on the individual concerned. In MID, however, these infarcts occur in greater abundance. Sufficient areas of the brain are progressively affected, leading to an irreversible state of dementia. Although infarcts occur relatively randomly, the cortex and other areas controlling higher function, tend to be severely compromised. It is known that a number of cardiovascular illnesses can induce MID. There may also be a familial link.

Although Stuart-Hamilton (1991) and Odenheimer (1989) suggest a difficulty with diagnosis because MID may mimic the effects of other types of dementia, the main difference between this and other dementias is the progress of the disease. There is a stepwise, uneven rate of decline. Memory is often affected early in the illness and, in some instances, intellectual deficits are lacunar in nature (Stuart-Hamilton, 1991, p.125). The physical examination will often give evidence of cardiovascular disease and the patient may demonstrate a labile affect, together with other symptoms. The prevalence of MID is uncertain but may be as much as thirty per cent in dementia related conditions (Holden, 1995).

Lewy body disease (LBD)

LBD is now becoming more widely recognised with some research suggesting an association with other dementias (Holden, 1995). Presenting symptoms commonly include hallucinations which are mainly visual, together with paranoid delusions. Holden argues that research into this illness is of utmost importance as it requires different treatment to other conditions. There appears to be a negative and potentially dangerous response to neuroleptic drugs (McKeith et al., 1992).

Less common dementias

Less common types of dementia can include Parkinson's Disease (PD) which is primarily a disorder of movement. Scott et al. (1985) suggest that the ultimate cause of this neurological illness appears to be the degeneration and loss of neurones in the dopaminergic systems. There are strong indications that a proportion of PD sufferers do have dementia. It is not clear if the dementia arises from the same cause as PD or whether the two conditions occur by chance (Woods, 1989, p.24). Other less common dementias include: Alcohol Related Dementia, Pick's Disease, Binswanger Disease, Neurosyphilis, Huntingdon's Disease, AIDS Related Dementia and Jacob-Creutzfeldt Disease (JCD). JCD, a human prion disease, is rare, affecting less than one person in a million, normally before the age of sixty. However, it is now more widely known due to its association with Bovine Spongiform Encephalopathy (BSE).

American studies indicate that nearly four million of their citizens have some type of dementia (Thal, 1988). Scott Hinkle (1990) argues that recognition, diagnosis, assessment, and treatment of these disorders have become a major concern for all health care professionals. At present, Woods (1989) estimates that there are about seven hundred and fifty thousand sufferers in the United Kingdom. These older adults have SDAT and/or Vascular Dementia, in about seventy per cent of those elderly with some type of dementia. With increasing world wide numbers comes increasing costs in terms of community support services, hospital and residential provision. It is a progressive illness that destroys the life of the sufferer and devastates the family involved (Woods, 1989, p.13). There is a need to adopt alternative coping strategies in the face of overwhelming loss.

The importance of psychological processes in dementia

Laing (1967) suggests that there is an argument that all human thought and actions are meaningful if related to the person's situation. Laing argues that all action is intelligible if only we take the pains to understand it. Laing is primarily concerned with functional rather than organic mental illness, but Busfield (1986) suggests that the proven case for demonstrating the cause of dementia as organic does not rule out any psychological processes that may precipitate or generate such biological changes.

Kitwood has suggested two `vicious circle´ theories of the dementing process that are based on [one] the neurological impairment and [two] some assumed psychogenic causation of neurological impairment. He argues that the `labelling´ or medical diagnosis of neurological impairment produces a type of `malignant´ social psychology imposed on the neurologically impaired individual that can damage the fragile self esteem and `personhood´ of the older person (Kitwood, 1997a). He suggests that this aspect of the dementing process should be investigated by medical science research, which has undervalued the importance of this concept. Kitwood (1990b) points to the unexplained variance of some seventy per cent between neuropathology and dementia, and suggests that medical science verifies this viewpoint. He further suggests that there is considerable overlap between the observed condition of the brains of mentally well-presented and those of demented elderly people (Kitwood, 1989). Moreover, Damasio et al. (1990, p.98) state that "the issue of when enough impairment is enough, is important and unresolved".

The impact of irreversible dementia on the individual

In dementia, the sufferer will gradually begin to lose memory and learning ability. The ability to plan and to "understand how to work things out" will also be affected. As the condition worsens, the person will become less able to care for themselves (Woods, 1989, p.38). Do sufferers have any insight into their condition? He argues that a large proportion of older people with this type of illness, are, "vaguely aware that something is wrong" (p.46), and suggests that it is this sense of loss which produces the sadness and distress which is so common in the early stages of this disease. Failure to produce successful coping devices may also increase this distress and despair.

My own work with people with dementia indicates that they do know that they are `different´. The personal acceptance of this illness can be seen as akin to the process of grief and bereavement. I have seen people experience sadness, anguish, anger, denial, depression, and eventually, acceptance. Some people may never complete this process and may stay permanently locked into a state of denial and anger. For these people, it is always `other people´ who are responsible for the loss of belongings or who have muddled their lives. Other older dementing people seem to comfortably accept that their memory is poor.

This process of successful adaptation to the dementing process is a central theme of the writings and research of Kitwood, who has been largely instrumental in bringing this issue into the forefront of academic and practitioner discussion. In some of his earlier writings, he innovatively focuses on the previously neglected areas of the psychological relationships within dementia, and explores the relationship between the experiential or feeling self and the adaptive self, which is formed through our social interactions with others. Dementia removes the cognitive supports that surround the adapted self and leaves the experiential self exposed and vulnerable. This vulnerability may be enhanced by an immature and wounded experiential self. It is, of course, this self that is sought and supported within most forms of psychotherapy.

Kitwood (1988, p.129) further suggests that "the psychological precondition of dementia is an underdeveloped experiencing self, while the adapted self is seriously undermined". This `personal´ framing of dementia indicates the personal nature of the illness. It is an existential plight of persons, which cannot be defined solely in a managerial and technical framework. This thesis has had profound influences in the developing paradigm of dementia care and, indeed, forms part of the basic theoretical and therapeutic arguments for this study.

Through these arguments it is possible to understand the inhibitions posed by the great medical barrier reef, which has created a sharp divide between patient and professional carer. As these technical barricades fall away, understanding grows and good care skills assume the prominence long denied. This process of instrumentalisation creates a personal environment in which the sufferer of dementia is free to be him or herself, albeit with the help and support of others. This empowerment of a person with failing cognitive processes restores personhood, integrity, and a sense of the individual uniqueness of being.

The personal environment has been compared by Kitwood (1990b) to that of Winnicott's (1971) maternal facilitating environment, where the needs of the child's emerging self are met. This life task begins through a created `reality acceptance´, although Winnicott suggests that no human being is ever free from the strain of relating inner and outer reality. At times these strains can be so great as to lead to a psychotic illness. Kitwood (1990b) perceives the state of unattended dementia as similar to that of a semi-psychotic state, which would benefit from psychotherapeutic interventions. These observations have also received the agreement of others (Cheston, 1996; Hausman, 1992; Mills, 1991; Mills and Walker, 1994; Sutton, 1995; Woods et al., 1992).

Psychotherapeutic interventions

Scrutton (1989) suggests that counselling, as part of psychotherapeutic strategies, is essentially an approach to human communication. Counselling is a much overworked term for what is, in essence, a complex process, for it requires the possession of intuitive and learned skills. It is a helping process that enables the respondent or client to explore an area, or areas, of their lives that has caused loss of well-being. The loss of well-being may be so great as to manifest itself in actual mental and/or physical illness.

Egan (1975) and Webster and Young (1988) suggest that counsellors, or `skilled helpers´, must have a variety of skills, in order to help respondents or clients explore painful experiences. They need to be attentive and active listeners, aware of verbal and non verbal responses and orienting self towards the client through positive body posture. This approach calls for dynamic understanding, respect, trustworthiness, basic and advanced empathy, insight and a non-judgmental stance. Egan (1975) argues that it also involves listening to the client's affect, the feelings and emotions that are, in any way, connected to the client's experiences and behaviours. Nelson-Jones (1993, p.66) further suggests that counsellors should be genuine, spontaneous and "able to resonate and respond appropriately to clients' feelings".

This latter personal attribute is part of empathy which is defined by Reiser and Rosen (1984, p.27) "as the ability to fully understand and share in another's feelings, coupled with the ability to know that those feelings are not identical to one's own". Much of the research and literature on empathy has resulted from the work of Carl Rogers, one of the founding fathers of Humanistic Psychology. Rogers sees empathy as crucial when the other person is "hurting, confused, troubled, anxious, terrified, and doubtful of self worth" (Rogers, 1975, p.9). Many practitioners involved in the care of dementing elderly people have seen them experience these painful states all too often.

The use of these skills by the psychotherapist should enable a trusting and effective relationship to develop between two people in an appropriate interview situation. A counselling interview is assumed to be a reciprocal influencing process, which indicates that both the client and counsellor will be affected by the therapeutic process. Much of the research on factors affecting client change yields inconsistent and non significant data. However, a small study undertaken by Davies (1993) for a Health Authority in England, indicates that all one hundred and two clients felt better following therapy. Over ninety-two per cent felt they would return for further counselling if necessary and seventy-six per cent felt they would be able to cope with life more effectively in the future. Further, most clients expressed positive views regarding their working relationship with the counsellor.

Highlen and Hill (1984) suggest that the personal qualities of a counsellor are difficult to identify and measure accurately. Further, Parloff et al. (1978) argue that the data regarding the relationship between therapist experience and counselling outcomes are unclear. It would appear that counsellors in training may be more effective than experienced colleagues and vice versa. Moreover, Barkham's (1996) review of the literature suggests broadly similar outcomes for different types of counselling therapies. Against this background of inconclusive findings, it must be said that most counselling services are stretched to capacity. Counselling is a service that is much in demand.

The demand for this service includes few requests from elderly people, although Butler and Lewis (1982) suggest that mental health concerns tend to increase with advancing age. Kramer et al. (1975) point out that at least twenty-five per cent, and perhaps as many as sixty-five per cent, of all older persons, have some kind of treatable mental health problem. Flemming et al. (1986) indicate that these needs are not met in America. There, it is estimated that the elderly form twelve per cent of the population, but only form six per cent of the case load of community mental health practitioners and two per cent of the case load of private practitioners. Further, Roybal (1988) argues that older people who are housebound have little access to mental health services.

A number of reasons have been proposed for this lack of adequate provision of mental health care to older persons. It is noted that many older people will seek the help of their doctor as opposed to mental health care organisations. Myers (1990) suggests that this may be due to the negative stigma associated with such services from their youth, when only the severely impaired received help. There is probably also a desire to retain independence and privacy, with a corresponding lack of vocabulary for emotional issues in old age. Most older people come from a generation which is not used to discussing feelings.

Further, as Myers and Blake (1984) comment, there is lack of sufficient training to meet the needs of older people. Butler and Lewis (1982) suggest that there is also an issue of bias against older clients, although there is an increase in therapists advocating work with this client group (Orbach, 1996; Twining, 1996). Other social and economic factors may prohibit providers from accepting older people as clients (Knight, 1986a). Scrutton (1989) argues that social provision for the elderly is under resourced and many problems associated with ageing are closely linked to the injustice of social provision. It would be quite wrong, however, to assume that older people have concerns that are only associated with the ageing process. As Orbach (1996), Scrutton (1989) and Twining (1996) point out, they are individuals with a unique set of experiences. These experiences have been gathered over many years, giving them the resource of a wealth of experience and coping skills, to use in the changing circumstances of later life.

The knowledge that older people are reluctant to seek help from mental health services has lead Myers (1990) to suggest that help must be proffered using different terminology such as life review discussions. However, it must be recognised that there may be areas of an older person's life that are too personal to be discussed. This should not be treated as resistance, but rather as a reluctance to participate. The use of the life review in working with older clients is not a new concept. It is a function of reminiscence which Butler (1963) argued was a normal activity in old age, in that it could lead to life review which is a process that people may have to undergo, if they are to come to terms with their `lived´ lives. Hagberg (1995), Scrutton (1989) and Waters (1990) among others, suggest that the goal of life review therapy is to help clients recall past events and relationships, consider their meaning and ideally develop a sense of pride in their accomplishments. This process creates a climate for the development of ego integrity, which is the final life task of Erikson's (1963) concept of the stages of life.

Thus, within the counselling discipline for older people, there is a school of thought which advocates the use of life review techniques with some elderly people. Coleman (1986b, 1994) suggests that not all older people will want to engage in the life review process, or even in that of reminiscence. However, reminiscence therapy has become a major tool for many practitioners engaged in various aspects of work with this client group.

Reminiscence

Reminiscence, according to the literature, is the recalling of past life experiences. Molinari and Reichlin (1985) define reminiscence as a process of recollection that is carried out internally or in the presence of others. Webster and Haight (1995, p.286) suggest that it is "a multifaceted, multipurpose, naturally occuring mental phenomenon manifested across the life span in a variety of forms and contexts". Reminiscence, then, is not an activity solely ascribed to the elders in our society but is a normal function of the life process. The study of reminiscence work with the elderly would indicate that the use of reminiscence/life review therapies does produce some long term beneficial effects in non dementing elderly people.

Nonetheless, this positive view of reminiscence in old age is comparatively recent in origin. Previously it was felt to indicate organic impairment of the intellect (Dobrof, 1984). Further, Cummings and Henry (1961) suggested that it could be seen as `disengagement´, a process by which the elderly `withdrew´ from concerns with the outside world. However, Butler's (1963) seminal paper which argued that reminiscence was a normal activity in old age, which may lead to life review, fell on fertile ground. Although Coleman (1986b) points to the difficulty in one article, changing attitudes within a particular field of study, Butler paved the way towards a greater understanding of reminiscence. Reminiscence became acknowledged as a normal activity for the elderly with suggested therapeutic and beneficial outcomes. Nonetheless, Butler's arguments, that most individuals need to justify their existence and hence the need for life review, found some detractors. Erikson's (1963) life stage theory, with the final stage being concerned with the achievement of wisdom, seemed to attest to the usefulness of reminiscence. Carlson (1984), Castelnuovo-Tedesco (1978) and McMahon and Rhudick (1964), argue

14

that reminiscence could also be seen as a preservation of self in threatened or actual loss.

Coleman (1986b, p.35) suggests that it is possible for "someone whose life has worked out comfortably" to be less inclined to be critical about their past. Nonetheless, it would seem to make sense to argue that no person can have lived a life which contains no regrets. Some of these regrets may be so strong as to become unresolved conflicts. Lewis and Butler (1974) suggest that reminiscence is a psychotherapeutic function in which an older person reflects on their life in order to resolve, reorganise and reintegrate concerns. Although recurring memories may simply be part of the recall process, Kaminsky (1984) argues that they can also reflect repeated attempts to resolve painful memories. Feil (1985, 1993) perceives the confused ramblings of the demented elderly as an attempt to resolve past conflicts. Following the work of Erikson, she describes this as a new life task in a new life stage.

Reminiscence, therefore, can serve a variety of functions. It is `story telling´ (McMahon and Rhudick, 1964; Wong and Watt, 1991). It is a story that justifies existence (Lieberman and Tobin, 1983; Wong and Watt, 1991). It is a psychotherapeutic function that can resolve a troubled past (Coleman and Mills, 1997; Lewis and Butler, 1974; Feil, 1993; Sutton, 1997; Wong and Watt, 1991). These studies of reminiscence suggest the existence of three major types of reminiscence, although Wong and Watt (1991) have suggested a new taxonomy of reminiscence that indicates six types of reminiscence. Some of these, however, closely parallel existing theory.

a) Story telling reminiscence/informative reminiscence McMahon and Rhudik (1964), Lo Gerfo (1980) suggest that this type of reminiscence is associated with nostalgia, oral history, and an enhancement of self esteem. It permits older people to act as teachers/guides to the younger members of society as they act as informants/interpreters to past societal, social and familial processes. Wong and Watt (1991) argue that this is similar to their concept of instrumental reminiscence. The defining characteristics of this type of reminiscence include recollection of past goals and achievements, together with a sense of an internal locus of control, which Rodin et al. (1985), Schulz (1976), and Slivinske and Fitch (1987) suggest is related to life satisfaction and subjective good health. Billings and Moos (1981), Folkman et al. (1986), and Lazarus and Folkman (1984) further suggest that it indicates the use of problem solving strategies, which have been shown to be a buffer against emotional distress.

b) Evaluative reminiscence/life review reminiscence   This type of reminiscence must have an evaluative component in order to allow the commencement of the life review process. Butler defines life review as a "naturally occurring, universal mental process characterised by the progressive return to consciousness of past experience ... prompted by the realisation of approaching dissolution and death, and the inability to maintain one's sense of personal invulnerability" (Butler, 1963, p.66). Wong and Watt (1991) regard this as similar to integrative reminiscence. Lo Gerfo (1980), McMahon and Rhudik (1964), and Wong and Watt (1991) argue that life review reminiscence is, therefore, very different to story telling reminiscence, in that it is a personal struggle to come to terms with the past.

c) Defensive/obsessive/escapist reminiscence   This type of reminiscence allows the past to be defined as more important than the present, in order to reduce the anxieties produced by declining social, physical and mental states, and/or the feelings of guilt produced by an unsatisfactory life review (Lo Gerfo, 1980; McMahon and Rhudik, 1964; Wong and Watt, 1991). Life review can therefore be defined as a "form of reminiscence in which the past is actively evaluated and conflict is necessary for resolution to occur" (Molinari and Reichlin, 1985, p.83).

Haight's (1991) review of the literature on reminiscence suggested that much of the published work has clouded research issues. However, a more recent review (Haight and Hendrix, 1995, p.8) indicates a greater clarity in descriptions and methodologies "with the value of the life story appreciated". Certainly, Wong and Watt (1991) have made progress in the task of defining those types of reminiscence that are associated with successful ageing. They suggest that successful agers show significantly more integrative and instrumental reminiscence, but less obsessive reminiscence than their unsuccessful counterparts. Wong (1995) argues that these positive forms of reminiscence are adaptive and preserve a sense of mastery.

Thus it is possible to view reminiscence in a variety of ways for, as Haight (1991) indicates, it is a multi-varied concept. It is also necessary to see reminiscence as a total process that may encompass all or part of the identified categories. The use of reminiscence, either in groups or on an individual basis, is also important. Haight (1991) identifies forty-one research reports published since 1960. Of these, twenty-one were discussions of group reminiscence, while the remaining twenty were with individuals. Wong and Watt's (1991) study focused on a large group of carefully screened informants (one hundred and seventy-one) who were interviewed individually. Although most articles and reports of the use of life review/reminiscence therapy focus on group work with non dementing elderly people, this approach has also been used with older people who have failing cognitive functioning.

Applied reminiscence/life review therapies used with dementing elderly people

Most published works detailing reminiscence work with the confused elderly have focused on group reminiscence work with these subjects. Some, such as Isohanni (1990) have seen reminiscence as part of a `coping strategy' that allows demented elderly to function as part of a therapeutic community model of care. Another study by Holland (1987) has postulated that the semantic realities of present day, time, place and people, would become salient and memorable if linked with the past.

Kiernat (1979) argues that group reminiscence work with confused elderly people allows the group leader to become the learner with the group providing the learning material. Yet a further paper, by Cook (1984) suggests that group reminiscence work, with confused nursing home residents, led to positive changes in behaviour and demeanour. The most apparent change was the gradually increasing length of time that members spent in socialising before and after each session. Cook acknowledges that as this project was not a controlled scientific experiment, the findings are tentative and must be confirmed by a formal study.

Farran and Keane-Hagerty (1989) suggest the best way of seeing the real person behind the dementia is the use of validation and reminiscence therapy. This, the authors suggest, will help to clarify the context of confusing statements. Bornat's (1985) article on the use of reminiscence aids to help recall the past, leads to the importance of the work by John Adams (1986) on the need to surround patients with dementia with articles of their past or of a past era. Adams argues that personal reminiscences, prompted by the use of such cues, enable individual identity to be restored. Moreover, reminiscence allows the expression of the patient's own perspective (Adams, 1994). In an earlier article, he suggests that it is not important if recalled experiences are not reliable in every respect, because "they recreate a world we have lost and they help to furnish the milieu from which the patient came" (Adams, 1984).

This viewpoint is echoed in the work of Webster and Young (1988).

They argue that accuracy of recall and authenticity of specific detail is not a chief concern. Rather, it is the subjective meaning and relative importance the memory represents for individuals in their current context which are of concern. They see this as a process through which individuals attribute meaning to the past in three interactive and overlapping steps. These are recall, evaluation and synthesis. They suggest "painful memories necessitating ego defence activation are either accepted with great reservation (resigned acceptance) or rejected and ruminated over, perhaps contributing to a sense of despair (unaccepted) ... Further, some memories will be associated with positive emotional connotations - happiness, pride, love - while others will be affiliated with the converse, such as guilt, helplessness or hate". They also suggest that the practice of life review uses some of the conditions and techniques which are part of counselling.

Woods et al. (1992) reviewed the literature and the results of their own findings on reminiscence and life review work with this client group. They suggest that these activities are beneficial and should form part of the assessment and care giving process by providers of care for dementing elderly people. They perceive this as an activity that can be accomplished during the time spent meeting patients' personal needs. It is probable that recalling the past may have positive effects on some elderly people with dementia (Gibson, 1994). Kitwood (1989) suggests that there are "certain kinds of psychological `strength´ that may enable an individual to remain intact as a social and communicative being, despite the presence of pathological processes in the brain".

The use of psychotherapeutic/counselling skills in reminiscence therapy

Woods and McKiernan's (1995, p.242) review of the literature indicates that "the use of reminiscence with people with dementia is relatively untapped". The literature concerned with the use of reminiscence therapy with psychogeriatric subjects tends to suggest that it is mainly used with small groups rather than on an individual basis. Little has been outlined of the approach used by the group leaders / innovators / investigators of these groups (Adams, 1984; Cook, 1984; Goldwasser et al., 1987; Holland, 1987; Isohanni, 1990). This situation is now undergoing some change. Feil's Validation theory advocates the allowing of very old confused elderly to speak of their past and the feelings they have, without correcting them by the use of reality orientation therapy. Therefore, one does not collude with the confused person by agreeing with what they are saying, but rather listening to what they are trying to say. She sees this stage as Resolution - the final life task, with humanistic psychology therapies as a crucial part of in this work (Feil, 1985, 1992, 1993). Jones and Burns (1992) reminiscing disorientation theory, also follow much of the work of Feil, in that this approach validates feelings and permits the reorientation of the confused elderly person.

Farran and Keane-Hagerty (1989) have outlined the necessary communication skills for use with demented elderly people. These techniques are actually basic counselling skills. The literature outlining effective interviewing techniques stresses the importance of listening, observing, absence of threat, role, presentation of self etc. (Berg, 1989; Chernitz, 1986; Hargie et al., 1981; Lofland and Lofland, 1984). Again, these are all part of effective counselling strategies. Feil (1982) suggests that use of Validation therapy as a therapeutic tool needs specific skills. She argues that it means listening with the third ear, seeing with the mind's eye, genuine empathetic touching, eye contact, and travelling with the very old, disorientated person. Goudie and Stokes (1989) follow the work of Feil in that they argue of a present, as opposed to past meaning, behind the `confused´ messages of the dementing elderly. They see the use of Rogerian counselling skills as crucial in allowing clients to `resolve´ their present needs or distress.

Hausman (1992) advocates the use of dynamic psychotherapy with individual demented elderly people. This approach focuses on the treatment of internal factors which determine each older person's way of adapting and finding restitution within the demented state. Individual psychotherapy attempts to address and resolve internal stress. Many of the techniques used can be taught to care givers which will promote well-being for those people in their care. Kitwood (1990a) writes convincingly of the need for a psychotherapeutic approach with this client group. He argues that the malignant social psychology (MSP) which surrounds the dementing process can be removed by psychotherapeutic interventions. It would appear, therefore, that allowing elderly people with dementia to talk of their meaningful past life experiences within a therapeutic structure, can promote feelings of well-being. The pilot study which formed the basis for this present work produced similar findings.

The pilot study

The sample

This investigation was concerned with the ability of some demented elderly people to recall past life experiences. Although five elderly people had originally agreed to participate, the eventual number of informants who took part in this study were four, three male and one female, all medically diagnosed as suffering from moderate to severe dementia. They were patients in a long stay, twenty-eight bedded psychogeriatric unit of a small psychiatric hospital. The unit appeared to be a warm, friendly, noisy environment with high levels of staff interaction. Patients' well-being seemed of paramount importance to the staff, who displayed attitudes of respect, patience and kindness to those in their care.

Method

A series of weekly individual interviews were held on the same day and, approximately, at the same time, in order to allow the elderly person to speak about his or her past experiences. There was a total number of twenty-one recorded and transcribed interviews which lasted from twenty minutes to one hour. The informants dictated the length of the interview, which was drawn to a close when it became apparent that informants were tiring. Permission to undertake the interviews was sought and obtained from close relatives, the hospital consultant, nursing staff and the district research ethics committee. Since it was not possible to obtain permission from the elderly informant in advance, an invitation was extended on each occasion and the individual was free to participate or withdraw. The fifth informant did, in fact, choose to leave the study. On being asked if he would like to talk to the interviewer about his past life, he said `No!´ very firmly and walked off. He died some weeks later.

In order to aid the investigation, some information about significant past events was obtained from staff in the setting and close relatives. This information was used as prompts and cues to aid retrieval of past memories. Information obtained from informants was reported back to close relatives in order to ascertain whether or not it was based upon real events. The approach used during the interviews combined Rogerian counselling skills with the use of reminiscence/life review therapy with elderly dementia patients. The series of individual interviews with informants, in which they discussed/described their personal past, permitted the development of trust and security which is necessary for disclosure.

Analysis of data

Transcripts of the interviews were subjected to analysis using grounded theory in which common emergent categories and themes were identified. These data were considered, together with field notes and ethnographic observations, in order to locate the behaviour of the informant in the context in which it occurred.

Findings

All informants managed to recollect significant past experiences concerned with significant others, places and events. Further analysis of the data indicated that not only could informants recall significant past memories, but also the appropriate emotions associated with these memories. That is, they displayed happiness during the recall of happier times and sadness when remembering unhappy events. This core category was labelled as appropriate affective response.

Staff enjoyed discussing the informant's past with the researcher, and were touched by the feelings displayed by all informants during the interviews. The senior charge nurse, who listened to some of the tapes, said that listening to informants talking in the privacy of his home had given him a new perspective on his residents. He felt that it would be a good idea to record all residents on the ward which would be especially valuable for new staff. This investigation was too short to effect noticeable long term change in the informants. Theorists, such as Bromley (1966), Chertkow and Bub (1990), and Hanley and Hodge (1984) suggest that various measures, or indices of change in the behaviour of the confused elderly, do not readily lend themselves to the measurement of this type of intervention. However, short term change was noticeable with all informants. It was found that informants readily and openly shared their concerns, experiences and feelings with the interviewer. Further, they appeared to enjoy/welcome the experience of talking about their past life to another person.

Discussion

This investigation indicated that some elderly people with dementia could recall their past and reminisced. It further indicated the value of individual interviews with these informants. The importance of the use of counselling skills in this study cannot be overestimated. The strong emotions expressed by some informants could have been overwhelming without some knowledge of counselling strategies. A natural defence is to 'block' or deny strong feelings in others, if the recipient feels unable to cope with them. This investigation recommended increased training in use of counselling skills amongst professional carers of older people with dementia.

This investigation further indicated that a more complete social history of each informant would have been useful. This was shown in the main body of the work, when additional information given on one informant produced probes and cues which allowed her to remember much more of her past. She was also able to use whole sentences and keep to the subject under discussion. Furthermore, this informant found this final interview to be the most enjoyable of all the interviews (Mills and Chapman, 1992).

Perhaps the most significant finding in this work was the importance of memories and emotional response. The emotional memories of the informants ran like a rich vein throughout the investigation. This suggested that the emotional intactness of response in dementia was worthy of further investigation. It is probably fitting to close the discussion of this study with the words of one of the informants, Mr Lamb, who described how he felt when speaking of his past experiences.

And I tell you what! I felt happy when I was telling you about them!

Conclusion

This chapter has clarified the background to this study. The demographics of ageing have highlighted the numbers of elderly who have and will have some type of dementia. The dementias themselves have been the subjects of some explanation, although the extent of the limitations of our present knowledge is painfully apparent. A discussion of psychotherapeutic interventions, especially with older people with dementia, indicates some interesting and beneficial lines of inquiry. The literature suggests that reminiscence is a useful tool in the work of dementia care, and can be combined with psychotherapy. The findings of the pilot investigation further suggest that there are some beneficial effects in the use of this combined approach (Mills, 1993; Mills and Chapman, 1992).

An examination of the present understanding of the dementias indicates how much entrenched positions and attitudes are changing. Dementia is no longer perceived as being an entirely negative state of being. It is now possible to argue that older people with dementia can be enabled to retain/return to a state of personhood and well-being. It is not that the sufferers of dementia have changed but rather it is we, as theorists, practitioners and providers of care who have undergone a change in attitude and perceptions.

The key to this sea change is a greater understanding of these illnesses, their management and the shattered personhood of most older people with dementia. As Kitwood (1997a), Kitwood and Bredin (1992) remind us, it is we who often have more of a problem than those in need of care, for we simply participate in the unacknowledged `pathology of normality´. Those older people who exist in a state of dementia, often exist in a state of greater authenticity than those who care for them. The demented person who stands before us is a simply devastated but highly sentient being (Kitwood, 1990a).

It is suggested that a growing understanding of another is linked to the sharing of emotions. Denzin (1989a) argues that this lies at the centre of the process of understanding. Possibly the commonality linking dementia, reminiscence therapies and psychotherapeutic interventions, may be centred in the expression, acceptance and understanding of emotion and emotional responses. This issue will be explored in greater depth during chapter two of this work, together with a discussion of the relationship between emotion and memory processes in dementia.

2 Autobiographical memory and dementia

Introduction

This chapter is concerned with a discussion of the developing emotional life in older people with dementia, together with the relationship between memory and emotion. This is not a simple task, due to present incomplete knowledge and understanding. Within the discipline of cognitive psychology emotions, per se, have received little interest. However, there is a growing literature on the relationship between emotion and cognition. Moreover, the relationship between memory and emotion has been the topic of extensive research, although largely devoted to the relationship between negative emotions, memory and neuroses.

   In addition, studies of dementia have largely been concerned with the failure of memory. There is little in the literature which seeks to combine the phenomena of emotion and memory in dementia. However, there has been substantial research in brain structures associated with memory processes. Further, there is a rising interest in the role of autobiographical memory. It is this aspect of memory which is deemed to contain emotional memories of a personal past. This chapter will, therefore, discuss emotion theories and the theoretical relationship between cognition and emotion. However, the main focus of this chapter will be concerned with theory and research gained from studies on the effects of dementia in brain structures concerned with memory processes, together with a discussion of theories of autobiographical memory and the implications for this study.

The emotions

The emotions have traditionally been associated with the Arts. Their influence in such areas as literature, painting, sculpture and music is manifest. Psychoanalytic/counselling work, too, is concerned with emotions that are part of problematic events in a person's life. In these contexts, a wide range of emotions is expected to be displayed and experienced. In many of these instances a full understanding of the psychology of emotions is not always necessary. The subjective/experiential component of emotions is normally sufficient. However, within a more scientific context, such perspectives require further explanation. There have been many attempts to attach theoretical understanding to the emotions. Theorists have endeavoured to explain their development and function from a physiological stance (Ekman, 1984; James-Lange, 1895; Tomkins, 1984; Watson and Morgan, 1917).

The emotions are also regarded as numerous and varied social constructs, who owe their existence to the influence of culture, social experience and learning (Averill, 1986; Harrè, 1986; Wetherell and Maybin, 1996). Other theorists regard them as psychoevolutionary and fundamental to all human beings (Izard, 1991; Plutchik, 1980). The phylogeny and ontogeny of emotions would indicate that emotions have evolved because of their adaptive functions in the instinct for survival, which is the basis for all aspects of human behaviour (Darwin, 1872). It is the strength of this instinct which forms part of psychoanalytic theory (Freud, 1920) and which suggests that survival and the emotions are intertwined. Thus, a living human being is an emotional being (Izard, 1991).

Theoretical arguments suggest that dementia sufferers have a rich and powerful emotional life (Kitwood, 1993, 1997a). Moreover, it is suggested that these emotions are not merely labile, but recognisable states that seemingly correspond to present experiences and events (Mills and Walker, 1994). However, much of the literature associates dementia with emotional problems. These include disinhibition and blunting of emotions, together with a lability of emotions and lack of self control (Bromley, 1990; Williams, 1987). Kitwood and Bredin (1992) suggest that many of the behaviours seen in older people with dementia, which include emotional issues, are more of a problem for their non demented carers and others. Further, they perceive sufferers of dementia as being `generally more authentic´ about their emotions. This, too, was a finding from the pilot study (Mills, 1991), in that all informants who took part showed honest emotions related to the topic under discussion. Further, there was little evidence of marked disinhibition and lack of self control during any of the interviews with informants.

In the search for appropriate theory to offer some explanation for the presence of emotions in older people with dementia, it is necessary to specify the dominant characteristics required. In this particular study, emotion theory had to account for the presence and durability of emotions in older people with dementia. At present there are over a hundred theories on emotion (Thompson, 1988). The most applicable theory of emotions in this context is the psychoevolutionary perspective which states that emotions are fundamental and are derived through evolutionary-biological processes (Izard, 1991; Plutchik, 1980; Tomkins, 1981). However, the social construct theory of emotions cannot be lightly dismissed. Emotions are learned and shaped through societal influences, but, it is argued, are not solely created within such interactions (Toates, 1996; Williams, 1989).

Moreover, it is suggested that emotions, in evolutionary terms, emerged prior to increased cognition (Maclean, 1990). Tomkins (1981) argues that emotions are strongly present in the neonate who, at this time, has immature cognitive processes. This theory is of interest as it suggests that the fading of cognitive abilities within dementia might precede the fading of emotional structures. It is further argued that fundamental emotions have a distinct and specific feeling that achieves awareness. The fundamental emotions that meet these and other criteria are interest, enjoyment, surprise, sadness, anger, disgust, contempt, fear, shame and guilt (Izard, 1991). Certainly, some informants displayed these emotions within the pilot study (Mills, 1991).

Emotions may be viewed as a tripartite system of neurophysiological-biological, motor or behavioural-expressive and subjective-experiential components. Generally, theories which seek to explain emotions more in neurophysiological terms, stress the effect that an external event will have on an individual with regard to bodily responses, particularly specific avoidance or approach reactions, together with responses of the autonomic nervous system (Mandler, 1987). Current thinking suggests that the facial feedback hypothesis might fill the information gap left by a purely visceral theory of emotion (Lazarus, 1991). This argues that response to a prototypic event triggers facial and postural responses which, in turn, trigger both the emotional state and the autonomic responses (Ekman et al., 1972, p.173). These theories of arousal include the functionality of neuroendocrine systems, which produces a hormonal response to stimuli. Nathan (1988) argues that hormones both form behaviours and are formed by behaviours, in that they produce needs and desires which do not occur until the particular hormone reaches the brain. In turn, behaviour influences the brain and this affects the secretion of hormones.

All emotions, however expressed, are founded in brain structures, which, according to Siminov (1986), comprise of a system of highly complex and interrelated interdependent structures, with many of their functions, as yet, unknown (Luria, 1973). Moreover, the emotional circuitry of the brain is still poorly understood (Thompson, 1988), and it is unwise to perceive the emotions as being a function of particular locations in the brain, for, as Buck (1988, p.569) argues, the nervous system is so interconnected that no structure works in isolation. However, cognitive psychological theory posits a relationship between the emotions and cognition, and is of interest in the study of emotions and memory in dementia.

Emotions and cognition

The apparent differentiation between cognition and emotion has long been recognised as a false divide. For many years, within the cognitive psychological discipline, emotions were seen as the result of cognitive appraisal. The emotional feeling was experienced and labelled accordingly (Schachter and Singer, 1962). Lazarus (1982, 1984a) perceives cognitive appraisal as an integral feature of all emotional states, although Zajonc (1980, 1984a, 1984b) argues for the supremacy of emotions over cognition: "affect and cognition are separate and partially independent systems and ... although they function conjointly, affect could be generated without a prior cognitive process" (Zajonc, 1984b, p.117). This theory is of interest to this study, in that emotions may be seen, in some circumstances, to have a certain freedom from cognitive appraisal and processes.

Emotion and memory

Further arguments linking cognition and emotion have been hypothesised in the network theory of affect (Bower, 1981; Bower and Cohen, 1982; Gilligan and Bower, 1984). Their theory indicates that emotional nodes in memory structures, connected to cognitive structures, will be `triggered´ by similar emotional stimuli such as mood. Blaney (1986), in a review of the collected evidence presented

27

for both mood-state-dependent recall and mood-congruence, finds that there is an argument for mood congruence effects as against that of mood-state-dependent recall, "what seems clear is that there exist either mood-congruence effects or state-dependence effects disguised as such, the former being the more likely of the two". Other reviews of the evidence also confirm some mood-congruency effects in a clinical context (Baddeley, 1990; Williams et al., 1988). A convincing explanation of the inconsistency in mood-congruent retrieval effects is given by Williams et al. (1988). They suggest that not all material encoded during these experiments was concerned with reference to the self. Further, both Isen et al. (1978) and Teasdale and Russell (1983) used self referent material and found evidence of mood-congruent recall. In reports of experiments, Bower (1981), Bower et al. (1981) and Hasher et al. (1985) did not use self referent material and no effect of mood-congruent recall bias could be demonstrated.

The research on mood-congruent effects in memory has largely been in a clinical context with depressed or highly anxious patients and has shown mixed results. Williams et al. (1988, p.166) suggest that emotional disorders bias cognitive processing. They conclude that "attention is biased, memory is biased, and judgments are biased". It appears that different emotions may be more specific on cognitive processing than was originally thought. They suggest that one possible interpretation of the data is that anxious subjects orientate their attention to threat. Depressed subjects may selectively remember negative material (Williams et al., 1988, p.168). Baddeley (1990) indicates support for these arguments. Further, some findings from the pilot study offer some evidence of mood congruent recall in dementia, the recalled memories of informants were largely negative when mood was low (Mills and Walker, 1994).

Other theorists who adopt a less cognitive stance to the relationship between cognition and emotion include Singer (1973, 1974), who posits the concept of interrelated/intertwined systems of cognition and emotion. This relationship is rooted in the infant's early efforts at accommodation to its novel and ever-changing environment. Thus, emotional and cognitive processes are intertwined from birth. This intertwined relationship will, in some instances, allow emotional processes to function independently (Izard, 1971, 1984, 1991; Leventhal, 1984; Tomkins, 1962, 1963, 1981; Zajonc, 1980, 1984b). Thus, within cognitive psychology there is an embryonic framework that links thinking to feelings (Averill, 1986; Lazarus, 1982, 1984b). This framework includes the relationship between mood and memory and has led to the formulation of cognitive approaches in emotional disorders (Teasdale and Barnard, 1993). Williams et al. (1988) suggest that theorists recognise the need for further progress to be made in understanding how perception, attention and memory contribute to this phenomena.

There is, therefore, within the cognitive school of thought, a posited association between memory and emotion (Averill, 1986; Baddeley, 1990; Bower, 1981; Bower and Cohen, 1982; Eysenck and Keane, 1990; Gilligan and Bower, 1984; Leventhal, 1984; Teasdale and Barnard, 1993; Williams et al., 1988). There appears to be no significant body of literature associating cognitive impairment with emotion, other than emotional disorders. However, there has been substantial research in the loss of memory due to cognitive impairment as the result of trauma, or congenital influences. Such studies include the effects of dementia on brain structures and processes, known to be associated with the learning, storage and retrieval of information.

Moreover, the loss of memory in dementia continues to decline as neurones cease to function. The progressive nature of dementia eventually affects all aspects of cognitive functioning. The timespan for this rate of decline is variable although Reisberg (1983) suggests that there are six phases in the dementing process. These range from forgetfulness, to confusional states and to the very severe cognitive decline found in late dementia. Diagnosis tends to become more common at the confusional stage leading to institutionalisation, and not infrequently death within a subsequent two-five year period (Reisberg, 1983). Similar findings are reported by Shapiro and Tate (1991).

However, there is some dispute over the stage at which mood changes occur, particularly with regard to AD (Bayles, 1991). Reisberg (1983) suggests that emotional changes are more typical of the latter stages of dementia and are associated with severe cognitive impairment. Other theorists suggest that disturbances of mood are usual (Lishman, 1978), together with dysphoria (Merriam et al., 1988). Nonetheless, most theorists agree that mood change is common in dementia, but typically appear subsequent to memory dysfunction (Bayles, 1991).

Memory and dementia

The brief description of brain changes associated with dementia given in chapter one suggests that this is a disease of neuronal death that is selective or modular in nature. These neuronal networks include the hippocampal formations which are known to be closely involved in retrieval and recall. It must be stated, however, that the hippocampal formation is not the seat of memory traces, but appears to be an important substrate for memory processes. Nonetheless, Squire (1992) argues that it is a complex structure which performs a critical function at the time of learning, if declarative memory is to be established in an enduring and usable way.

In early DAT, atrophic changes have been associated with the medial temporal lobes that particularly disrupt the hippocampus and hippocampal cortical links. Mayes (1992) and Parkin (1993) suggest that these atrophic changes contribute to memory loss within these illnesses. Squire (1992) further indicates that the CA1 region of the hippocampus is particularly vulnerable to ischemic damage. His studies on global ischemia in the hippocampal formation in the rat and monkey found evidence of selective neuronal loss in the CA1 region, together with memory impairment (Zola-Morgan and Squire, 1990; Squire, 1992). This, of course, has implications for multi-infarct damage associated with Vascular Dementia.

Moscovitch and Umiltà (1990) and Squire (1992) suggest that gradual reorganisation of memory storage occurs, so that storage and retrieval is eventually possible without the participation of the hippocampus or related structures. As the result of gradual processes that are still poorly understood, the organisation of memory storage is slowly transformed after learning. This transformation may involve rehearsal, additional retrieval opportunities, or the acquisition of related material. It may possibly be largely endogenous. Squire (1992) argues that concurrent changes in neocortex ensure possible re-representation of material in a more efficient form. In addition, Moscovitch and Umiltà (1990, p.41) argue that "there is a non hippocampal route to memory traces that also uses working memory ... alternate routes to those traces can be established that use central processes, or the traces can be revived and their content delivered to working memory, by newly established automatic associations for frequently retrieved pieces of information".

Squire (1992) offers some support for this argument, in that work with experimental animals provides direct evidence that the hippocampal formation is essential for memory storage for only a limited period of time. The role of the hippocampus then gradually diminishes, and a more permanent memory is established elsewhere that is independent of the hippocampus. These arguments are of some significance for this work, in that they offer a possible explanation of how some older people with moderate to severe dementia can recall some meaningful memories of the past. Further, Mills (1991), Mills and Chapman (1992), and Mills and Coleman (1994) suggest that these recalled meaningful memories of dementia sufferers are significantly emotional.

The hippocampal formation is part of the limbic system although limbic neuropathology within DAT is not confined to the hippocampus, but also to the entorhinal cortex and amygdala (Van Hoesen and Damasio, 1987). The area most severely compromised, however, is the nuclei closely interconnected with the hippocampal formation. Damage to higher order cortices indicates that feedback projections to other, less recent, brain structures are critical for recall, recognition and consciousness. Thus, the defect in retrieval of past events is not merely due to dysfunction in the hippocampal complex, but largely to dysfunction in higher order association cortices (Damasio et al., 1990). However, these affected cortical areas are still permitted to function for long periods during the course of the disease. Again, a comment that has some significance for this present investigation.

It is possible to see from these arguments that old memories may be perceived to undergo different retrieval processes compared to those of more recent memories. Moscovitch and Umiltà (1990) suggest that if these memories were of a frequent experience and/or often recalled, then the process would be relatively rapid and automatic as it travelled well established non hippocampal pathways. The cortex has approximately some 10^{10} neurones with perhaps, more than 10^4 synapses for each neurone (Rose, 1987). Further, according to Parkin (1987), a fully developed neurone can average over a thousand dendritic and a thousand axonal synapses, which gives some indication of the enormity of the level of interconnections between neurones. Thus, it is probable that there may exist any number of pathways and circuits, which can be modified through neuronal plasticity, by the functioning of learning and experience (Parkin, 1987). Further, the complexities of this vast system suggest that it may be tentatively possible to visualise, within dementia, the use of alternative emotional/cognitive networks to long term memories that have remained intact, despite inhibiting changes to neural structures and pathways.

Aspects of long term memory

The discussion of memory processes involving a non hippocampal pathway, suggests that the memories which will travel this route are more likely to be well established or long term memories. Within early dementia, there are more noticeable deficits in short term memory (STM), although long term memory (LTM), itself, will eventually show signs of decline. LTM can be seen as encompassing two memory systems, that of episodic and semantic memory (Tulving, 1983). Episodic memory can be generally categorised as a store of the record of individual life events, the temporally dated autobiography. Semantic memory may be seen as memory organisations that hold abstract knowledge such as concepts, facts and vocabulary. It has no necessary temporal landmarks. Bayles and Kaszniak (1987) suggest that loss in this area of memory is widely considered to be central to the communication problems experienced within later DAT.

Chertkow and Bub (1990) indicate that there is evidence to suggest that a semantic processing deficit exists within DAT, with significant loss of conceptual knowledge. However, although both STM and LTM function are disrupted within AD, Parkin (1987, p.136) suggests that episodic memory would appear to suffer greater disruption than that of semantic memory. Conway (1990) and Tulving (1983) suggest that a possible explanation for these differing arguments is that memory of past events is represented at both episodic and semantic levels, as these two systems are perceived to closely interact. Thus, autobiographical material may be represented in both episodic and semantic systems. Emotion is more closely associated with episodic memory, in that emotional experiences are personal events. It is, of course, possible for the memory of events to be low in emotional content. However, Conway (1990) suggests that autobiographical memories are closely intertwined with knowledge of emotion. The difference between these two types of memory would appear to be that event memory (episodic) can be associated with low levels of emotion, and personal event memory (autobiographical) is more likely to be associated with high levels of emotion. Conway (1990) argues that there are also timespan differences. Episodic memory may only last a few days whereas autobiographical memory can last for many years.

Autobiographical memory

Current interest amongst cognitive psychologists in the study of autobiographical memory is a comparatively recent phenomenon. Data were regarded as anecdotal in nature and unable to satisfy the requirements of objective science (Robinson, 1992). Although this debate still continues, there is increasing interest in this area.

Autobiographical memory may be seen as part of the memory system as a whole. The preceding discussion will have indicated that autobiographical memory is not a separate or distinct type but a memory for biographical information and life experiences. Robinson (1992, p.224) suggests that this type of memory comprises of several qualitatively different memoria, such as general versus specific. Conway (1990) also perceives autobiographical but not episodic memory as possessing sub-divisions.

Brewer (1986) suggests that all autobiographical memory is memory of information relating to the self. He further identifies four sub-divisions or types of autobiographical memory. He perceives them as being self referent and interpretations of complex events. Johnson (1983, 1985) offers a model of at least three basic memory sub-systems: the sensory, perceptual and reflective. His multiple entry (MEM) approach proposes that all memories are represented in the various sub-systems. Autobiographical memories, therefore, suggest a pattern of distinguishing characteristics which can be shared with other types of knowledge, although most clearly typifying autobiographical memories.

Conway (1990, p.14) identifies seven such characteristics, most of which are strongly present within such memories. Perhaps the most important of these is that of self reference, for autobiographical memories are significantly concerned with the self (Brewer, 1986). Another characteristic, the experience of remembering is, according to Conway, always present, as is context specific, sensory and perceptual attributes. Yet another is the duration of these types of memories. Autobiographical memories can, and will, exist for years. This, too, was an important finding from the pilot study.

Conway perceives the characteristic of interpretation (personal), as being frequently present, together with imagery. Veridicality, however, is variable. It is suggested that autobiographical memories represent interpretations or meanings of experienced events. Neisser (1981) demonstrates this quite clearly in his account of the testimony of Nixon's aide, John Dean, concerning the Watergate affair. He suggests that when Dean was wrong in the accuracy of his recall, there was a sense of truthfulness in what he was saying. He did recall the common themes of conversations, but reconstructed them into inaccurate memories of single events. Thus, Dean had faulty recall for isolated incidents, but he certainly remembered the `message´ of Watergate.

Bartlett (1932, p.204) would support this finding, for he proposed that memory was fundamentally reconstructive as "literal recall is extraordinarily unimportant". However, Brewer (1986) suggests that memory is only partly reconstructive for, as Conway (1990, p.25) points out, memory is certainly reconstructive but there must be something with which to construct. Which memories of the self are more likely to be encoded? Research indicates that it is distinctive events as opposed to routine happenings which are more likely to be recalled (Conway, 1990; Linton, 1982). This was, again, a finding from the pilot study. Significant events concerning the self were recalled by all informants (Mills, 1991). Conway (1990, p.104) argues that the emotional intensity and personal significance of an event give rise to autobiographical memories, which are detailed, highly available for recall and comparatively resistant to forgetting. This suggests that emotional memories have a great strength and that some may well survive for long periods throughout the process of dementia.

Conway (1990, p.164) further suggests that autobiographical memory is hierarchical in nature. Within this structure, knowledge about activities, people and places are focal points for memory. It will be recalled that the categories assigned to memories of informants in the pilot study, closely followed these themes. Bromley (1990, p.233) also perceives autobiographical memories as strongly associated with emotional significance which have been organised into schema, in ways that permit ready access. Autobiographical memories, therefore, have an interdependency with cognition and emotion. Again, findings from the pilot study suggest that this interdependency would appear to be maintained for long periods within the dementing process. This interdependency was present in different types of medically diagnosed dementia, such as Vascular Dementia (Mills, 1991; Mills and Coleman, 1994) and in DAT (Mills, 1993; Mills and Walker, 1994).

Memories of a personal past are associated with reminiscence, which has been the subject of much discussion in the preceding chapter. Salaman (1970, 1982) suggests that these memories can be involuntary or spontaneous. Some may be the detailed recall of whole events, whereas others may be fragmented pieces of the past with fragmentary `factual´ knowledge not spontaneously or involuntarily recalled. Conway (1990) offers the explanation that these snippets of factual knowledge are not accompanied by a feeling of remembering. Other types of knowledge can be so strongly remembered as to allow the person to momentarily relive past experiences. This, again, was a finding from the pilot study. Occasionally, informants appeared to be able to see their very old, past emotional experiences with great clarity (Mills, 1991).

Salaman (1982) strongly suggests that autobiographical memories carry personally relevant important meanings. In maturity these meanings may become clearer and resolution may occur following a period of life review. Conway (1990, p.157) suggests that: "It seems likely that the purpose of the life review, and the role of autobiographical memory in this process, are determined more by the existential problems set by the past and nature of current circumstances, than by any predetermined cognitive process". Thus, the role of emotion in recalling the past has been given some prominence in recent research.

Conclusion

The discussion of the emotions, together with a discussion of emotion and memory in dementia, has indicated the scarcity of the literature that actually pertains to these topics. It has been necessary to define emotions from a simplistic stance in order to aid clarity. The many theories concerned with the emotions are not particularly helpful in the study of emotions in dementia. However, the psychoevolutionary theories on emotion do offer some insight in to the presence of emotions in this client group. Further, the named and specific number of fundamental emotions is of importance. Their presence in older people with dementia gives some indication of the strength of these emotions which have endured in spite of neurophysiological changes to brain processes and structures.

There is progressive neural damage associated with dementia. However, it is not yet known how much neural damage individuals can tolerate before brain function is compromised. Moreover, although the hippocampal formation is under attack within dementia, there is some evidence that there is a non hippocampal pathway which is involved in the laying down of long term memories (Moscovitch and Umiltà, 1990). Some of these memories may fall into the category of autobiographical memory. Theoretical suggestions that emotion and memory have an intertwined and interdependent relationship leads to the importance of present interest in autobiographical memory. It is this concept of the recall of memories relating to the self which was of significance for this study.

Conway (1990) suggests that autobiographical memories may be emotional. Further, they possess some durability and are comparatively resistant to forgetting. They are also concerned with memories of the self. Life review and psychotherapeutic interventions are also concerned with emotional memories of the self. It would seem, therefore, that there is a relationship between emotion and memory which is made evident in the recall of a personal past. Moroever, findings from the pilot study suggest that all informants had memories which were strongly emotional. Thus, the phenomena of dementia, memory and emotion have been shown to have a common meeting place, both theoretically and therapeutically, within the recall of autobiographical memories or life story. This chapter suggests that the emotions associated with this life story continue throughout life, throughout old age and even throughout dementia.

3 The single case-study method

Introduction

The aim of this investigation was to investigate the characteristic features of emotional memories in older people with dementia. The research aims focused on an area which has a unique singularity, for memories themselves and their associated emotions are the particular property of individual people. In addition, dementia presents with no standard cognitive profile. Sufferers of this disease present differently, they themselves are singular. Therefore, this was a study of individuals and of individual phenomena. The chosen methodology should encompass this concept of individuality and allow a close examination of informants' recollections of their past lives and of the moving stories they told. A review of the literature suggested that these demands would be met by the single case-study method. This chapter, therefore, will discuss the strengths and weaknesses of case-study methodology, together with methods used to analyse the data generated from the investigation. Ethical issues are of great importance in this type of inquiry and will be carefully examined. A brief description of the sample will also be given. Finally, there will be an examination of the procedures used during the collection, analysis and presentation of data.

The case-study method

Runyan (1982, p.121) states that the single case-study method involves the presentation and interpretation of detailed information about a single individual. It is an in-depth investigation of a single person, which can be conducted over a lengthy period of time (McAdams, 1990; Yin, 1989). Allport (1937) and Runyan (1982, p.175) suggest this idiographic method is concerned with that which is particular and specific to the individual, rather than a search for general laws arising from studies of large samples or groups. Runyan (1982, p.152) states that case-study methodology can effectively portray the social and historical world that the person is living in. Yin argues that it can illuminate the causes (and meanings) of relevant events, experiences and conditions. Indeed, Campbell (1975, p.179) states that the case-study may be the only route to knowledge of human behaviour and experience, "noisy, fallible and biased though it may be".

Bromley (1990) argues that a case-study is concerned with a single slice/episode in the life course with a longer term approach being the life-history method. In contrast, Rosenthal (1993, p.61) argues that life story and life history are continuously and dialectically linked. They produce each other. Yin (1989, p.23) suggests that the case-study should be regarded as an empirical inquiry that: investigates a contemporary phenomenon within its real life context; when the boundaries between phenomenon and context are not clearly evident; and in which multiple sources of evidence are used. Further, case-studies may be exploratory, descriptive or explanatory, with a wide degree of overlap between these characteristics.

Case-study methods can be seen as solely qualitative in nature but Yin (1989) argues that case-studies can be based entirely on quantitative evidence. For example, this investigation could have used the experimental single case-study method which involves the establishment of baseline behaviours for informants, applying treatment and testing for post-treatment effects. Equally, computer assisted methods of content analysis might have been helpful in establishing changes that occurred throughout the series of interviews, with particular reference to the relationship between cognitive contents and the associated emotional reactions. Such an analysis would have generated quantitative measures and possibly revealed some sort of trend over time. Case-study methods, therefore, can incorporate both qualitative and quantitative measures. Runyan (1982) suggests that the structure of life history narrative can be explored from many different perspectives. Indeed, Yin argues that the case-study, as a research tool, is distinct from other research strategies and can be seen as a separate methodology with a clearly defined structure and having specified procedures.

Criticisms of the case-study method

Case-study methodology has a controversial history. Although widely used for many years in a variety of settings and disciplines, its value for scientific investigation has been questioned by Kratochwill (1978), Kazdin (1980), and Liebert and Spiegler (1978) among others. Such arguments see case-study methodology as non scientific and having a lack of rigorous methodology (Yin, 1989). Critics of case-study methodology, such as Kratochwill, have also suggested that it is an impressionistic and non-verifiable method. Further criticisms of case-study research include biased data. Case-studies may be reports on a single individual by another and, as Runyan (1982, p.151) suggests, can contain biased interpretations or inferences. However, Rosenthal (1966) and Yin point out that bias may also enter in experimental methodology.

Runyan (1982, p.124) suggests that case-studies are further perceived to have low internal and external validity. The single case-study provides little basis for generalisation. Yin (1989, p.21) argues that the criteria involved in the problem of generalisation within the single case-study method might also apply to a single experiment. He points out that scientific facts are normally based on a multiple set of experiments which have replicated the same phenomena under different conditions. This leads him to suggest that case-studies, like experiments, are generalisable to theoretical propositions, and not to populations or universes. In this sense, the case-study, like the experiment, is not representative of a `sample´. Moreover, the investigator's goal within a case-study, is to expand and generalise theories, not to calculate the number of particular occurrences. A further criticism of this approach is that it is all too easy to produce a bad case-study. The production of an exemplary case-study certainly requires the following of methodological procedures. However, it also requires insight and interpretation of human processes. Yin (1989) suggests that it is this insight which differentiates the exemplary case-study from those with a less discerning content.

General characteristics of good case-studies

Runyan (1982) suggests that it is necessary to consider methods which will improve case-study methodology. Yin (1989) posits five general characteristics of an exemplary case-study. Many of his concepts are included in the suggestions advocated by Bromley (1986). Bromley's guidelines are, however, more specific and give six rules for the preparation and writing of a psychological case-study. These rules are based on ten procedural points, concerned with ten kinds of information about the person. Bromley suggests the use of a quasi-judicial procedure in the preparation of this type of case-study. This allows the evidence, inferences and arguments to undergo a critical examination by others.

A case-study is, by its very nature, high in informative content and, as such, is high in the number of ways its conclusions can be shown to be unjustified. Popper (1980) argues that highly falsifiable statements/theories are also highly testable. Magee (1985) suggests that it is this testing of conjectures in an attempt to refute them, that leads to advance in science. This concept is not free of criticism. Baddeley (1992) argues that many concepts and models are fruitful, without being in the final analysis, testable. He points out that in the field of cognitive psychology it is often possible to generate many parallel interpretations of phenomena. In principle, each of these interpretations is testable, but the lack of adequate techniques does not allow the principles of falsification to be applied. Baddeley's comments, however, would appear to be more concerned with practicalities than refutation of principle.

It seems appropriate, therefore, to consider the concept of falsification in conjunction with the use of the information rich case-studies of this particular investigation. Throughout this particular study, the investigator acted as a researcher and as an interviewer. Hawker (1982) suggests that these roles both complete, but also compete. Further, it is in this presentation of results that the final interplay between the researcher and the interviewer occurs and encourages the reader to consider their validity. It is argued, therefore, that following Bromley's (1986, 1990) precepts, where possible, will allow a greater stringency, structure and internal coherence to this work and permit a strong scrutiny of the evidence and interpretations offered by the researcher.

The preparation of a psychological case-study

Bromley's six basic rules for the preparation of a psychological case-study suggested that all case-studies prepared for this investigation should be reported truthfully and accurately, with clear aims and objectives. They should also contain an evaluative element in which the extent of the achievement of the aims and objectives will be discussed. Bromley further suggests that if the inquiry deals with episodes of deep emotional significance to the person, then the investigator should be someone who is trained and equipped to establish and manage a fairly long and possibly difficult relationship. This was an important precept for this investigation as it was anticipated that the single case-studies would contain many memories of emotional events. Further, individual relationships with informants were to be of long duration. Fortunately, researcher background and previous training/qualifications met the needs of this guideline.

A further precept points to the importance of informants being understood in the context of their specific historical, social and symbolic world. Finally, Bromley suggests that this knowledge of the informants must be written in good plain English, as objectively and directly as possible without, however, losing human interest as a story. This task should be accomplished with sympathy and imagination, and with due regard for high standards of evidence and argument (Bromley, 1986, pp.24-5). This approach offers a more scientific approach to case-study methods. McAdams (1990, p.108) argues that scientists judge theories according to the criteria of comprehensiveness; parsimony; coherence; testability; empirical validity; usefulness and generativity. He suggests that if these criteria are adopted, then a good case-study should take into consideration a comprehensive body of case information; should be simple and straight forward; show internal coherence and consistency; provide hypotheses of human behaviour which is empirically testable; is in accord with documented valid empirical studies; is useful and generates new ideas. Runyan (1982) further suggests it is possible to have an evaluative case-study which would focus on assessment of the effects of treatment.

Case-study design applied to this investigation

Case-studies may be experimental or naturalistic, but all may have three foci. These foci are the assessment-formulation of the problem, either in terms of a current baseline and/or a reconstruction of its origin and course through life history; a description of the treatment processes, techniques used and of the interactions between client and therapist; or an assessment of the effects of treatment (Runyan, 1982, p.146). These focal points were the basis of all case-studies used in this study although emphasis varied. Points one and two were seen as more significant than point three. Runyan suggests that the difference between single case experimental designs and naturalistic case-studies is the relatively different emphasis within an array of possible goals. It is probable that no one category adequately describes the specific type of naturalistic case-study used during this investigation. The aims of this study and the broad based descriptors given by Yin (1989) suggests that the single case-studies pertaining to this investigation were both exploratory and descriptive. These case-studies are considered unlikely to be `explanatory´ due to the lack of knowledge surrounding the phenomena under investigation.

Advantages in the use of case-study methods

The advantages of the use of the case-study method in this investigation were many. The use of open-ended, informal interviews permitted a descriptive and exploratory approach. These interviews allowed the informants time to use as they wished and to choose any topic for discussion. There is some evidence provided by Mishler (1986) and Paget (1983) that client-led interviews, in which both the interviewer and interviewee work together in trying to understand important client life experiences, encourages searching, reflective and extended responses. Further, the longitudinal nature of this investigation meant that informants experienced the forming of new and stable relationships with myself. Over time, this new relationship was held in informants' memories, and allowed me to be greeted with warmth during my visits to the setting. This led to an increase in the informant's well-being and trust and enabled the generation of rich data.

A final consideration in the use of this method is that the presentation of this data, in the form of a narrative, allowed the informants to speak to a wide audience. Much of the clinical research with demented elderly people tends to focus on the negative aspects of this illness. The findings of such research tends to be presented as numerical tabulations of endured loss. The use of the informants' personal narrative in a single case-study permits sufferers of this illness to share their thoughts and feelings with others, to allow their listeners to marvel and wonder at their recollections of the past, rather than stress the fading of their cognitive abilities.

It is this sharing of emotional experiences, suggests Denzin (1989a) that leads to a greater understanding. Understanding is an interactional experience which requires the interpreter to enter into the experience of another. Denzin (1989b) further suggests that the relating of an experience to another is a self story, which places the self centrally in the narrative. Self stories are, therefore, personal narratives, or the person's story of his or her life. It is this concept of a life history told in the form of a story or narrative, which is worthy of further discussion.

The study of narrative

Telling stories about past events appears to be a universal human activity that begins early in life. White (1973) suggests that it is a method of making sense of experience, whether it be satirical, tragic, humorous or romantic. Denzin (1989b) argues that personal narratives are similar to oral histories, personal histories and case histories. They define one another only in terms of difference. The meanings of each spill over into the meanings of the other. Further, Denzin (1989b, p.28) suggests that stories of a life consist of two phenomena: lived experiences, and a person who is both a self conscious being and a named cultural creation. Bruner (1986) argues that the representation of experiences which form the narrative can be understood as a way in which realities of life present themselves to the consciousness of the human being. Personal experiences form part of a person's life story, but no self story ever stands alone but is always embedded in a cultural, ideological, and historical context (Denzin, 1989b). It is necessary, therefore, to have some understanding of these contextual issues in order to have greater understanding of a life. A hermeneutical approach aids this understanding of a life through an interpretation of the text of the narrative. Thus, Widdershoven (1993) indicates that the relationship between life and story can be characterised as interpretative.

As social constructionists, Wetherell and Maybin (1996, p.258) suggest that narratives are widely used to create and interpret the self in face to face interactions. Riessman (1993, p.5) argues that narratives are, therefore, essentially meaning making structures, which are constructed, creatively authored, rhetorical, replete with assumptions and interpretive. She suggests that interpretations are inevitable because narratives are representations. Further, Riessman points out that investigators, themselves, have only indirect access to informant's experiences through ambiguous representations of talk, text, interaction and interpretation. The narrator tells his or her story through the filters of language, para-language and significance of meaning. The story is, according to Merleau-Ponty (1964, p.119) a representation of facts and the description of facticities, or how these facts were lived and experienced by interacting individuals.

Riessman suggests that the idea of representing experience in the research process may be perceived as a series of transformations which begins with the primary experience itself. During this investigation it was expected that an informant would narrate some past meaningful event. According to levels of cognitive impairment, the informant then selectively recalled the experience (attending). This is the first level of representation which is followed by the second level, that of narrating the story (telling). This, again, depended on informants' levels of cognitive impairment and/or the levels of desired disclosure. The narrative is inevitably a self representation (Goffman, 1959). For all of us, there is an unavoidable gap between the lived experience and the telling of it. Mishler (1986) suggests that the researcher will often influence the form and content of the narrative, through the process of interaction. Further, Helling (1988, p.235) points out that the interview text is, itself, an interactive product, even before it is read and analysed.

The next stage of the research process is the transcribing of the conversation from the taped interview (transcribing). Again this involves representation of the conversation into text, which is an interpretive process. There were times, in this investigation, when it was difficult to understand informants' words. It was often impossible to understand confabulated sentences and it was necessary to indicate in the text where I failed to understand informants' speech.

The fourth level of representation is the evaluation of the transcribed text (analysing). It is at this stage that the researcher endeavours to impart a sense of coherence to the whole. Developing theory must support and be supported by the narratives of informants. As Denzin (1989b, p.81) argues, our texts must always return to and reflect the words persons speak, as they attempt to give meaning and shape to the lives they lead. The narrative must also fit the requirements of the written document. It is this sense of editing that creates a false document, as it is represented in a different format to the original (Behar, 1993).

The fifth and final level of representation occurs when the reader encounters the written report of the investigation (reading). Again, the reading of the text is, according to Riessman (1993, p.15), open to varied interpretations. Meaning is ambiguous because it arises out of a process of interaction between people: self, teller, listener, analyst and reader. Meaning is fluid and contextual, not fixed or universal. All we have, suggests Riessman, is talk and texts that represent reality, partially, selectively and imperfectly. It is this discussion of representation that gives some understanding of the problematic nature of narrative truth. Narratives are interpretive and, in turn, require interpretation. Stivers (1993, p.424) argues that analytic interpretations are partial, alternative truths that aim for believability, not certitude, for enlargement of understanding rather than control.

Denzin (1989b) describes a truthful narrative as one that is faithful to facticities and facts. Denzin (1989b) together with Freeman (1993) argue that a truthful narrative creates believable experiences for the reader, who reads the text through his or her own life. Schafer (1981) and Spence (1982) suggest that the interpretation of texts and single cases aim for narrative truth. Spence (1982) suggests that this is attained by interpretations which are internally coherent; have a continuous structure in which early events logically relate to later occurrences; embody closure or a sense of things fitting into a final form; and finally, are aesthetically pleasing. Riessman (1993) contends that validation of the narrative rests on the concept of trustworthiness. It is this concept that moves the process of validation into the social world. Riessman gives four criteria that can be used to validate a narrative analysis. The first criterion is that of persuasiveness which is related to plausibility. This enables the reader of the narrative to perceive it as reasonable and convincing, when theoretical claims are supported by evidence from informants' accounts of their lives. However, the literary and interpretative skills of the researcher may unduly influence the reader. Texts, suggests Riessman (1993, p.66), have unstable meanings and that the written report can be verified by those who have given an account of their lives. This would appear to be desirable where possible. However, in the case of this investigation it was not practical due to most informants' poor short term memory. Indeed, Riessman maintains that human stories are not static, meanings change. In the final analysis, it is the researcher who is responsible for the truths of the narrative.

A third criterion, that of coherence, assumes that the coherence can be considered to consist of three types: global; local; and themal. Global coherence refers to the overall goals of the narrator. Local coherence stresses the way in which the narrator links events within the narrative. Themal coherence is concerned with content, the themes of the narrative. Agar and Hobb (1982) suggest that if discourse can be shown to be understood in terms of the three kinds of coherence, then the interpretation is strengthened. However, Riessman argues that these concepts of coherence are difficult to apply to all investigations. Finally, she posits a future validation criterion, that of acceptance by the scientific community. This does not, however, aid the researcher's argument for validation prior to this acceptance. The problem of validating the narrative cannot, therefore, include a set of formal rules or standardised technical procedures. There is, she suggests, no canonical approach in interpretive work.

This discussion of theoretical considerations for the validation of narrative analysis suggests, therefore, that an unambiguous adherence to the text should minimise false representation. The present investigation was a longitudinal story of individual experiences and the emotionally meaningful memories of informants. Allowing informants to tell their own stories, to be the authors of the text, permitted a more authentic interpretation of their meanings. A repetition of these stories, over the life of the investigation, strengthened verisimilitude or plausibility. In many ways, repetition of these memories suggested that the authors of the text `agree´ that these accounts are meaningful and contain a global and thematic coherence. The criterion of local coherence, which permits the use of linguistic devices to relate events to one another, is not too easily met in this study. Some informants did not easily link events in order to give their stories a further and deeper meaning. According to Denzin (1989b), the primary obligation in the presentation of any narrative is always to the people whose stories we study, not to the project or larger discipline. The stories that are given to the investigator to share with others are testimonies to our human ability to endure, to prevail and to survive. Denzin (1989a) argues that narratives should establish the significance of an experience. The voices, feelings, actions and meanings of interacting individuals should be heard.

As with the pilot study, it was envisaged that these characteristics of interacting individuals would be more easily observed in an individual interview situation. These interviews, then, were unstructured in an effort to allow informants more freedom in recalling their own personal narrative, with the assistance of interviewer counselling skills. As the introduction to this work discussed, the generation of rich data rested heavily on the relationship between myself and the informants. However, the informal interview format appeared to enhance both the development of relationships and generation of data.

Description of informal interview format used during this investigation

Most interviews in this investigation were recorded on a small, powerful, battery controlled and unobtrusive audio-cassette recorder. This method of data collection is perceived by Hammersley and

Atkinson (1983) as reducing reactivity. Further, the previous study had shown that some informants could not sit still for any length of time and would wander through the setting. This method of recording allowed me to wander with them and even use it as we walked in the grounds together. I frequently played back a portion of the tape at the closure of an interview, so that informants could hear themselves speak. Without exception, it made them laugh. I had considered videoing interviews, but I decided that it was inappropriate because of the aforementioned reason. Ethically, it was also unappealing for me. I felt that in earlier years many informants might have found it objectionable. I also felt it was too obtrusive and the setting did not readily lend itself to this method of data collection. Clients who visited the setting would often wander into rooms when the interviews were taking place. It was always simple to switch off the audio-cassette recorder without too much disruption. It would have been far more difficult to do this with video equipment. It was also ethically important to remember that I had been given permission to interview selected informants but not others.

Prior to the commencement of any interviews, informants were always asked if they would like to talk to me. After agreement had been reached, they were then asked if they would like to go somewhere quiet, or stay in the main day room with other clients. Most informants chose to go into the small quiet lounge or the empty dining room. Sometimes, if other rooms were occupied, we used the staff room if it was free. Interviews that took place on a one to one basis, in quiet surroundings, always yielded more significant data. The interviews themselves began with a brief `warming up´ period and, similarly, a short closing session on completion of interview. All interviews were informal and open ended. There were no set questions.

As with the pilot study, some knowledge of the informant's past life experiences was of significant importance during the interviews. This knowledge permitted me to locate past experiences in the `here and now´, especially during seemingly confabulated talk. Most relatives and staff gave descriptions of informant's past life experiences and provided cues and prompts in the form of photographs. One informant's wife actually provided a short account of their life together, complete with pictures of houses, family and friends. Interviewer knowledge of the informant's past, was the primary resource used during this investigation. The opening remarks from an informant would often dictate the content and flow of the conversation. If informants did not provide cues, then I introduced a significant topic from their past. This was usually concerned with their childhood. This was often provided by the informants themselves during a previous interview, but was occasionally supplemented by an interview with relatives and/or staff in the setting.

The main counselling techniques used were exploratory questions, with the use of attentive and active listening. The use of advanced accurate empathy, building on primary level empathy, also formed part of these techniques. Egan (1975) suggests that primary level empathy focuses on relevant surface feelings and meanings. Advanced accurate empathy is an interpretative response which focuses on feelings and meanings that are somehow buried, hidden, or beyond the client's immediate reach. Other counselling techniques used were respect, non judgmental probes and stance. I consciously used an appropriate tone, pitch and rate of speech for individual informants and the topic under discussion and this appeared to aid informant response. Nelson-Jones (1993) argues that the voice message frames the verbal message and all research interviews are `conversations with a purpose´ (Berg, 1989; Bingham and Moore, 1959). The use of appropriate interviewer skills aids the `purpose´ or the collection of data.

Chernitz (1986) argues that qualitative informal interviews require the researcher to possess interpersonal skills that facilitate the easy flow of conversation. Lofland and Lofland (1984) further suggest that effective interviewing techniques contain such skills as careful listening, observing, ensuring absence of threat and respect for the informant. I tried to adhere to these precepts and practice these skills during all interviews with the informants, relatives and staff in the setting. The length of the interviews depended on informants. If they were tired or uninterested, interviews would be short and might only last for ten minutes. If informants were enjoying the process, then the interviews would be longer and might take up to an hour. There were a few informants who were reluctant to let me go.

Analysis of data

All recorded interviews were transcribed. This was an arduous task as these transcribed interviews produced nearly seven hundred and fifty pages of text. Another difficulty was that some informants had severe speech defects, combined with confabulated speech. The meaning, however, was usually very clear. In spite of the time consuming nature of the task, there were many benefits to this method. It was often easier to understand the complete `message´ as I transcribed data. It was also possible to actually hear what they were saying. Some informants spoke very quietly, but I could adjust the volume as I listened to their recorded voices alone.

I frequently experienced feelings of amazement as I transcribed their words. Often I had `intuitively´ grasped the meaning of their message, even though I had misunderstood words and sentences. Equally, I felt quite de-skilled when I heard myself give inappropriate responses in some situations. Berg (1989) however, would disagree with this concept of intuition. He argues that interviewer skills are not based on intuition or insight. They are based on the interviewer's ability to respond appropriately to cues and prompts in a `drama´. In this drama the interviewer performs the roles of actor, choreographer and director. He suggests that these skills are used in a self conscious social performance, that allows informants to feel comfortable in the interview situation. As an actor learns a role, so too will the interviewer learn these skills.

I did feel that the interviews with informants were `conversations with a purpose´ but I rarely felt `in command´ of the interview situation. I perceived my own role to be of lesser status than that of a director or choreographer. It was normally the informants who controlled events. I felt as if I had been given special permission to accompany someone on a journey. I was permitted to share the mundane and meaningful experiences of this journey. I was not permitted, however, to choose our destination. This deductive stance, possibly enhanced the richness of data. Analysis of this data generated by the interviews, allowed for a number of qualitative methods of analysis (Banister et al., 1995). One such approach was that of content analysis, which is a method of handling narrative, qualitative material. Content analysis, however, has some disadvantages. It is a very time consuming method with some risk of subjectivity.

Another possible method was that of analytic induction. This method has several similarities to that of grounded theory. It has, however, some important differences. Analytic induction is concerned with the testing of inductively derived hypotheses. The grounded theory method is concerned with the generation of categories, properties, and hypotheses, rather than testing them. Other researchers concerned with the analysis of transcribed interviews from single case-studies have also used grounded theory methods for data analysis. One such researcher has written of the value of grounded theory to psychological research (Rennie and Brewer, 1987; Rennie et al., 1988). Rennie commented that it was the sheer amount of generated data that drew him and his colleagues towards qualitative methods. Further, his study, although larger than this present investigation, was concerned with client's representation of experience in a psychotherapeutic relationship (Rennie, 1992). There were several similarities between his reported account and this present inquiry. Both were client led, were concerned with the narrative and with the use of psychotherapeutic interventions.

Rosenthal (1993) also used the basis of this method in her interpretation of the life of a former member of the Hitler Youth organisation. This particular study is interesting in that the recorded interviews were transcribed in their entirety, word for word with no respect for the rules of written language. Again, this was a procedure which was largely adopted during the transcribing of interviews for this investigation. Rosenthal perceives the narrated life story as a sequence of mutually interrelated themes. These themes between them form a dense network of interconnected cross references. A global analysis of all interviews was undertaken according to the model of theoretical sampling found in grounded theory methods. Her study focused on the in-depth interpretation of one case-study. Rennie's (1992) inquiry is concerned with fourteen informants. This investigation has a sample of eight informants. Grounded theory, therefore, appeared to be an appropriate method for the analysis of data generated from the transcribed interviews in this investigation.

Grounded theory

Grounded theory, according to Glaser and Strauss (1967), is the discovery of theory from data. It is a systematic method of developing theory that is `grounded´ in the phenomenon under investigation. One of the fundamental features of this approach is that data collection and data analysis occur simultaneously. Hutchinson (1986) suggests that the method is circular, allowing the researcher to change focus and pursue leads revealed by the ongoing data analysis. Noerager Stern (1980) argues that grounded theory can also be described as a form of field methodology, which aims to generate theoretical constructs, which explain the action in the social context under study. According to Tesch (1991), a single research project does not produce an entire social theory, but it can develop a set of theoretical propositions. Strauss (1987) argues that it is this construction of theory which produces concepts which seem to fit the data. Noerager Stern (1980) further suggests that grounded theory is especially useful in areas which have been the subject of little research, as is this investigation. It is obvious that where no theory exists then no theory can be tested. It is also argued that this particular methodology can give a fresh perspective in a familiar situation. Hawker (1982) argues that it would appear to be of particular use when applied to data obtained from semi-structured or unstructured interviews.

During this investigation, data from each set of informant's transcribed interviews were compared and conceptualised in terms of commonalities. Each piece of data was examined and coded. Coding took place in three stages. The first stage was that of open coding, or level one. Level one coding was concerned with the generation of as many codes as possible in order to insure full theoretical coverage. Level one coding broke the data into small pieces, whereas levels two and three refined the data to more theoretical levels. In this investigation, the data from each interview was broken and coded into themes. Each theme then generated more codes, with `the constant comparison´ of data allowing the grouping together of similar concepts. Indeed, grounded theory is often thought of as the `constant comparison method´ (Glaser and Strauss, 1967).

Level two coding or categorisation saw some level one codes subsumed into a larger category. Decisions about categories are reached by constant scrutiny of similarities between incidents. Finally, the emerging categories are compared to ensure mutual exclusiveness and cover the behavioural variations. Level three codes or theoretical constructs are a combination of academic and clinical knowledge. Hutchinson (1986) suggests that these constructs create theoretical meaning and scope to the theory, by conceptualising the relationship between the three levels of codes. The conceptual tasks involved in the analytic component of this investigation involved the reading and re-reading of all transcribed interviews.

Glaser and Strauss (1967) argue that it is these reflective periods which allow the researcher `time out´ from data collection and permit the uninterrupted consideration of the field experience. Further, it allows the researcher to reflect systematically about the data in accordance with basic analytical categories and to consider the interplay between the two. The properties from identified categories in this investigation were defined and individual categories were then written on small colour coded cards. The collected data was coded and categorised as coded data that seem to cluster together in recognisable concepts (Hawker, 1982; Noerager Stern, 1980). The categories elicited from the data were constantly compared to data obtained earlier in the data collection, so that commonalities and variations were determined. Most individual interviews from this investigation were transcribed shortly after recording and before I entered the setting again. I was, therefore, highly sensitised to the emotional responses surrounding informants' themes. This made it possible to reintroduce a meaningful theme with individual informants and, if appropriate, to cross check this with other informants.

As the data collection proceeded, the inquiry became increasingly focused on theoretical concerns. Main categories or variables began to emerge to undergo constant comparison with all other data, and to see if they were central to the emerging theory. This process of selective sampling is deductive but also inductive. Noerager Stern (1980) suggests that it seeks not only to prove or disprove the importance of categories, but also to study in depth the properties and dimensions of these categories. Lofland and Lofland (1984) and Tesch (1991) further suggest that these categories may be compared to the conceptual equivalent of file folders, for they serve to organise pieces of data. Selective sampling led to the saturation of categories which occurred when nothing new concerning identified categories was discovered. It is at this point that categories began to be collapsed. For instance, there were several categories relating to memory, but it became apparent that only two categories were significant. This was the categories of semantic and autobiographical memory. Finally, it was recognised that only the category of autobiographical memory was significant, in terms of this investigation. This was confirmed by the literature (Conway, 1990). He suggests that the importance of semantic memory is less significant in autobiographical recall.

This process of reduction enabled the integration of the categories into possible core categories (Glaser and Strauss, 1967). The identification of a core category or categories imposed a responsibility on the part of the investigator to verify the significance of the core category through the assistance of an authoritative figure in the field. Verification for this part of the investigation was sought and obtained from two psychologists and from three accredited counsellors. Ongoing with the discovery and identification of the core category was the memoing and theoretical coding (the thinking of descriptive coding in theoretical terms of data). Strauss and Corbin (1990) suggest that memos are the written records of analysis related to the formulation of theory. They are kept separately from documentation concerned with categories. Thus, memoing is the writing down of any idea that seems connected with the data. Ideas were therefore grounded in data. Memos themselves, argue Strauss and Corbin (1990) hold the key to order.

The sorting of memos is a vital part in the analytical process. The reading, rereading and sorting of memos allowed a descriptive story to be written. This descriptive story was then translated into analytical concepts. According to Hutchinson (1986) it is the discovery of a core category or variable which is an essential requirement for a quality grounded theory. This requires continuous reference to the data, combined with rigorous analytic thinking. The core category possesses three characteristics: it occurs frequently in the data, it links the various data together and it explains much of the variation in the data. It was this category that became the basis for the generation of theory during this investigation.

Strauss and Corbin (1990, p.121) suggest that each study should possess only one core category in order to achieve the tight integration and the dense development of categories required of a grounded theory. Further, Glaser and Strauss (1967) argue that the investigator should possess theoretical sensitivity, which will permit the conceptualisation and formulation of theory as it emerges from the data. Constant immersion in the data allowed me to have some theoretical insight into the particular area of research and to perceive links with existing theory (Glaser and Strauss, 1967).

Hutchinson (1986, p.126) indicates that the process of grounded theory is not easy for the investigator "who experiences alternating periods of confusion and enlightenment". It is not an orderly linear process. There is a possibility that small samples can become even smaller. This is especially true of research into people with incurable illness, as in this present investigation. No informant died during the main period of the investigation, but it was an ever present possibility that this would happen. The investigator using this method, learns to live and work with uncertainty. The investigator can also feel in the midst of total chaos as the investigation, memoing and categorising of data simultaneously proceed. The use of grounded theory produces a great mass of information which must be organised. The advantages of the method for this investigation were many. The use of grounded theory was instrumental in the discovery that all of the elderly people with dementia who took part in this investigation possessed a significant number of `very old´ emotional memories. Thus this method enabled the investigation to focus on specific categories of dominance and to indicate new areas of potential research.

After the sessions were completed, the tape was dated and indexed to show the names of all recorded informants. All interviews were transcribed onto cards that were part of a card index file, with each informant having a card containing personal information such as name, date of birth, date of admittance to setting, next of kin and primary nurse. All recorded interviews were transcribed as discussed previously. All significant data found in the text of transcribed interviews were transcribed onto cards under appropriate headings. The text, or transcribed discussions between myself and the informants, was the sole source of data used for analysis.

Memo cards for each interview were also developed as each interview was analysed. Each interview memo card was numbered with the initials of informant, number and date of the interview. They contained an overview of the interview and the ideas that seemed to be connected with the data. Appropriate headings or categories also developed as the interviews progressed. Analysis and constant comparison of interview content allowed the development of these headings or categories, which were then transcribed on colour coded cards. Each card, as for the memo cards, was numbered and included the informant's initials, number and date of the interview.

The final categories were themes, significant others, significant events, emotions and feelings, general memory, autobiographical memory and semantic memory. These categories may appear to be rather limited, but it must be remembered that the area under study was that of informants' emotional memories. It was necessary, therefore, to have broad sweeping categories that would include any type of emotional memory. Perhaps the most broad sweeping category of all was that of `themes´. This category acted as a base or lower order category (Rennie, 1992) whose properties formed part of all other categories.

The concept of `a significant other´ comes from the work of Mead (1934) whose contribution to the theory of Symbolic Interactionism led him to see the growth of personality as directly attributable to the responses of significant/generalised others. Symbolic Interactionists argue that we can only know our own self, our social identity, through the responses of others. Significant others, therefore, appeared to be a highly meaningful category for this investigation. It was not until the process of data analysis was quite advanced that I had some theoretical understanding of this category. Although each informant had a varying number of `significant others´ in memory, the most significant person mentioned was that of the self. All autobiographical memories, as indicated by the literature, were highly self referent. Again, this category became a base category which generated a more significant category, that of self.

The nature of this investigation gave importance to the category of emotion and feeling, and to the categories concerned with memory. As the analysis of data progressed, categories were reduced and others expanded. The category of general memory was abandoned as it became obvious that this was repeated in the category of autobiographical memory. It was also repeated in varying degrees within the category of semantic memory. This was also true of the category of significant events. As the investigation advanced, the category of semantic memory and significant events shrank, but the category of autobiographical memory grew in importance. A further category emerged from the reduction and expansion of these categories. This was the category of self stories or personal narratives of informants, related to meaningful and emotional life events. It was this category that possessed the three characteristics of a core category. It occurred frequently in the data, it linked the various data together and it explained much of the variation in the data. It was this core category that was felt to hold significance for the questions posed by this investigation. The analysis of data from this investigation commenced from the beginning of this work in April 1992, with the recording and transcribing of interviews. It continued until the end of the investigation in January 1994 and included further interviews with informants to test generated theory.

Presentation of data analysis

The question of how to present the findings of any investigation requires considerable thought and this investigation was no exception. The decision to use single case-study methods was made in order to allow each informant to tell his/her story or personal narrative to others. Further, the following of specific rules enables the reader of the case-study to be able to enter the `world of the other´. However, there was some danger that the voices of informants could be muffled by the amount of background information needed to meet the demands of these precepts. In addition, analysis of the data had indicated a number of significant categories. From these categories emerged the core category which was grounded in the generated data. Again, it was necessary to clearly indicate the contextual emergence of these concepts. Consideration of these points suggested that each case-study might form a single chapter of this work. However, the total word length made this an impractical suggestion. The findings, therefore, are presented as a critical comparison of all case-studies, using second order analysis.

Ethical considerations in the use of qualitative methods

Banister et al. (1995), Berg (1989), among others, argue that the use of qualitative methods requires the investigator to consider such ethical issues as informed consent and confidentiality. The issue of informed consent may be difficult as in the case of this investigation. Informed consent was obtained from the professional and relatives of the informants and implied consent by the informants themselves. Privacy of the setting and informants must be maintained by the use of pseudonyms, as was the case in this investigation. In all qualitative research it is the expected duty of the investigator to ensure a high degree of confidentiality. Another possible source of difficulty may be that the nature of the investigation could lead to overdisclosure by the participants. The investigator must then decide if it is ethical to include these views in the written work. If it is not, then they must be excluded. This was the policy adopted during this investigation. The ethical considerations for each piece of qualitative research must be considered in great depth. Ethically, each situation is different and must be viewed as a separate issue. The question of ethical considerations in the use of qualitative research places an individual burden of responsibility on all researchers. In many instances, it is often the researcher who alone must define what is ethical in research (Berg, 1989).

Ethical considerations for this investigation

Permission for this investigation to take place was sought from a variety of sources. Permission was sought and granted from the local Ethical Committee for Research. Permission was also sought and granted from the Clinical Services Manager (Elderly) for the investigation to take place in the hospital. An interview took place with the hospital Consultant Psychogeriatrician in which details of the investigation, including the methodology, were discussed. The Consultant Psychogeriatrician gave permission for his patients to be used in the investigation. There was a further meeting in March 1992 with the senior charge nurse of the setting. During this meeting the investigation was again discussed in some depth. Proposed informants suitable for the study were discussed at length, including the most appropriate days and times for the research to take place.

Permission was also sought from the proposed eight informants. I was introduced to three of them informally during this first visit to the setting. During this meeting they were asked if they would like someone to talk to them about their past lives on a regular basis. All agreed. It was felt that if they did not wish to take part then this would become quickly apparent during the course of the interviews. Following the initial meeting with the senior charge nurse in the setting, it was agreed that I should write a general letter explaining the purposes of the investigation. This was pinned on the notice board in the setting for all to see. It was further agreed that I would write to each of the informant's relatives explaining the purpose of the investigation and asking permission for their relatives to take part. All gave their permission and expressed interest in the project. As with the pilot investigation, they indicated that they felt it would be beneficial for informants to take part. Relative co-operation was very high, a fact that has been discovered in other health care settings (Hawker, 1982). As these permissions were given, I returned to the setting at various times throughout March/April 1992 to meet the remaining informants who agreed to take part in the study. Interviews began in April 1992.

After some months into the investigation, another man began to attend the setting. He was frequently in tears and seemed to be very unhappy. He often wanted to talk to me. I approached the senior charge nurse to discuss the advisability of including this man in the study and he felt that it would be appropriate. I wrote to the elderly man's wife for the necessary permission. After discussion with the charge nurse and myself she gave her permission for her husband to take part. By this time one of the informants had left the investigation as it was felt to be too much for her. She was aged ninety-five years and became quickly tired during the interview process. Finally, it must be noted that all members of the Health Service and informants' relatives were extremely friendly, helpful and cooperative throughout this investigation.

The sample

The investigation used a small group of eight elderly people, with moderate to severe medically diagnosed dementia. The decision to use eight informants was not fixed at the commencement of the investigation as I was unsure of how many informants would be manageable. As the number of informants grew to eight, it was felt that this was an appropriate number for the investigation and for myself. The initial group comprised of three females and five males, the final group of two females and six males. They were selected from the forty clients who attended the setting, from between one and five days per week. Of these forty clients, twenty-one were men and nineteen were women. This ratio constantly changed throughout the investigation as clients left the setting to move into long term care, or died and new clients took their place.

Although the group consisted of more males than females, the uneven balance between male and female informants was co-incidental. The initial selection of informants was made by the senior charge nurse of the setting. This also reduced the possibility of bias on behalf of the researcher. The basis of selection was that they could respond verbally to questioning, could speak about their past life and that they would enjoy one to one interaction with the investigator. The senior charge nurse said that there were other participants for the investigation if there proved to be any difficulties with those he had selected. He was concerned that two informants who had quite severe speech impediments might not be suitable. After some discussion we decided to include these two informants as it was felt that they would benefit from the experience. Further, all informants presented very differently. They had different personalities, interests and varying symptoms of dementia. They appeared to be an interesting group of people. As is indicated in the previous discussion of this section, pseudonyms are used throughout this report.

These people were: Mr Robert Biddley; Mrs Agnes Charlton; Mr Charles Clerkenwell; Mr Andrew Coxley; Mrs Bessie Pinks; Mr Melvin Rider; Mr Ronnie Silverthorne and Mrs Abigail Woodley. These people attended a psychogeriatric day care hospital situated in the grounds of a local psychiatric hospital. All informants attended the setting at least two days per week. After some weeks and three interviews, Mrs Agnes Charlton retired from the investigation. Her place was taken by Mr Hugh Raft. Of these eight informants, seven were selected by the senior charge nurse and one, Mr Hugh Raft, by myself. The following chapter contains more detailed information on each informant, together with the setting.

Procedures

The nursing staff were asked to provide description of procedures used in the setting. I was particularly asked to avoid disrupting organised group activities. The interviews, therefore, took place prior to, or after, these events. Staff were also asked to describe individual informants' personality, mood and behaviour prior to the investigation. Nursing staff were also interviewed regularly to comment on any change in mood and behaviour during the process of the investigation.

All relatives, or key people such as social workers with an in-depth knowledge of informants, were interviewed. This allowed me to explain the purpose of the investigation and to define my role as a researcher. Some relatives felt in some undefined way that I was part of the Health Service and as such had access to resources. The main purpose of these interviews however, was to gather biographical knowledge of informants and to seek for possibly meaningful events in their lives which could be used for prompts and cues during the interview process. Interviews with informants' relatives tended to last for about two hours, although some were longer. Relatives were also contacted at regular intervals throughout the investigation, to discuss any observed changes in behaviour of informants and for general comments on the investigative process.

The collection of data from informants took place through a series of regular interviews, usually on a weekly basis although occasionally more frequently. Sometimes the timespan was longer due to illness or absence of informants from the setting. On some occasions, informants did not want to talk to me. Initially, the interviews took place in the afternoon, when I was less likely to upset the routines of the setting. This, however, proved difficult as informants were very tired by this time and were often too anxious to enjoy the interview process. I discussed this with the senior charge nurse who agreed that the interviews could take place in the morning, prior to most group activities. The interviews then took place between 9 am and 10.30 am. This meant that my visits to the setting became more frequent, approximately three to four times each week. Although this was time consuming it did mean that informants began to remember me and to greet me with pleasure.

I had learnt during the pilot investigation that the length of the interviews would depend on how the informant was feeling on that day. Consequently no set time was given to individual interviews. My first visit to the setting was for an informal meeting with the informants and ward staff. These conversations were not recorded or transcribed although I took notes of the setting and informants for general use. There was eventually a total of one hundred and forty-one recorded and transcribed interviews. These varied in length from approximately ten minutes to one hour. There were fourteen recorded and transcribed interviews with Mr Robert Biddley, seventeen with Mr Charles Clerkenwell, fifteen with Mr Andrew Coxley, nineteen with Mrs Bessie Pinks, thirteen with Mr Hugh Raft, sixteen with Mr Melvin Rider, twenty-two with Mr Ronnie Silverthorne and twenty-five with Mrs Abigail Woodley.

Interviews with informants commenced in April 1992 and continued until December 1993. Three informants, however, were seen for a final interview in January 1994. During this period, two residents died, two were moved into a private sector psychogeriatric nursing home, one was in the assessment ward of the setting waiting for a vacancy in a suitable residential home and one became an in-patient of a long term psychogeriatric hospital. At the time of writing, three remain living in a psychogeriatric nursing home.

Conclusion

It is evident that the description of the methodologies used during this investigation is based on relationships. This is, of course, true of all research methods, but has a deeper significance when focused on the relational aspects of naturalistic investigations. The instigator and `holder´ of these many relationships is the researcher alone. This is possibly one of the many reasons for the scarcity of research in the field of emotions, memory and dementia. There is a heavy emotional burden placed on the researcher by this type of research and use of these particular methods of data collection. Bromley (1986) argues that case-studies in general should not be undertaken by unqualified investigators. Yin (1989) also maintains that case-study methods are extremely difficult to do well, due to the levels of skills needed by the researcher.

These relationships are concerned with instigation (getting in) maintenance (staying in) and endings (getting out). But it is more than this, because the researcher not only has a duty to maximise his or her data collection, but should minimise any possibility of negative impact in the field situation. This was not accomplished without some difficulties because the relationships that I formed in the field were many and varied. The prime relationships were, of course, those with the informants, but other relationships were important. These included the hospital administrators, both individually and in groups. They also incorporated the nursing staff, again, both individually and as a team. Other professionals such as unit managers, social workers and care staff were also involved. I was also concerned with relatives as individuals and their own relationships with informants. Relationships were also implicit in my dealings with other clients in the settings for wherever I went, I spent time with other `non informants´ who wanted to talk to me. For the length of this investigation it was found to be necessary to keep a great many people happy, without compromising data collection. This relational aspect is also reflected in the method of data presentation and analysis, for what is the single case-study method if not a story of a relationship? What is grounded theory if not an analytic method concerned with clusters of relational data? It is, however, the personal aspect of `relational methodology´ that is perhaps underdefined and undervalued in descriptive studies. It is important to state that the quality of relationships enjoyed by the researcher and others had some bearing on the quality of data generated by this investigation. The degree of `researcher personal skills´ therefore, has great bearing on qualitative studies that involve relational research. Chernitz (1986), Hawker (1982), and Lofland and Lofland (1984) indicate that these skills are notoriously difficult to describe. Nelson-Jones (1993), however, suggests a number of helper attributes, applicable to the counselling relationship, that might be perceived as being a valued part of the researchers' skills. These are altruism; humanism; intellectual curiosity; worked-through emotional pain; commitment to competence and people orientation. This latter attribute is concerned with Holland's (1973) taxonomy of personality or profiles of personality types. It is this social personality type which predominates in the profiles of counsellors. The characteristics of this profile suggest that they might well predominate in the personality profiles of researchers engaged in naturalistic inquiries.

This is not to suggest that I felt in command of this immense repertoire of skills, but rather had some knowledge of their existence. Indeed, I was often made aware through practice and the literature (Sinason, 1992; Sutton, 1997) of my many shortcomings. However, these skills, even partially grasped, appear to influence the outcomes of any naturalistic studies. They form part of the methods used for this particular investigation which have been discussed throughout this chapter. These methodologies have been scrutinised in some depth in order to establish their suitability for the task.

There will be further opportunities to study the contextual and relational aspects of this work during the next chapter which is concerned with the informants and the various settings visited during the period of research. Ensuing chapters concerned with the findings from this investigation will indicate the relationship or `fit´ between proposed theoretical considerations and the generated data from this inquiry. The interpretation of these findings, through the combined use of case-study methods and that of grounded theory methodology, should allow critical considerations of their validity.

4 The settings and the sample

Introduction

The main setting used in the investigation was a psychiatric hospital situated near the centre of a small town which cares for all adults with mental health problems. At present there are three wards that specifically care for older people, the Roycroft Assessment Unit, Willow ward and Rosewood Annex. There is also a psychogeriatric day hospital, The Mary Walker day hospital. Although informants were seen at different times in these and other settings, such as nursing and residential homes, it was the day hospital which acted as the main setting for this investigation.

The settings

The day hospital is a single storey detached building whose large windows allow views of the grounds and other hospital buildings. It is built in the shape of a double `L´ with the main rooms sited at each end of the structure. (See Figure 4.1.) The building was opened ten years ago and client needs have changed during this time. Staff in the setting, however, felt that the building largely met client needs. They saw the importance of the friendly `homely´ atmosphere provided by the staff team as overcoming any inadequacies in the environment. The setting can accept a maximum of twenty-five clients per day with a total client population of forty. Clients attend between one and five days per week from Monday to Friday between 8.30am and 4.30pm. Referrals are instigated by the consultant, social workers and community psychiatric nurses.

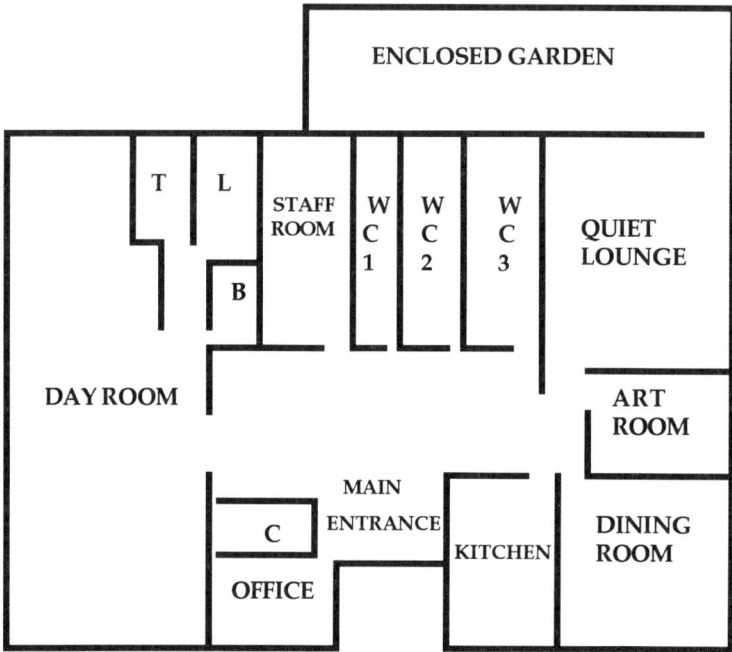

| | | | | ENCLOSED GARDEN | | | | |

DAY ROOM

T   L

STAFF ROOM

W C 1

W C 2

W C 3

QUIET LOUNGE

B

ART ROOM

MAIN ENTRANCE

C

OFFICE

KITCHEN

DINING ROOM

T = TREATMENT ROOM
L = LAUNDRY ROOM
B = BATHROOM
C = COAT CUPBOARD

WC1 = STAFF WC
WC2 = WOMEN'S WC
WC3 = MEN'S WC

Figure 4.1 The Mary Walker Day Hospital

During the investigation there was a team of six staff, the senior charge nurse, two qualified nurses, two nursing auxiliaries and one part time occupational therapist. Minimum staffing levels require at least four nursing staff, one of whom must be qualified.

Each day began with one member of staff reading the newspaper to the client group, with news items discussed according to client interest. There was a large board on the main wall of the day room containing a large calender, together with a description of the weather. A lunch menu was also displayed. Each day, two or three more structured group activities took place. These activities consisted of art work, pottery, cooking and various discussion groups which focused on a specific theme such as gardening. The setting presented as a warm lively and friendly place. All visitors were made welcome by all staff who displayed attitudes of kindness and humour, no matter how busy they appeared. Often on entering the setting I would see clients sitting in the office, or with staff during their breaks. I was given permission to use any unoccupied room, but occasionally the venue was dictated by client's poor mobility. The quiet lounge or the dining room were some distance from the day room. Equally, if they were unable to settle, we would pace the main corridor together.

Description of other settings

Two clients entered the same nursing home during the latter course of this investigation. This was a large psychogeriatric nursing home with a purpose built wing for those who were severely demented. It was situated in large grounds, some miles from the nearest town. Another client was moved, at his own request, to day care at a local authority home for the elderly. I visited this setting for some months at weekly intervals. I found all staff helpful and friendly.

The informants

All informants, bar one unmarried male, lived with their spouses in the community. He lived in a local authority home for the elderly. Background information about informants came from social workers, friends or colleagues but, as would be expected, mainly from close kin. The results of the various cognitive and behavioural tests came from informants' hospital notes. Although many of the informants were taking some form of psychotropic medication, it was decided not to include this information as their drugs regime underwent a number of changes throughout the series of interviews. It must be acknowledged, however, that psychotropic drugs will have an effect on mood and recall. The following descriptions of each of the informants were largely gathered from partners, one sibling, one childhood friend and one retired colleague during single in-depth individual interviews.

Mr Robert Biddley

Mr Biddley was a small, dark haired man, aged sixty-six years and the second youngest of the informants. He had never married although he had been engaged when he was forty to a girl aged eighteen, but this engagement had been broken. He lived alone, about three miles from the setting, in a bungalow built in 1966 for himself and his future wife. Before this, he had lived with his mother. Immediately prior to the commencement of the investigation, he had moved into a psychogeriatric wing of a local authority home for the elderly.

Mr Biddley was the youngest of five. He had two brothers and two sisters. His father was a plasterer who according to a childhood friend "was down the pub most nights" and died young, due to alcohol abuse. The family suffered because of his drinking habits and often went without. Mr Biddley was close to his mother and cared for her until her death in 1984. He maintained regular contact with his two sisters who were very fond of him. He worked all his life for British Rail, except for a short period in the Army during the war. He worked long hours and was always willing to do overtime. He was always careful with money. He appeared to have few friends and his childhood acquaintance described him as a loner. He received early retirement on medical grounds, after forty-four years of service, due to pre senile dementia.

He was known to the setting, having been treated for depression in 1981, due, it was felt, to the strain of caring for his mother. In 1987 he was diagnosed as having mild depression and possible pre-senile dementia. In May 1988 he went into a large teaching hospital for a series of neurological tests, one of which was a CT scan. This indicated primary degenerative dementia. He continued to have regular monitoring appointments and in August 1989 he told the registrar, "My memory is not as good as it used to be". He then began attending the day hospital but his behaviour quickly gave cause for concern. His home began to be dangerously neglected. He hoarded everything, including perishable foods. He continued to walk everywhere but was unable to remember where he lived. In March

1992 the decision was made to legally admit him to residential care. In September 1992 a mental test was applied and his mental test score (MTS) was 3/10. In October 1992 the situation broke down due to his increasingly difficult behaviour. In November 1992 he was admitted to a psychogeriatric nursing home where his sisters continued to visit him regularly.

Mr Charles Clerkenwell

Mr Charles Clerkenwell was a charming, tall, eighty-one year old man who was arthritic and registered blind. He lived with his much younger second wife about a mile from the setting. He had been widowed in 1965 and remarried in 1975. There were no children from either union, although his present wife had four grown children, no longer living at home, from her first marriage. Mr Clerkenwell had been born in a large city with important dockyard facilities. His father worked for a shipping company and was often away on long voyages. Mr Clerkenwell had one older sister and a devoted mother, whom he adored. Mr Clerkenwell went to the local grammar school on a scholarship and had various jobs until he was old enough to join the Army. He joined when he was twenty-one and left when he was forty-five years of age. During this time, he fought in the second world war until captured by the Japanese. He was interred in the infamous Changi prison camp where he was a POW for three years. His war experiences haunted him for many years and his wife said that he still suffered severe nightmares about the camp.

After leaving the Army, he worked as a clerk for a large company. Although he hated it, he remained there for twenty years, until his retirement in 1975. His wife described him as a cautious person, reluctant to take risks. However, she described him as:

A lovely fellow when we first married. He treated me like a lady. He has been a wonderful husband.

They had been married for seventeen years at the commencement investigation but Mr Clerkenwell's behaviour had begun to deteriorate two and a half years ago, when his eyesight began to fail. His wife said he had become "awkward and nasty" and he had began to complain when her children visited. She felt very torn at these times. In 1991 his GP referred him to the psychogeriatrician who visited him at home in October 1991. During the interview the Mini-Mental State Examination (MMSE) was applied giving a score of 11/27, having a cut-off point of 23. He was diagnosed as having SDAT and began to attend the setting two days a week, gradually increasing to five days a week. Mr Clerkenwell also had regular respite care. In February 1993 when his mental abilities were tested, the MTS was 4/10. Mrs Clerkenwell was not well. She had an osteo-arthritic hip and suffered considerable pain. In the summer of 1993 she underwent a hip replacement operation. During this time Mr Clerkenwell was cared for in Willow ward but his physical and mental condition slowly worsened. Mr Clerkenwell died in Willow ward in October 1993, aged eighty-three years. His wife was a regular and devoted visitor until the end.

Mr Andrew Coxley

Mr Coxley was a pleasant, mildly confused man, aged seventy-six years, who lived with his wife in a small isolated village, approximately five miles from the setting. They had been married for nearly fifty-one years and had two children, a boy and a girl. Both children had married and had left home. Mr Coxley had a hard life. He was the eldest and had two younger sisters, one of whom died in childhood. His father was a farm labourer and they lived in a tied cottage, deep in the countryside. His mother appeared to have had a severe, intractable post natal depression following the birth of her second child. Mr Coxley thought she had "milk fever and it turned her brain". She was ill for most of his childhood, often going missing with the family having to look for her. On one occasion she was found face down in a stream but was rescued before she drowned. The railway line and other dangerous places, such as the well, were searched when she disappeared. After spells in various institutions, she was admitted to one of the wards in the setting when she was in her fifties. She spent some years there and died when Mr Coxley was in his forties. He visited her regularly until her death, riding his bicycle each way.

Mr Coxley became a farm labourer when he left school. Although poorly paid, he loved the work. However, after twenty-one years, he was forced to leave owing to severe ulcerative colitis. The hard physical work was too much for him. He tried to work in agricultural retail outlets but his illness made this too difficult and embarrassing for him. In 1978 he underwent surgery, leaving him with an ileostomy which he and his wife saw as "a blessing". Shortly before the operation Mr Coxley was opening his bowels some twenty+ times a day and this had severely restricted outings of any kind. In 1990 Mr Coxley had a small CVA. Although he appeared to recover well, it left him with mild memory deficits. In 1992 he was referred by his GP to the psychogeriatrician who saw him in April 1992 in his outpatient clinic. An MMSE was administered giving a score of 14/30 and he was diagnosed as having MID. He began attending the setting two days a week which gradually increased to three days a week. His wife was devoted to her husband and would keep him at home if he showed any signs of ill-health. Their daughter visited regularly, performed any task required and was on call for any emergencies. One gained the impression of a tight knit and supportive family unit. Mrs Coxley made it clear that she would care for her husband for as long as she was able. At the completion of the investigation, Mr Coxley remained living in his own home, due entirely to the unceasing efforts of his wife.

Mrs Bessie Pinks

Mrs Pinks was a small round lady, aged eighty-five years, who lived with her husband approximately two miles from the setting. She had been born in the locality and had two older brothers. Her mother was a young widow and according to Mr Pinks, she raised her family in some poverty:

> She was one of the best. It was a horrible bloody life.

When Mrs Pinks was thirteen, although still at school, she began to help out at the local vicarage. Before leaving school at fourteen, she eventually moved into the vicarage as a part time maid of all work. On leaving school she remained at the vicarage as a full time worker. She married from there when she was in her twenties but this union foundered, leaving her with a son who sadly died of multiple sclerosis in his early thirties. Mr and Mrs Pinks had known each other since their childhood and were married in 1940, shortly before Mr Pinks was posted abroad. According to Mr Pinks, their honeymoon "was a cup of tea at the local railway station". After the war, Mr Pinks continued to work abroad as a heating engineer, mainly in the Middle East. Mrs Pinks accompanied him on his travels and revelled in the warm climates. He described his wife as a shy person when younger but felt he had given her more confidence.

When he retired in 1975, they moved to their present address. Her grandchildren visited them regularly and Mr Pinks appeared to be very fond of them. One gained the impression of a couple who had a long and happy marriage. However, Mr Pinks was now quite ill and had just had a major operation. Mrs Pinks forgetfulness had began to manifest itself in 1991. Her GP then referred her to the psychogeriatrician and she was seen in July 1991. On examination, her MTS was 2/9 and a diagnosis of dementia was given. She began attending the day hospital one day a week and this steadily increased to five days a week. Mrs Pinks also had regular respite care. A mental test was given again in September 1991, her MTS was 5/10. This rise in score may have been due to her more settled mood. In August 1992 she was again tested, using the Crighton Royal Behavioural Rating Scale (CRBRS) which gave a dementia score of 3 and a dependency score of 13. In September 1992, during a period of respite care, a mental status questionnaire (MSQ) was applied, giving a score of 5/10. Mr Pinks found life hard, but his sense of humour helped him to cope. He tended to let Mrs Pinks "poodle about the place" although he said he could never find anything afterwards. He chose her clothes and laid them out for her each morning, making sure they were colour co-ordinated. His health continued to deteriorate as Mrs Pinks' behaviour began to decline. In February 1993, Mrs Pinks entered the same long stay psychogeriatric nursing home as Mr Biddley, approximately eleven months after our first interview. Her husband was happy about this move and continued to visit her regularly.

Mr Hugh Raft

Mr Raft was a short, grey haired man, aged seventy-two years, who lived with his second wife in her house approximately two miles from the setting. The house itself was comfortable and immaculately maintained. Mr and Mrs Raft had been married for one year, having lost their previous partners, Mr Raft's wife to AD. Both couples had been friends for forty-two years. Mr Raft's present wife had three children from her first marriage and Mr Raft had two children. One was a daughter and the other was a son whom he and his wife had adopted. His daughter visited her father on a weekly basis but the son maintained little contact with Mr Raft.

Mr Raft had an unhappy childhood. His mother was unmarried when he and his sister were born to different fathers. His mother had then married and had several children. His stepfather appeared to have been a drunken bully who beat Mr Raft regularly. Mr Raft was terrified of him. His mother did not intervene. Their home circumstances were very poor. Mr Raft escaped by joining the Army and eventually rose to the rank of sergeant major. After leaving the Army, he became a caretaker for a social service setting until his retirement. As his wife's condition worsened, they moved to a warden assisted flat where his future second wife visited regularly. After his first wife's death in 1990, she began to look after Mr Raft. He spent much of his free time at her house, going home only to sleep.

When he asked her to marry him in 1991, six months after his first wife's death, Mrs Raft agreed. She had lived alone for nine years since the death of her husband and was lonely. She felt she could care for Mr Raft but she was adamant that she did not know that he was suffering from dementia. However, it was a matter of record that she had been told of this probability by the psychiatric services, but had chosen to ignore their warnings. His behaviour since their marriage horrified her. She found his personal habits totally repugnant. She had made it clear, prior to their marriage, that there was to be no intimate relationship between them. Mr Raft, however, frightened and disgusted her with his unmet demands for a "full married life".

His GP referred him to the psychogeriatrician in November 1991 and he was seen in the setting on January 10th, 1992. An MSQ was administered giving a result of 6/10. He and his wife also attended the memory clinic in January 1992. A Cambridge Examination for Mental Disorders of the Elderly (Camdex) was applied and his scores were 72/107, having a cut-off point of 80. His MMSE score was 20/30. He was diagnosed as having DAT with no evidence of Vascular Dementia, but his blood pressure was 180/95. In view of the problems experienced by Mrs Raft, a case conference was called in which Mrs Raft spoke openly of her problems. Mr Raft was prescribed medication which quietened his libido, but his behaviour continued to worry her. She described herself as "being full of nerves". She regretted marrying him very much. She said that she had lost many of her friends and that she felt on her guard the whole time.

Mr Raft began attending the setting in July 1992, three times a week and was often to be seen crying quietly. After some months in the setting, he asked "to be somewhere where he was more useful". He was then offered day care in a psychogeriatric wing of a local authority home, which also offered respite care. He then began to experience "little blackouts". During the autumn/winter of 1993 his behaviour became increasingly disturbed. His blackouts began to increase in severity and his wife could no longer cope. He was transferred to the assessment ward of the local psychiatric hospital and, at the beginning of 1994, it was decided to place him in the same psychogeriatric nursing home as Mrs Pinks and Mr Biddley, when a bed became available.

Mr Melvin Rider

The youngest informant was Mr Rider who was a large, tall man, aged sixty-five years and who lived with his wife, in a pleasant house approximately one mile from the setting. They had been married for thirty-nine years and had two children, a boy and a girl. Their son was a lieutenant commander in the Navy and was unmarried, their daughter was a mathematician who lived in the north of the country. She was married with two children. Mr Rider was born an only child in Yorkshire. His mother was a teacher and his father was a railway clerk. His mother had high expectations of her son who won a scholarship to an Oxbridge university where he read physics. After university, he joined the Navy and had various postings all over the world including a spell at NATO. He left the Navy in 1966 and commenced his teaching career, culminating as the head of the physics department in a local grammar school.

In February 1983, aged fifty-seven, he was referred to the psychology department of the psychiatric hospital by his GP. He had been very depressed throughout 1982 with long periods of sick leave. He tried to return to work but he could not cope with the demands of his job. His wife described him as "a perfectionist, always trying to give every endeavour one hundred per cent". In March 1983, he underwent a battery of tests which indicated patchy but severe memory deficits. The tests included a CT scan which indicated no abnormal changes in brain structures. In 1985 he had an isotope scan and again the results were inconclusive. In 1986, his wife, having read of the symptoms, felt that he might be suffering from dementia and asked if her husband could see the psychogeriatrician. He was seen in April 1986 and his hospital notes indicate that he answered most informal questions which tested recall but with noticeable hesitancy. Further, there was marked evidence of repetitiveness with good recall of the distant past. A diagnosis of DAT was given. Mrs Rider described this period of her life as:

> *A muddily horrible time. It's no good tearing yourself apart. You put your emotions away and pull down the blinds.*

She wished her children lived nearer to give her more support. Mr Rider began attending the setting three times a week which gradually increased to five times a week. She also used the sitter service one afternoon a week. Mrs Rider used this time to socialise with her friends. Prior to Mr Rider's illness they had a wide variety of interests. They belonged to the amateur operatic society and often went to concerts. They were committed and involved Anglicans. Mr Rider had also enjoyed DIY, car maintenance and gardening. As with other carers, Mrs Rider saw the future as bleak. Her own health began to deteriorate as her husband grew more dependent. Mr Rider's condition continued to worsen over the next year and a half and very reluctantly, Mrs Rider decided that she could no longer manage. Mr Rider entered Willow ward in September 1993. Mrs Rider had managed to care for him at home for eleven and a half years.

Mr Ronnie Silverthorne

Mr Silverthorne was a tall quiet man, aged eighty years, who lived with his wife in a well maintained bungalow three miles from the setting. He was born in London and was one of five children. Mr Silverthorne and his wife had been married for forty-four years but had no children. However, they maintained close contact with their nephews and nieces. Mr Silverthorne had spent most of his working life in the retail trade, commencing with an apprenticeship at Harrods. He joined the army during the war but returned to his work as soon as he was demobbed. When he was working as a buyer at a large London department store, he met his wife, who was the managing director's secretary. Mr Silverthorne was the manager of several large department stores until his retirement in 1978. At this time he was the general manager of a prestigious department store in the locality. A working colleague described him as being the best manager she had ever known. He was fair and well respected by the seventy to eighty people who worked under him. She further described him as a man who was very set in his ways, one who "you could set your watch by". She thought his work and his wife were the two most important things in his life. These two areas, however, were strictly compartmentalised. No member of staff had ever visited him at home.

Mr Silverthorne had been diagnosed as having diabetes in 1961 and cataracts in the early 1980s. He had his first cataract operation, by laser, in 1986. It was during a routine visit to the diabetic clinic in January 1991 that the doctor casually told Mrs Silverthorne that he felt her husband had AD and referred her to the psychogeriatrician. This was a great shock to Mrs Silverthorne; but worse was to follow. Mr

Silverthorne was due to have a necessary second cataract operation but, as he could not remain still, he would have to have a general anaesthetic. Mrs Silverthorne was told that this could increase his confusion, but she alone had to make the final decision. She felt under great strain but, as his eyesight was very precious to him, she said the operation should take place. Following the operation, Mr Silverthorne's mental state severely deteriorated. His wife said:

It blew the lid off it. I felt I had been kept in the dark.

His GP referred him to the psychogeriatrician who saw him in June 1991. During the interview an MSQ was applied giving a score of 2/10. He was diagnosed as having MID enhanced by diabetes. After diagnosis, Mr Silverthorne began to attend the setting two days a week, gradually increasing to five days a week. Mrs Silverthorne also used the local domiciliary sitting service for one afternoon a week until day care was extended. However, she had many feelings of hopelessness and despair:

I could cope if I knew when it would end. I'm in a sort of limbo.

In October 1992, Mrs Silverthorne finally agreed to her husband having planned respite care. Mr Silverthorne continued to live in the community until December 1992 when following a period of respite care he became too ill to go home. He died in Willow ward in March 1993, aged eighty-three years. Mrs Silverthorne had managed to care for him for six years in their own home.

Mrs Abigail Woodley

Mrs Woodley was a pleasant arthritic lady, aged seventy-six years, who lived with her husband in an immaculate semi-detached house, approximately one mile from the setting. They had been married for nearly fifty years and had two daughters, aged forty-six and thirty-nine years old. Their widowed daughter lived in the vicinity and saw her parents at least three times a week. The other daughter, who was married, lived some distance away but still maintained close contact. The impression was of a close caring family who pulled together in times of crisis.

Mrs Woodley was one of seven girls and had always lived in the locality, apart from a short time during the war. Her father owned a prosperous family bakery and her upbringing appeared to be untainted by poverty, but marred by her poor relationship with her mother. Her family were also staunch supporters of the Salvation

Army Church. Her husband described her as a worrier with a tendency to depression, which was attributed to the tragic death of her son-in-law seventeen years earlier. This seemed to deepen some five to six years prior to the diagnosis of AD in 1990.

Mrs Woodley's hospital notes showed that she was an in-patient at the general hospital in 1987. The reason for admittance was not given. Her clinician administered a cognition test during this time giving a score of 6/10. However, she refused to be referred to the psychiatric hospital for further assessment. In April 1990, her GP referred her to the hospital psychogeriatrician. In May 1990, Mrs Woodley was seen as an outpatient where her Camdex test scores were 55/107 and her MMSE score was 15/30. The clinician gave a diagnosis of SDAT with possible vascular component. Her husband who accompanied her found this to be a particularly distressing experience. He said of it:

> It's like being told you've got cancer. They take you to a hospital, a place you've never been before and you think, what's it all about? You're just left to get on with it.

Following this, a community psychiatric nurse was assigned to Mrs Woodley who continued to remain at home until April 1991 when she was admitted to the Assessment Unit for assessment procedures. A mental status questionnaire (MSQ) was administered, giving a score of 4/10. As Mr Woodley gradually became more familiar with hospital processes he adjusted to the many changes brought about by his wife's illness. Mrs Woodley began to attend the day hospital two days a week, although this gradually increased to four days. Further, Mr Woodley used the respite bed service for his wife every few months. During respite care in August 1993, an MSQ was applied. She was asked four questions and gave one correct answer. She became distressed and irritable and the test was abandoned. Mr Woodley endeavoured to keep Mrs Woodley's anxieties low by "adhering to a stable routine and never reprimanding her". He seemed a dedicated carer whose personal strengths permitted Mrs Woodley to remain in the community.

Conclusion

It is hoped that this brief description of the settings has described the resources available to the informants and their families. The short descriptions of the informants will have given a brief thumbnail sketch which will be expanded in their case-studies, when all informants tell their own stories. Their narratives suggest, in many cases, different perspectives to those offered by their main carers. Their transcribed words permit some understanding of the world of the dementia sufferer through the recall of their narratives, the recall of their own life stories.

5 The storied self - the study of individual narratives

Introduction

This chapter contains an account of the case-studies produced during this investigation, together with an evaluation of the method used to generate such findings. There will then be a meta analysis of the arguments contained in each case-study. Finally, the conclusion to this chapter will draw together the findings of the individual case-studies.

General characteristics of the case-studies

Eight case-studies were produced from the series of recorded and transcribed interviews conducted with the eight informants (Mills, 1995). The number of interviews with each informant varied between thirteen and twenty-five, over a period of five to seventeen months. However, the meetings between the interviewer and informants took place over a twelve to twenty-four months period. The quantity of interviews depended on a number of variables. These were the severity of the illness, the ease of access to informants and the death of informants. The case-studies, too, varied in length from approximately nine thousand to twelve thousand words. Neither does their length reflect the degree of cognitive impairment of informants, or the timespan of recorded and transcribed interviews. The longest case-study concerns the most severely impaired informant, who was interviewed over a period of seven months.

The format of the case-studies followed the interviews. The introduction gave a brief description of the informant and the date of the first meeting. The context and content of the first interview are described in some detail. By the second or third interview, possible emergent themes from informant's conversations are discussed and are validated, or refuted, during subsequent interviews. Not all themes were clearly identified at this stage, but developed as the investigation progressed. These themes are related to the emotional memories of informants and are validated through the informants recalling them on a number of occasions. These memories, therefore, occupy a central place in their narratives. Although all informants recalled emotional memories, there was a variation in clarity, content and recall. These differences were reflected in the informants' backgrounds.

Dissimilarities between informants

Although all informants suffered from some form of dementia, there were dissimilarities. Some informants were more severely compromised by their dementia and, in some cases, speech was affected. Background information suggested that no informant lived in a state of poverty or hardship. Most had attained a comfortable standard of living through their commitment to hard work, but many had had unequal opportunities in education and advancement. Mr Rider had achieved academically due to his intelligence and family encouragement. Mr Coxley did not have this support. Further, family traditions may have encouraged him to become a farm labourer. Mr Raft also experienced poor life chances and their consequential effects. However, even Mr Coxley and Mr Raft's traumatic childhoods were dissimilar. Mr Coxley's deprivations were caused by his mother's long standing illness, whereas Mr Raft's deprivations were caused by deliberate abuse. Nonetheless, both were victims and suffered hardships.

Close relationships, too, were qualitatively different. Some had good relationships, others were of a poorer quality. Mrs Woodley and Mr Coxley were fortunate in their relationships, which were enhanced by the physical well-being of their spouses. These were the only two informants who remained living in the community at the closure of the investigation. Mr Biddley, on the other hand, had few significant relationships and was the first informant to enter into long term residential care. This brief discussion of the dissimilarities between informants gives some indication of their singularity. They had, however, many commonalities.

Similarities between informants

There were similarities between informants, other than the nature of their diagnosis and use of the setting. The findings suggest that all informants recalled emotional, albeit fragmented, memories from their past. Over time, these memories cohered into parts of their life story, or narrative in which they occupied the central role. These stories of the self gave informants a sense of narrative identity which was lost as the illness progressed. Moreover, it is also suggested that all informants, with some variations, appeared to enjoy the process of the interviews. Further, all informants experienced a marked increase in levels of well-being. For some, this continued after the conclusion of the interviews.

Therapeutic outcomes are difficult to measure other than through anecdotal report. However, most investigations within this area require more precise methods to evaluate therapeutic outcomes and to meet the needs of scientific appraisal. The extended single case-study method may be one such approach. Within the investigation, the beneficial effects narrated by all informants were clearly indicated through the use of this method. Again, although anecdotal in nature, these self reports were given over a long period of time by a group of cognitively impaired people who, according to Kitwood (1990a), are less capable of deliberate subterfuge.

An evaluation of the method

The effectiveness of the method chosen for this study must be questioned. Was it appropriate for this investigation? Did it work? A generalised examination of the findings indicates that the approach used by the interviewer allowed all informants to recall their past and that these memories were able to be shared with others through the use of case-study methodology. An overview of the findings, therefore, suggests that this method was appropriate, given the nature of this research. Moreover, the use of grounded theory for data analysis indicated several significant themes and categories. Further, the method led to the emergence of the core category, that of the importance of informant's self stories or narratives during dementia. This method, therefore, appeared to be an appropriate and effective tool for the task.

A detailed examination of the case-studies suggests that the structure of these reports are based on Bromley's (1986) guidelines for the preparation of a psychological case-study. However, his stringent requirements for truthful, accurate and evaluative accounts, are the subjects of further scrutiny throughout this chapter. Although the case-studies are `truthful´ and `accurate´ in the sense that the reported conversations did take place, through the recording and transcription of data, the concerns of truth, accuracy and evaluation form part of narrative truth, which itself rests on informant and researcher interpretation. The interpretations of informants' meanings, offered by the researcher/interviewer, may well be open to alternative points of view. Another area of possible concern is interviewer bias. All informants were interviewed over a substantial period of time. Most interviews began in April 1992 and some continued until 1994. Therefore, the case-studies are not only a record of informants' narratives, but also an account of interviewer/informant relationships. The strength of these long standing relationships may have exerted a positive bias on interviewer accounts of informants. These are important issues which will be addressed throughout the examination of individual case-studies.

Further areas of consideration

Other considerations are the possibility of bias in the interviewer's interpretation of informant's responses. Moreover, it could be suggested that there were leading questions asked which encouraged the informants to give answers/replies which would conform to the interviewer's own expectations. However, the discussion of the counselling techniques used in this investigation suggests that exploratory questions can be asked to aid client disclosure. These exploratory questions, together with the use of advanced accurate empathy, can sound like leading questions. However, interviews with informants were not solely psychotherapeutic in nature. They were, primarily, investigative interviews which contained elements of counselling principles. Nonetheless, the suggestion that the informants may have been `over led´ is worthy of examination. An evaluation of the evidence indicates that this may have occurred during interviews with Mrs Woodley and others:

> **Int.** *And then you worked on the burns unit.*
> **AW** *Mm.*
> **Int.** *You must have seen some terrible burns there.*
> **AW** *Oh the burns were horrible!*

Mr Silverthorne disliked some of the activities in the setting. The interviewer asked if he found them childish. He agreed they were:

> Int. *Do you not like playing things, if you think they're silly?*
> RS *Of course they are!*
> Int. *Of course they are?*
> RS *Yes.*
> Int. *So some of the games are silly?*
> RS *Yes.*

Mrs Pinks was encouraged to say that she liked children:

> Int. *So that was your job was it? To be a nanny?*
> BP *Yes. That's right!*
> Int. *So you've always liked children.*
> BP *Yes ... I quite enjoyed looking after children ...*
> Int. *You seem as if you would. You've got that kind of personality.*
> BP *Perhaps so!*

However, there were many times when this did not happen. For example, it was felt that Mr Biddley might feel some anger over his present situation. Mr Biddley denied this:

> RB *Yes, because most people in my predicament, they get to know the other people and, you know, they do the best they can! And that's all there is to it, isn't it!*
> Int. *So it doesn't make you angry?*
> RB *No! because I used to be as really sharp as a tack!*

Mr Raft, the final informant, did not agree that he might have seen the Army as a safe place. He was quick to deny this:

> Int. *Did that make you feel safe being in the Army?*
> HR *Not particularly. No ... I just ... I loved the Army! I joined when I was seventeen I think it was.*

Although informants may have appeared to have been led on occasions, the evidence suggests that these questions were more exploratory in nature. Thus, there are strong indications within the case-studies that the major outcomes of this work rest on meanings given by the informants. Moreover, all informants' conversations and stories should be considered against the backdrop of their narrative.

To select partial extracts is, itself, misleading.

Further considerations of the approach used by the interviewer

The value of the approach can be questioned. Is this particular interviewing technique needed to discover the life story of older people with dementia? One might argue that if no narrative is present in memory, interviewer skills assume a lesser relevance. The final interviews with Mrs Pinks and Mr Biddley, where the dissolution of their narrative is clearly shown, indicate some support for this argument. It is possible, therefore, to view the presence of story as all important and the approach used throughout this study, as a necessary tool. Further, did interviewer approach bias the interviews and subsequent interpretations? All eight case-studies portray the informants as very likeable people. Although interviewers engaged in this type of research are expected to have high levels of respect for informants, it might be said that here the informants were viewed with too kind an eye. In addition, the strength of the relationships led to a deep understanding of the informants and it is difficult for dislike to flourish in these circumstances. These and other analytic concerns will be addressed throughout a discussion of the case-studies of the eight informants who took part in this investigation. The informants will be presented alphabetically. The first case-study to be examined is that of Mr Robert Biddley.

Mr Robert Biddley (RB)

At sixty-six years of age, RB was the second youngest participant in the investigation and his illness progressed more rapidly than with other informants. There were thirteen recorded and transcribed interviews with RB which took place between May 1992 and August 1993. As with all of the informants, there were more meetings than this number would suggest. He greatly enjoyed the social aspects of the interviews. He frequently said that he liked talking to others:

RB *Oh, I've always em, have a chat with anybody, you know.*

Int. *I've seen that! You like chatting don't you?*

RB *Yes. If you don't do that, then what's life?*

RB *I like the fun of talking to people that, you know, not trying, they're not trying to be big! or anything like that. That's what I like, because they have a good laugh, and you have a good laugh, and that's the best thing isn't it!*

RB found it difficult to show his emotions. The interviews indicated that he tried to accept his changing circumstances and loss of mental abilities, but this was very painful for him:

RB *I used to be really sharp and do any job, you know. But er it's no good to apologise! Er ... (There were tears in his eyes.)*

RB *People, lot of people ... Just because it's er, you're being not being quite 100% you know, it makes it's ... it easier. There's a lot of people in the same ... illness. The same predicament coming ...*

It is suggested that this sadness over his failing cognitive abilities was a significant theme in his conversation. Further, there were indications of a strong desire to move towards a state of acceptance. He continually spoke of the importance of accepting life and others:

RB *Yes! I'm ... I always try to have things easier really! There's no sense, you know, trying to make it ten times more difficult. You don't want that do you?*

He felt that laughing at oneself and with others was important:

RB *Oh yes! But you've got to be able to laugh at yourself as well. Otherwise all ... I think that if you can have a good laugh, that's a lot of goodness.*

His memories of his childhood and his mother were significant. His experiences from this time suggested that he felt he had to make his own way in the world, to work hard and to be careful with money. His work was, therefore, of great importance to him. This theme was to be developed as the interviews progressed:

RB *I didn't want to get married. I'm one of seven children and that makes a big difference as well, doesn't it?*

RB *What being ... um one of seven children ... We're not going get a lot given you. So you've got to get what you can! And that's it!*

RB *We looked after my mother, you know. They all did, all the children. We did what we could. We didn't have a lot, but we did the best we could!*

RB *I did anything. Clerical.*

Int. *Clerical ... Who did you work for?*

RB *British Rail.*

Int. *British Rail? Did you work for them for a long time?*

RB *Quite a bit! Yes yes ...*

RB *Wants money.*

Int. *... Money?*

RB *Yes. Money is the only thing that can help.*

RB *Yes ... Yes. But apar ... apart from that, I don't think you can do anything ... without money!*

Interviewer interpretation of RB's comments concerning money, suggests that RB felt that not enough was being spent on medical care for people in the setting. However, they might also indicate the importance he attached to the possession of money. Certainly, other conversations cited in his case-study suggests that he was careful with his finances. He did not appear to have any major regrets about his past life, he felt he had done his best and had enjoyed his life:

RB *Everything that I've done, I've done purposely and that's it! So I've no sense in ... (gave a little laugh) ... I shouldn't have done that, or I shouldn't have done this ... You just do the best things you can, don't you?*

RB *I've ... I've enjoyed it! I've made mis mistakes, we all do. There's no one can tell me they've made no mistakes and things like that, but I know, I think I'm I'm just as good good as most ...*

Interviewer interpretations of his conversations suggests that RB was a kind man with many acquaintances and few close friends. Evidence from a boyhood friend supports this viewpoint. RB appeared to be a relatively private person who kept much of himself hidden. However, there were some indications of his inner self during a discussion on death:

Int. *Does it frighten you, the thought of dying?*

RB *No! Because it's ... it's got to happen! You you can't er avoid can you, really? If we could, we'd put a bit more in the kitty!*

RB *I'm not very keen on talking about it but it seems ... Well you ... you shouldn't ... Some people take it as a a matter of fact, don't they? It is! ... Well nobody's going to stay here for ever and ever and ever, are they?*

RB *Yes ... Yes ... It's sad but er inevitable, isn't it? You going to deathly go going yourself ... Yes ...*

Although the interviewer endeavoured to change the topic, he returned again to the subject of death:

RB *Mm ... Oh yes but ... doesn't matter where you're living ... it's ... you're going die ... You can't stop that can you? No ...*

It is possible that this topic could have been more fully discussed and might have led to further disclosures by RB. However, the interviewer chose not to pursue it further, possibly due to a reluctance to upset the informant. Equally, the interviewer may have sensed RB's concerns and felt reluctant to cope with potentially strong emotions. However, this is merely another conceivable interpretation of events. As the investigation progressed, together with his illness, RB's stories began to fade. Of some significance is the final interview that took place in August 1993, in the nursing home where he now lived. As with other informants, his memories had seeped away leaving a faint outline of the original contents:

Int. *Do you remember when you worked for British Rail?*

RB *Yes.*

Int. *You do? Was that a good job? (Pause.) Was that a good job working for British Rail? ... (RB did not reply.) Do you remember looking after your mum?*

RB *Mmm!*

Int. *Was her name Violet? ... Was her name Violet? (RB nodded) ... You looked after your mum for a long time ... (RB was silent and continued to pace the corridors.) But you remember working for British Rail?*

RB *Yes.*

Int. *A good job ... (No reply. RB continued to pace the corridors without pause.)*

RB was unable to sit for any length of time. Staff in the setting reported that he would only sit if there was food on the table. The interviewer noted that he appeared to be totally exhausted. Interviewer evaluation of this case-study suggests his sense of narrative identity was rapidly dissolving. However, RB had enjoyed the process of the interviews, and, for a long period into the investigation, experienced increased levels of well-being and personhood:

> **RB** *You and I talking our bits ... Quite decent isn't it?*
> **RB** *... It is! Well tis tis, I I can have a chat with people, I mean it's easier isn't it!*
> **Int.** *I think it makes you feel happy, would you say that?*
> **RB** *Oh yes! Oh yes!*

Although this informant was held in deep regard, the interpreted meanings are based on the informant's actual conversations, and, as this particular informant was able to express himself quite clearly for much of the investigation, it is not possible to offer alternative explanations. Although leading, albeit exploratory, questions were asked of this informant, the identified themes were frequently introduced by RB himself and remained constant over a long period of time. Further, the emotional memories possessed by this informant indicate a link between emotions and states of cognitive awareness. Finally, the disappearance of his narrative is clearly shown in the final stages of the investigation together with a loss of a sense of narrative identity in the closing interview.

Mr Charles Clerkenwell (CC)

CC was interviewed between June 1992 and October 1993, with a total of seventeen recorded and transcribed interviews. Although he had minor memory deficits, he was a very articulate person with a fund of self stories. However, he thought of himself as a shy man who had led a dull life:

> **CC** *I very often think that I've met a dull drool sort of existence ...*
> **CC** *... because I was a pretty shy person ... I have been shy in my time, yes ... Believe me!*

The most significant theme for this informant appeared to be one of loss. This was concerned with the loss of his father, loss of freedom during the war when he was a prisoner of the Japanese, loss of health and loss of independence due to poor eyesight and present illness. An examination of the evidence would appear to support these findings. CC spoke readily of these topics:

Int. *Do you remember what your father did? For a living?*

CC *... He mostly ran away, I think!*

CC *The other chap was never there to sing anyway! Unless it was in jail or something! No he wasn't a very er ... Oh he was a ha half sort of person. He would come on leave, dragging a hamper full of lovely rosy apples in the middle of the war ... pretty precious. But er what he did between polishing the apples, and polishing this woman behind the blackberry bush or something, that was the point! We had stuff given to us, we had all that, that's not everything ...*

CC *I suppose the worse thing it's done to me is I've near enough lost my sight, hence this ... And er, I can't see prop ... well ... It's still a strain to see ...*

CC found it very difficult to cope with poor eyesight:

CC *A blow comes with this thing. It's when ... specialist says "I'm ... I'm sorry it will never better, you know". Oh thank you very much!*

Int. *That must have been a terrible blow ...*

CC *What dear?*

Int. *That must have been a terrible blow ...*

CC *Yes, it is you think, well it'll be all right one day, you know ... And then this chap in his very ... e ... r what can I say his um ... thorough examination after several ... well, several months! ... And then I said, "Surely there must be some improvement" But, "I'm afraid not ... Not in your case! ... Just not showing any improvement! And, after a long examination, I'm sure there will not be one!"*

CC indicated that he felt `imprisoned´ in the setting:

CC *The trouble is, I'm chained in here you see. I can't just get up and walk out.*

Int. *Do you get fed up with coming here?*

CC *Only in the sense I like ... seeing people and so ... No I like coming here but what I object to is the doors clang behind me, and there's ... I have a feeling I've just walked in into Pentonville, or some similar prison. And I can't get out again until the warder er gives a nod, you know, and says, "Right you can ..."*

These themes continued throughout the investigation. The last recorded interview with this informant indicated that his memories of the war remained with him:

CC *... in that in that er er twenty odd people, women soldiers, ATS or what have you. And they were locked up, and they were raped, one by one, whenever the Japanese felt like it ... Not very nice!*

CC *You got to remember that they [Japanese] are completely and utterly different.*

Int. *Did you feel that you couldn't understand them?*

CC *Yes, Well you can't understand people the way they ... some of the things they did. Even ... so called ... um ... small things which I I mean aren't small to us ... Taking a dog and beating to death ... I mean we don't look upon that as being funny or careless or anything. It's downright bloody wicked, even if it is a dog ...*

However, in spite of his traumatic experiences CC still enjoyed life. He felt that he had had a good life:

CC *Yes! ... What's the good of being miserable when it's so easy to be happier?*

Int. *Do you think you have good life, Charlie?*

CC *... Yes! I can't complain at all!*

CC *Well ... I've had jolly good moments ... I've had calm and peaceful moments.*

CC enjoyed recalling his past memories and his relationship with the interviewer:

CC *Anything is interesting, discussing it with you.*

On one occasion, after an absence, he sang to prove he remembered her name:

CC *Marie, the dawn is breaking ...*

He said he felt happier than he perhaps looked:

CC *I look miserable, but I feel inside quite jolly ...*

Further, towards the end of the investigation he did not seem to have such a negative view of ageing:

Int. *Do you hate getting old?*
CC *... It's quite pleasant in its way.*

It is argued that this informant's life history possesses a certain clarity when compared to other informants, due to CC's relatively unimpaired memory. It is difficult to disagree with this. This case-study is full of quite complete self stories. It is also pointed out that it is highly likely that these stories were well rehearsed, owing to CC's skill as a raconteur. Again, the evidence would appear to support this argument. They were the type of memories which, as CC said, "live long in the memory of a mind", for they tended to be significantly concerned with the individual physical and psychological survival of the self. The interviewer also suggests that the intensity of effort to survive, may have created these durable memories which appeared to withstand the onslaught of dementia, almost until the end. However, it is equally possible to suggest that it is merely the rehearsal of these memories which may have led to their remaining in memory. Equally, this informant's present circumstances reflected his past experiences. In the present he was as much a `prisoner´ of his illness as he was as a POW. It may have been his present circumstances which led to this rich recall of the past.

Finally, the interviewer stresses the emotional content of CC's memories and notes the proposed link between emotion and cognition. One must agree with this conclusion, as the case-study contains a wealth of evidence to support this finding. It is also posited that CC's stories allowed him to be readily seen as a `whole´ person and that this gave him a sense of narrative identity. The interviewer argues that it is this sense of narrative identity which is lost during the process of dementia, and highlights the importance of the maintenance of the narrative during this illness.

Thus, it is possible to agree with most of the interpretations reached through this case-study and to suggest that the comparative ease of this exercise was due to the clarity of the informant's memories.

Moreover, the question of faulty interpretation of this informant's meanings are minimised throughout this case-study, due to the detail offered by CC. However, once more, this informant is seen in a most sympathetic light and as one who enjoyed the process of the interviews and the interviewer/informant relationship. The interviewer suggests that, as with other informants, CC experienced increased levels of well-being through the process of the investigation. These increased levels of well-being were evident throughout the case-study, but may have as much to do with the interviewer/informant relationship as with the recalling of the personal narrative.

Mr Andrew Coxley (AC)

AC was, probably, the least cognitively impaired of all the informants, although not such a skilled raconteur as Mr Clerkenwell. A small CVA had left him with minor memory deficits. AC was interviewed between June 1992 and January 1994, with a total number of fifteen recorded and transcribed interviews. There are several suggested significant themes in the narrative of AC. His work on the farm appeared to be an important part of his life. Certain aspects of this work, such as driving his beloved tractor, had been very enjoyable:

> **AC** *Yes. All the years I gone on the farm. Tractor man, and old tractors. Good old tractor wasn't he? Never let me down. I used to drive it every day ...*
> **AC** *Yeah. Open air wan it, yes. I used to love it.*

He would get his orders for the day from his employer when he arrived for work. It is suggested that this ordered routine appealed to AC:

> **AC** *Oh yes! I got on there alright! Well ... its long days, that the trouble ... But I didn't take no notice, you know. Used to know what we had to do. Used to get our orders in the morning ... And they'd last all day ...*

Further, the interviewer suggests that there may be some significance in the fact that driving his tractor was a solitary pursuit. Given his current situation, this time of certainty and order would be especially meaningful in the present. However, AC had had problems with ulcerative colitis for many years and he had to open his bowels many times during the day. An alternative explanation is that this solitary work allowed him privacy. AC gives some indication of this:

> **AC** *I didn't ... wasn't too bad when I first had, because I was on the farm, you see. I was out in the field I could go anywhere ... Used to be ploughing, when I used to plough up the furrow   and then go in that and bury, you know. I always liked to bury it! But t'was there all the time sort of thing ... Said, "I think I'll operate", he said ... I said, "Well the sooner the better" ...*

Thus, although it is possible that the uncertainty of the present may have idealised the orderly calm of his farm work, one might argue that the physical freedom of his working life `managed´ his very real physical problems. A further significant theme in his case-study was the disclosure of his mother's illness:

> **AC** *My mother was in here [the setting] for about eight years ... Died in here actually ... Over there in the ... (gestured towards another part of the hospital).*

As the interviews progressed, AC began to speak of his troubled childhood, due to his mother's ill health:

> **AC** *She had milk fever apparently. Went to her head ... Never got her right anymore, you know ... We tried hard with her. She used to get over it and then get attacked again and it was a bit of a struggle you know.*
> **Int.** *So you couldn't have had a happy childhood then, really?*
> **AC** *Not really, no as far as mother was concerned ... Yes.*

He indicated that he had never fully resolved his sense of grief and guilt concerning his mother:

> **Int.** *Mmm ... So all the memories of your mother, are they mostly sad memories really?*
> **AC** *Yes. They are really ... Wasn't really old enough to understand, you know ...*

He tried very hard to believe that he had done his best for her:

91

> **AC** *I done what I could, and well I got to the stage where you couldn't do anything else for her ... (Tears filled his eyes.)*

Towards the end of the investigation, he spoke of his feelings at being in the same setting as his mother:

> **AC** *She was then over there. (Looked out of the window towards the building where he used to visit his mother on Sunday afternoons.) That place haunts me, over there ... Well, it do when I come that ... no which ... where was she as it happens? Oh, it's that bit over there. (Pointed out of window to a building.) I hate coming ... round that bit.*

The interviewer argues that, although his narrative of this part of his life consists of a brief outline, it is possible that his mother's illness is a story of disorder. `Disorder´ was not only descriptive of her condition, but was also of her effect on much of his existence. It might be suggested, therefore, that AC had experienced strong elements of order versus disorder in his life. It is difficult to disagree with this interpretation. The elements of AC's story certainly suggest a traumatic childhood, with much uncertainty for the whole family:

> **Int.** *So you never knew ... you used to come home from school and you wouldn't know what she was going like?*
> **AC** *No, no ... Didn't ... Never had no tea ready or anything, you know.*

AC implied that his mother had tried to end her life:

> **AC** *... Fairly often ... No she couldn't help it see ... I used to ... get home from work at night and had to find her always ... Dad was still at work ... He used to work til five look and I used to come at five, near enough before five ... and she wasn't there, she was gone!*
> **Int.** *Mmm ...*
> **AC** *And you didn't know what to do! Had to go and look for her didn't you? And I knew ... she ... down where we used to live, just down the road a little way, there was a river ... It's shallow but good enough to do the damage ... I only had to walk down there and look in, and there she was, you know.*

This uncertainty continued into AC's adulthood and his own role as a father and provider. The evidence, therefore, would appear to support the interpretations offered by the interviewer. However, it is also possible that the process of the investigation may well have allowed AC to use this opportunity to explore his unresolved conflicts in a relatively safe manner. It might be suggested that the story of his mother was always ready to be told. Certainly, AC was able to discuss his unresolved feelings of sadness and grief during the course of the interviews:

> **AC** *Well that's what I've often thought that but ... I done what I could and well I got to the stage where you couldn't do anything else for her ... (Tears filled his eyes several times throughout this interview.)*
> **Int.** *No ... Sometimes you just can't win whatever you do ...*
> **AC** *No! I used to come in here and I don't know what she's going to be like today, and then she'd have one of her moods on, you know, and I couldn't get nowhere with her ...*

Further, AC was able to disclose his feelings concerning his mother's death:

> **AC** *She died in there. You see ... I went in there one afternoon and she was gone ... I sort of come out, went to get me bike ... I ... I didn't sort of realise it that she were gone, but I sort of thought, well that's er a lovely release.*

This story of his mother's illness and eventual death is full of strong emotions. However, there were other aspects of AC's life that were meaningful to him. He often reminisced about aspects of his life on the farm. He was aware that these days were never to return:

> **Int.** *Those were the days weren't they?*
> **AC** *Oh yes! All gone now though! ...*
> **Int.** *Everything changes though, Andy, doesn't it?*
> **AC** *Yes! ... Go over the years don't it? ...*

However, speaking of them gave him pleasure:

> **Int.** *So, were good days were they?*
> **AC** *Yes. Won't come back no more will they? I don't think.*
> **Int.** *I think when you think about them, they come back don't they?*
> **AC** *Well, they seem to. Yes.*
> **Int.** *Does it give you pleasure to think about them?*
> **AC** *Yes.*

Overall, he enjoyed the process of the interviews and appeared to have experienced increased well-being. He spoke of his interests, his family and of his concerns. His own health was a problem and he frequently discussed this with the interviewer. AC indicated that it had been helpful talking to the interviewer:

   AC *Oh yes! Makes a difference for the say, don't it?*

At the conclusion of the interviews and although more frail, AC was still able to recount his stories. However, it is argued that his mild loss of memory and often understated responses, created difficulty in defining a clear path through his narrative. Often, in cases of severe memory loss, the repetitive story indicates an area of significance. With other less cognitively impaired elderly people, this is not so readily perceived. Certain themes in the narrative of AC were identified over time, through the course of the interviews. These memories were emotionally significant and moving. The interviewer suggests that AC was searching for wisdom, as defined by Erikson (1963), during their meetings. His testimony would appear to support this argument. Much of AC's life appeared to have been spent searching for interpretation, personal understanding and acceptance. However, the link between emotion and cognition is not quite so clear cut with this informant, due to his relatively mild impairment of recall and understated manner of speaking. Nonetheless, his emotional memories were strongly present, especially those concerning his mother. Further, his ability to tell his stories in some detail, minimised the possibility of misinterpretation.

Mrs Bessie Pinks (BP)

BP took part in nineteen recorded and transcribed interviews between April 1992 and August 1993. She had severe memory deficits, with poor short term memory, together with impaired long term memory. She, too, was a natural story teller who had stories to tell but these were fragmented and repetitive. However, she enjoyed speaking of her past. The social aspects of the investigation appeared to give her pleasure:

BP *Oh, I I like listening to the other people ... I always hope to find ... who ... who chat along.*

BP *... Yes. That's right! And meeting such a lot of different people! I think I I ... like that part. I think it's nice to meet a lot of people.*

BP did not like to recall unpleasant memories:

BP *Yes, Oh yes! I'm ... I don't like being miserable ... No ... Just take things as they come ...*

The interviewer argues that the significant topics in this informant's life were, again, those of loss. These were loss of childhood, loss of her child and loss of her memories:

BP *... I lived in Borham Rectory before I left school.*

Int. *Before you left school?*

BP *Yes. Because they had a maid there called Mabel, and em she kind of took a fancy to me. So I used to spend my evenings after school there, you see. And in the end I finished up by living there.*

BP *I just sort of grew into the place. I used to ... I was still going to school. They had a maid you see, she was 30 years old. Mabel. And she took a fancy to me, you see. We used to play games ... card games in the evening time there. In the end I slept there, because they said I was going home late at night, you see.*

BP *Well of course I drifted into the rectory, you see. They had a maid there, Mabel. She was one of the old fashioned type maids, you know ... Mabel ... And when I came home from school, I used to go in there, and they used to give me all sorts of things to do ... And I've just faded in there, you see ... And then I faded in to where she [Mabel] went out. Although I was still at school, I still worked there.*

Int. *So you missed your home?*

BP *Oh yes! I missed playing outside and ...*

Int. *You became grownup before wanted to?*

BP *I ... I did! Actually I did! Yes. Because I was always looked on as a little girl, but all of a sudden I was turned into a grown woman! ... Just like that!*

She felt she missed a lot of her childhood by commencing work at such a young age:

BP *Because I er I er ... None of this running out and round the streets after school. That that was wiped ... wiped out absolutely ... I just stayed in.*

According to her husband, BP had had a son who died some years ago:

BP *Er ... yes ... I had the baby. I still went back to work, and my mother looked after the baby.*
Int. *What happened to the baby?*
BP *Er ... He a boy ... er, Richard! ... Richard ... My Richard!*
Int. *Your Richard ...*
BP *Yes ... Richard ... Er, he married. He's still around.*
Int. *Is he?*
BP *Yes. He married. Er. Had two grandchildren.*
Int. *Two grandchildren?*
BP *Yes and er, I know it's a sad story. I er I don't why he died. I don't know. I never really been able to work it out ... What ... What caused his death, I don't know.*

During the case-study, BP frequently made reference to her failing memory:

Int. *Do you worry about remembering sometimes? (BP responded immediately to this question).*
BP *Yes I I had ... Oh it's dreadful. I forget things! That is one of my downfalls! All my life I ... my ... forget!*
Int. *And it's got worse has it?*
BP *Yes!*
Int. *It's a shame isn't it? ...*
BP *Oh, Oh. From very young I was forgetful! ... One of my downfalls ... Being so forgetful ...*
BP *You know I'm ... my brain's so muddled now about Richard. Of what did he die of? ...*
BP *... It's awful when you get to certain age! Seem to forget things.*

The significance of these topics for this informant appears to be supported by the evidence. Further, this informant had a fund of stories concerning her work at the rectory. She remembered a great deal about the car she drove for the rector and his wife, Mr and Mrs Romney:

BP *Yes It was ... and then they brought ... Do you know if you remember the Trojan cars, the great make cars they first came out. They brought a new ... new Trojan car, and I used to drive it.*

Int. *Did you like driving?*

BP *Yes but it's er ... it's tricky on the steering, because it's got solid tyres.*

Int. *Really?*

BP *Yes not pneumatic tyres ... They're sol ... solid tyres, with notches in and it's a bit heavy on steering. Yes, but I used to get away with it. (BP chuckled.)*

Although some of her memories of past experiences appeared to be relatively intact, the repetitive nature of her stories concerning the rectory, her childhood and the Trojan car, suggests that these memories were well rehearsed and well established. They were, after all, very old memories. However, as with other informants, BP was still able to surprise the interviewer late into the investigation by recalling a new story, the story of her little village shop. This took place in October 1992. As with other informants, the progression of her illness and inability of her spouse to cope with her behaviours meant that BP entered into long term residential care. Of interest is the final interview with this informant in August 1993, in which it is obvious that only faint traces of her former stories remained in memory:

Int. *What about when you were at the rectory? Do remember that?*

BP *Oh yes ... That's wrong. It ... long time ...*

Int. *Mm! You worked there a long time ...*

BP *Mm ... Yes I did ...*

Int. *Do you remember the name of the vicar?*

BP *Yes!*

Int. *What was his name?*

BP *... Dear ... Don't remember ...*

Int. *You drove their car didn't you?*

BP *Er ... William ...*

Int. *William?*

BP *William Rom ... Ney ...*

During the discussion of this case-study, it is suggested that this informant had emotional memories of the past which were still available for recall during the process of the interviews. There is a posited link between emotion and states of cognitive awareness. In addition, although her stories were fragmented, it was still possible to see them as part of a whole. As with Mr Biddley, it is suggested that the life story or narrative of BP is of interest, because it gives some indication of the developing relationship between memory and dementia during the later stages of this illness. It was possible to trace the progress of some of these memories throughout the life of the investigation. Many of these memories appeared to lose content until only a faint trace remained. However, even at the very end of the investigation, knowledge of BP's past stories gave the interviewer some assistance and marginal success in prompting some recall. There is some evidence that the process and management of dementia might inhibit the preservation of a sense of narrative identity. Although staff in BP's nursing home reported that she occasionally mentioned the rectory, they were unaware of her story and thus were unable to supply prompts and cues which may have aided some recall. The interviewer further suggests that by the time of the final interview BP had appeared to have lost the ability to recall her stories and had lost this sense of narrative identity.

The process of the interviews and the relationship with the interviewer also gave BP enjoyment:

> **BP** *You know, it's lovely getting to know you.*
> **BP** *Now I've seen a smiling face ...*
> **Int.** *You look happier. That's good isn't it?*
> **BP** *Yes ... Yes ... Yes I've picked up your smile ...*

Although BP was asked leading questions by the interviewer, the identified themes and interpretations did remain fairly constant over time. Further, although this informant, too, is presented in a very positive light, it is difficult to envisage how this might be otherwise. BP said that she disliked being miserable and enjoyed the social aspects of her meetings with the interviewer.

Mr Hugh Raft (HR)

HR was perceived by the interviewer as an unhappy man who might benefit from the psychotherapeutic aspects of the investigation. The interviews with HR began in August 1992 and continued until January 1994, with a total of thirteen recorded and transcribed interviews. HR had mild cognitive deficits and, for most of the interviews, was able to remember his past with some clarity. This case-study is interesting in that it appeared as if the informant himself had made inaccurate interpretations of his own life experiences. For this reason, a more psychodynamic interpretation of his meanings is given.

RH had recently remarried for the second time. His relationship with his new wife was poor. At the commencement of the investigation he frequently cried, and did so throughout many of the interviews. Life for him was not happy:

> **HR** ... *But er ... it is a good I think you if you can get dead somehow!*
> **HR** *I am sad! (Tears filled his eyes). I've been sad a long time darling.*

During the first interview, he spoke of his present wife:

> **Int.** *Are you happy in your second marriage or not really?*
> **HR** *Well ... Yes I think I am. She gets a bit funny now and again, but you got to put up with that at the moment haven't you?*
> **Int.** *But you're not as happy as with your first wife?*
> **HR** *Definitely not! No ...*

The story of his second marriage continued throughout the investigation and formed a significant theme. As the interviews progressed, it became obvious that his wife was giving him very mixed messages. She would tell him that she would never let him go but at the same time would tell involved agencies that she could no longer cope. This uncertainty caused HR some distress. Another significant theme was the story of his abused childhood. HR and his sister were illegitimate. They had different fathers. His mother had subsequently married and there were several children from this relationship. HR began to speak of these times during the first interview:

> **HR** *Cause it was a very hard life when I was a kid anyway.*
> **Int.** *You did?*
> **HR** *Oh yes! Hit about terrible!*
> **Int.** *Did you?*
> **HR** *Yes. Drunken father ... step father ... terrible man!*
> **Int.** *So you ... That would have frightened you to death when you were a boy ...*
> **HR** *No it didn't frighten me death, no. I just scared of keep getting good hidings. I sorry I got to tell you this sort of way, bu ... but it's all true!*

He also spoke of his time in the Army where he was a sergeant major. This again was very important to him and continued to be mentioned in many interviews:

HR *... I loved the Army.*
Int. *Had a good life really ...*
HR *Well! Up to the army ... It was good in the Army, honestly it was, very good indeed! Well I had had eight hundred and eighty men in my company!*

The interviewer suggests that period of his life was made more significant by his present uncertainties. It is argued that HR continued to remind himself, and others, of a time when he had authority, respect and his basic needs of security were met. His story of his ill-treatment at the hands of his stepfather, continued to develop in further interviews:

HR *Yes ... He's [stepfather] dead now he is, Thank God! (gave a short, harsh laugh). You see the great problem is he's ... I'll get something for his ... for the shops or something and I always made my mind up that I was going get it! But sometimes you wouldn't get it ... When I used to go home ... use some bloody good hidings! It was terrible, honestly!*
Int. *Was he a big chap?*
HR *No! He weren't much bigger 'n me! ... much bigger 'n me ... But he was always scrumpying [drinking cider] ... "Where's the little bastard to" he used to say! Oh ... I shall never forget that as long as I live ... (Bastard was said with great venom.)*
Int. *It must have been terrifying for you ...*
HR *Yet the other kids, you see, there was about nine ... eight or nine of us and he never touched them cause they weren't his kids ... Well they were his kids! But ... not ... not like I was ...*
HR *... Til it wasn't wasn't for five minutes. It was sometimes an hour he was hitting me about.*

Several interpretations of the themes both from a psychoanalytic and other, less interpretative, viewpoints are offered. It is suggested that most psychoanalytic theories from Adler to Winnicott, including Klein and Freud, to name but a few, were applicable to this informant. The significance of his abused childhood might explain much of his present personality. From a fairly young age, HR had been unloved and devalued. His unresolved memories of this time were with him still. He could tell his story but was unable to face the true reality of this abuse, it was too frightening for him to face the depths of his vulnerability. Using psychoanalytic theory, the interviewer suggests that he coped with this trauma by `splitting´ which is a defence mechanism that enables the self to disown `the bad self´ and to project it on to others. HR retained the `good self´. He continually praised himself for his achievements in order to feel better about himself and to deny that he was unworthy. He saw himself as a very good and kind person:

> **HR** *My great problem is I'm too gentle ... I personally feel that I'm ... I'm a bit too good.*
>
> **HR** *... I'm n' in the habit of getting in trouble with any ... not even the police or nothing. Touch wood I've never been in trouble. Though I thought I would have been done by now. But no, I've never stole nothing ... I was ... To be truthful, I was a little angel! I shouldn't say that really but I was! To myself!*

He felt his kindness to others was not reciprocated:

> **HR** *I'm silly like that ... I I help anybody, but the little buggers don't seem to want to help me! (Laughed nervously.)*

These explanations do follow the psychoanalytic school of thought. However, HR may well have wished merely to stress the fact that he did not deserve to be treated like this. It is possible that both explanations may hold some validity but will depend on the reader's own beliefs and background. Moreover, his view of his personal qualities seemed at variance with his role as a sergeant major. Further, HR had an unrealistic grasp of current concerns. During a period of great unrest with his second wife, he did not seem to appreciate the gravity of the situation:

> **HR** *Wasn't much of a tiff. Just ... just to say she didn't want me [to remain living with her] and that sort of thing.*

Less complex interviewer interpretations suggest that HR had some clearly defined themes which gave structure to his narrative. His grief over the loss of his first wife was evident and this may have re-emerged, due to the uncertainty of the present and the difficulties with his second relationship. His childhood memories occupied much of the interviews and he returned to them time and time again. His service career was a significant part of his life. He associated this time with very positive emotions. He continually reiterated his pride in his past role as a sergeant major.

The evidence appears to support these simple interpretations. Nevertheless, the approach used throughout these particular series of interviews suggests that it was beneficial for this informant. As the interviews progressed he gradually became happier. He possessed sufficient insight to acknowledge that the investigation had been partly responsible for this:

> **HR** *Any rate, thanks to you ... Thanks to everybody else, I'm here. Especially thanks to you ...*
> **Int.** *Well, I don't think I've done a lot.*
> **HR** *Yes you have! You you coming along cheers me up don't it?*

Nevertheless, he still saw his childhood as unhappy. When the interviewer asked him if he had a good life, he replied:

> **HR** *Noo! Not not family wise, no.*

However, he appeared able to see his childhood experiences more objectively. He appeared to become less of a victim:

> **Int.** *What did he [his stepfather] look like?*
> **HR** *Er ... He tall. He had his hair brushed back pretty thick and he walked on his on his toes quite a lot. As he walked along he he used to go up and down like this (bounced his hand up and down). He ... he had a beery complexion ... He was a right sod, he was. The only one good thing I had about it is my stepfather and his name was Wyatt. And police come and say, "Hugh that's not your dad there is it?" I said, "No, that's my stepfather."*

Towards the end of the investigation, he saw himself as a different person. His relationship with his wife had been relatively tranquil after a very upsetting period, and he felt happier:

HR ... *You done a lot for me, haven't you?*
Int. *Why?*
HR *What a different man I became! Be truthful!*
Int. *How do you feel about life at the moment? Is it quite good?*
HR *It's been very very good.*
Int. *So you've been happy? You're feeling happier?*
HR *Yes. Yes.*
Int. *But life's better for you now?*
HR *It's a 100% better, yes ...*

His memories of his first wife appeared to be less grief stricken. He told the interviewer, calmly, of a visit to the cemetery to lay some flowers on his first wife's grave. He did not cry. Indeed his tears had lessened as the investigation progressed. In November 1993, HR's wife finally decided she could no longer cope and HR entered residential care, after an initial period in the assessment ward of the setting. His memory was more obviously impaired and he had forgotten much that had previously caused him great distress. He no longer remembered being married to his second wife. He thought that he worked in the setting and felt useful.

Although the more obvious psychotherapeutic approach adopted by the interviewer has allowed the informant to be presented in a more objective manner it might still be suggested that HR is presented in a very favourable light, given some of the comments made by his wife. However, the interviewer has endeavoured to present HR in a factual manner and to offer clear explanations of complex interpretations. The interviewer argues that HR displayed strong emotions associated with significant life events in that his memories of these times were intact and readily available for recall, in spite of the influence of the dementing process.

It is also suggested that addressing the emotional content of his memories allowed him to expand upon their meaning and significance. A review of this case-study appears to support this argument. It is indicated that this informant did have very significant emotional memories, again, indicating the relationship between cognition and emotion. However, the interviewer goes on to suggest that HR rewrote his narrative, in that he began to see himself in a more realistic, yet positive, light. The fact that HR appeared to move from a state of bewilderment and uncertainty towards the possession of a certain peace and acceptance, offers some support for this argument. This change remained with him in spite of the major changes in his life. The interviewer further suggests that this may be attributable to the acceptance and interpretation of his narrative by others. Although it is obvious that HR did rewrite his narrative, as is shown by his comments concerning his past and present experiences, the major difficulties of analysing outcomes of this nature are that they can be interpreted very differently. HR may have gone further into denial and shut off his more painful memories of the present and the past. Alternatively, HR may have developed a more positive self image due to the psychotherapeutic nature of this intervention. Equally, the process of dementia may have diminished his memories and/or his concerns.

It is probable that the outcomes were due to all of the above and not solely dependent on any one process. This case-study suggests that various psychoanalytic theories offer understanding at a deeper level. However, it is impossible to rule out alternative explanations. As with all informants, HR has a progressive illness which inhibits recall, insight and understanding. Complex interpretations, therefore, must remain speculative. Nevertheless, it is possible to propose that the psychotherapeutic benefits of this investigation led to an increase in well-being and personhood for this informant. HR did, indeed, move from a state of ill-being at the beginning of the investigation to a state of increased well-being by the conclusion of the study.

Mr Melvin Rider (MR)

MR, who was the youngest informant in the group, was sixty-five years of age at the beginning of the investigation. The interviews with MR began in June 1992 and continued until January 1994. There were sixteen recorded and transcribed interviews with this informant. The difficulties inherent in talking to MR were apparent from the first. His impairment of speech led to the interviewer experiencing great difficulty in comprehending his meanings. Many of MR's words were transcribed phonetically. Further, the interviewer admits that many of his words had to be replayed several times before any understanding was achieved. There exists, therefore, a greater possibility of misinterpretation of meaning.

The interviewer identifies several themes present during many of the interviews. It is suggested that MR liked to keep busy and wanted to do his best:

MR *Well it's n n n not. I do want want a sat sat something to do!*

MR *Mm! Wha what d do I do n n now? I I I nothing else, there's n not ...*

Int. *Do you get bored?*

MR *Yes!*

Int. *Very bored ... ?*

MR *It's awful bor er er er!*

MR *I wanted t t t die ve to b be de um good!*

Int. *So you wanted everything you do to be really good?*

MR *Oh, as much as much as I can!*

MR's wife gives some support for this interpretation. Mrs Rider junior said that his mother was also something of a perfectionist who encouraged her son to achieve. MR had gone to a famous Oxbridge college where he obtained a degree in physics. The interviewer commented on his academic achievements. However, MR knew that he was not as he once was:

Int. *You've obviously got a very good brain.*

MR *(Paused.) It's em, it's not g goo good ge good goby gone now!*

As the interviews progressed, further deterioration developed in his cognitive abilities. The interviewer makes no attempt to offer a deep interpretation of MR's words but seeks to show their developing relationship, together with a partial account of MR's narrative. Where other than simple interpretation is offered, it is stated that it is highly speculative. The possible strength of this case-study, however, lies in MR's anguished view of the present which was shared by the interviewer. During a necessary short stay in the secure ward of the setting, MR made his feelings concerning his `imprisonment´ very clear. His speech was also more distinct:

Int. *And you feel angry?*

MR *I do! Very! Very!*

Int. *Very angry ... yes ... Do you feel people are making you do things?*

MR *What!*

Int. *Do you feel people are telling you what to do?*

MR *N No!*

Int. *No ...*

MR *N N N N I can't can't can't do d told. I I I not not not said! I've never seen la seen er ... and anything else! And that's what's on on on my my my bad head! (MR sounded frustrated and angry.)*

Int. *That's what on your mind? ... All the time?*
MR *Yes! Yes! (Said quietly and calmly.)*
Int. *And you're very upset ...*
MR *I I am! (Again said clearly.)*

He felt angry and grief stricken that he had no control over his life and present situation:

MR *No! No so so so rotten! er er rotten.*
Int. *You're sad and unhappy ...*
MR *I'm ad de de yes!*
Int. *You're sad and unhappy.*
MR *I'm very happy happy!*
Int. *Very unhappy?*
MR *Very! (MR began to cry. Speech became incoherent.)*

He appeared to be very conscious of his diminishing personhood and well-being:

MR *Very very very un ... (He cried again) ... Is er is isi si choughed from me! I can't can it's either had **always always** all all wa wa wa there ... It's Rider doing this!*

Following this traumatic interview, MR returned home and there was a long period of relatively tranquillity. There were no further periods in the secure ward. He seemed less anxious and was able to see his life in a more positive manner.

MR *... And it was good good good!*
MR *Oh it's good good days!*
Int. *Good days? ... Good days.*
MR *Yes, yes yes yes ...*

He seemed to have no major regrets that he could recall, concerning his life. His deep love for his wife remained very much part of him:

Int. *You've had a good life?*
MR *Mmm.*
Int. *Do you have any regrets?*
MR *(Paused). No! Does it gain, no ... Good!*
Int. *And you've been married a long time ... It's good!*
MR *Mm! And we d don't go far. We w de go ... like e e each other.*

The interviewer suggests that MR largely told his story in the form of accomplishments. The case-study would appear to support this observation. Further, it was possible to trace the disappearing content of his self stories. They showed a positive decline over time. Again, the interviewer comments on the need for simple interpretation of MR's narrative, given the possibility that exists for error. The interviewer suggests that the strongest interview, which took place on the secure ward, offers support for Sinason's (1992) argument that anger unlocks memory.

A review of the arguments suggests that the interpretations, simple and generalised though they are, are correct. It is not possible to offer deeper interpretations of this narrative. Considerations of the contents of this case-study, once again, show that MR was seen in a very favourable light. However, the interviewer admits that this informant had a great effect on her. Possibly the deep regard and sympathy for this very vulnerable informant may have slanted the writing of this case-study. Moreover, although the reported conversations and experiences with him are truthfully and accurately detailed, the feelings engendered in the interviewer by this informant spill over into the case-study. The interviewer gives many examples of his kindness to her and to others. However, the conclusions drawn by the interviewer are stated objectively, albeit with compassion.

Mr Ronnie Siverthorne (RS)

RS was one of more severely impaired informants in this study. His command of language had been affected by the process of dementia, making the task of interpretation more difficult. However, on many occasions it is admitted that the imprecise nature of his speech meant that only the more obvious of his meanings could be interpreted. RS met the interviewer between April 1992 and January 1993 giving a total of twenty-two recorded and transcribed interviews. The interviewer found RS to be a reserved man who was not readily given to discussing his personal life or his emotional experiences. Further, his anxiety and concern about the present diminished his need to recollect a personal past. However, several themes appeared to hold significance. These were his work and the respect of his former staff. Moreover, his wife and his home were very important topics for him. They seemed to be his locus of safety in an unsafe present. He was frequently found to be anxious in the setting. His general attitude towards others suggested that he was a caring and responsible person.

The first interview with RS indicates that these themes were important for him and appeared to remain so throughout most of the investigation. He frequently spoke of his wife and recalled her name:

> **RS** *Lillian Rose, yes*
> **Int.** *Lillian Rose.*
> **RS** *Yes and a very nice smart word she is too.*

He recalled that he had worked as a manager for several large department stores:

> **Int.** *You actually er ... em ... worked. Your job was ... you worked at Sutors [local store] didn't you, and Harrods?*
> **RS** *Yes, that's right. That was ... That's only one though.*

RS also introduced the topic of his former staff, and of the pleasure he felt during their greetings when they met. He mentioned this during subsequent interviews:

*(?) in text indicates failure to comprehend speech.

> **RS** *Yes. Was general manager from, at the other ones. It would be er shall we say (?) I was stayed with er, with them longer than I would of done. I had a very good staff.*
> **RS** *They were all there ... and I er was walking across the road. They pick over the road, come across the road to say hello.*
> **Int.** *After you left?*
> **RS** *Yes, oh yes!*
> **RS** *Yes, for a long time they still come along and cross the road and say "Hello Mr Silverthorne". It very nice, it was pleasant! Think that they would do it! And then they carried on, but it's been a long time since I er ... done it.*
> **Int.** *Means a lot to you when your old staff say hello doesn't it?*
> **RS** *Yes.*

RS also indicated his concern over leaving the setting and his desire to return to his wife and home:

Int. *So do you worry that you will miss the bus?*
RS *I do of course! Cause I've been a long time on it.*
Int. *Do you feel you've been here a long time?*
RS *I know I've been here a long time, yes!*
Int. *Do you worry about missing the car to take you home?*
RS *Well yes 'cause you got me wife at home.*
Int. *So you miss her when you are here do you?*
RS *Yes.*

The discussion of hospital transport led him to remember the reasons for the giving up of his own car:

RS *... Er er ... the wife said it was a very good idea, er I had to agree with her em and get rid of it, but it was sim, it was quite a pull.*
Int. *Oh I'm sure it was a pull! Did it make you feel bad when you got rid of it?*
RS *No er side because if it hit somebody and killed em, I'd be **more** than sad!*
Int. *Yes. Yes ...*
RS *Wouldn't I?*

This apparent concern for others was substantiated by his story of the store that burnt down. RS implied that he was very relieved that no one was hurt:

RS *... so I went to er away from that. **(?)** very good ... came all the way. Saves. Thank God for that.*

Although RS was described as a caring person, the interviewer suggested that he had an authoritarian personality due, perhaps, to his former position. Occasionally he appeared to treat the interviewer as if she was a member of his staff. He made it clear when he wished the interviews to end:

RS *You Madam, sit there!*
RS *But now I think I'm going to stop, because I don't know how much I've said!*

The interviewer found RS to be a worried and unhappy man who found it difficult to cope with the loss of autonomy. His following words appear to support this view:

> **Int.** *Well you're used to being in charge aren't you? You're used to telling other people what to do.*
> **RS** *Oh yes! Well that's it's gone from glory hasn't it?*

However, RS was still able to able to assert his authority at times:

> **Int.** *... Do you think people make you do things?*
> **RS** *Like to!*

There is some evidence to indicate that he felt powerless:

> **RS** *Well it's ... I've left it off for a long time. I've said I'd like like to do it again, but I don't suppose I will!*
> **Int.** *You'd rather be at home?*
> **RS** *Well you don't get it as easy as that!*

As with other informants, RS appeared to enjoy the interviews and his relationship with the interviewer.

> **RS** *Anyway, it's pleasant seeing you for a spot!*

As the investigation progressed, facets of his conversations indicated an apparent lucidity when Mr Silverthorne was speaking of emotionally meaningful events. His messages were relatively easy to understand at this time, suggesting that strong emotions overcame his speech deficits. However, RS usually managed to make himself understood. His cognitive processes appeared more intact than his speech deficits would suggest. He could still recall giving up driving, with some assistance from the interviewer:

> **RS** *Yes, er I've got no ... co ... cart now.*
> **Int.** *No car no. You had to give it up didn't you?*
> **RS** *No.*
> **Int.** *Mm?*
> **RS** *No. Didn't gave it up. Happens sometimes ...*
> **Int.** *Do you miss your car?*
> **RS** *Oh yeah! It's long time ago now. I was thought about it and said I'd like to do it again, but em I well I first did it, I first packed it up and er cider er off straight away. I didn't want, didn't want re rill kill this other person sees.*
> **Int.** *Didn't want to hurt anybody?*
> **RS** *No! No!*

RS was also able to make the interviewer understand that he was cross with her for leaving him to talk to another informant, again indicating that his emotions empowered memory and speech processes:

> **RS** *It blissfully ... you blissfully take me these things, and you should really say Mr Silverthorne is such and such, and er you come in as if you come in from outside and go into the ziggles. It's way I can't do it. I stay pect stay in big outside there, and take all the pieces where we going and er n not happy!*

By the sixth interview, the interviewer noted that RS's self stories concerning his past experiences, appeared to be fading in importance. He seemed more preoccupied with present concerns. His stories concerning his work, his staff and his car were still there but were assuming a more shadowy substance. This fading of self stories seemed to be of some significance and caused problems for the interviewer as the following conversation indicates. The interviewer thought that RS wanted to run away from the setting but he wanted the `bus lady´ to take him home:

> **RS** *Now I wan, what I want. I really want! Most unlikely, is the er run run lady.*

With the fading of memories came the fading of concerns for others, a fading of conscientiousness. He began to talk about driving again:

> **Int.** *Do you still miss driving the car?*
> **RS** *Oh yes. I'd like to! Eventually I think I might have it ... with champagne ... yes.*
> **Int.** *You liked driving didn't you?*
> **RS** *I did, yes ...*

However, RS was still able to surprise the interviewer by giving more content to previously told stories, such as the store that burnt down:

> **RS** *... That was a game and a half.*
> **Int.** *A game and a half was it? ... It must have terrible when the police told you ...*
> **RS** *Mmmm, I can't put shooting along all wrong!*
> **Int.** *Got down there quick did you?*
> **RS** *Mmm ... Yes it bit tight ...*

Int. *Was it a bad fire.*

RS *Well, it was bad enough ... It went right to the opposite side of the road.*

However, all of his stories began to fade as his illness and the investigation progressed. He could not remember meeting his wife when they worked at Harrods:

Int. *That's where you met Lillian.*

RS *Long time!*

Int. *Long time ago ... You met Lillian there.*

RS *What work did we seek to be?*

Shortly after this conversation, the effects of his illness began to increase and RS was eventually admitted to the setting as a long term patient. He died in January 1993.

The interviewer suggests that the narrative of RS contained several important themes. He was not given to displaying his emotions as readily as other informants and he did not disclose to such a deep level, as did AC. The interviewer argues that this was mainly due to RS's personality, but she did meet his psychotherapeutic needs and, in part, encouraged well-being by allowing him to control the process and content of the interviews. This, it is suggested, helped to maintain higher levels of self esteem for RS.

It is, however, impossible to say if his reluctance to disclose was due entirely to this aspect of his personality. This may have been due to the process of his illness and loss of memories necessary for emotional disclosure. Equally, the approach used by the interviewer may not have been sufficiently experienced/skilful to encourage disclosure of these memories. Alternatively, RS's inability to recall more of his emotional past may have been due to all of the above. This is probably a more realistic assessment of the situation. Further, although it is possible to agree that the approach used during the investigation allowed RS to experience increased well-being and to retain/enhance his self esteem, it must be argued that his present circumstances did not allow him to do so. It is more realistic to suggest that this approach did not further diminish his levels of self esteem.

Finally, the interviewer discusses the significance of his fading self stories. The case-study does suggest that his stories slid away, until they remained only as a vague outline in memory. Again, the comment is made that his emotional memories were linked to states of cognitive awareness and that RS was able to recall tiny pieces of his personal past or narrative. These arguments appear to be supported by the evidence. Further, this case-study draws attention to the inherent difficulties in trying to gather such data from elderly people with fairly advanced dementia. It is, at this point, that one must question the charge that RS was asked leading questions. Did the interviewer cause RS to respond in such a manner as to conform to interviewer interpretations? Certainly, at times, RS was led by the interviewer. However, the total content of this case-study suggests that the themes of the discussed topics were offered by RS, himself, rather than the interviewer. Finally, again it is possible to see admiration and liking for this informant. However, the presentation and discussion of the data suggests that this is an honest account of the interviews held with this person. Although it is clear that the interviewer felt much sympathy for RS, it does not prevent the reader from having some understanding of the problems inherent in caring for this highly anxious and confused man.

Mrs Abigail Woodley (AW)

AW was seen by the interviewer from April 1992 until July 1993, with a total of twenty-five recorded and transcribed interviews. The narrative of this informant suggests that AW was a moderately demented, timid and fearful lady who had an uneasy relationship with her mother. Although her mother had died, AW persisted in seeing her as still very much alive. AW was extremely frightened of her mother, and the evidence suggests that the psychotherapeutic approach used during the interviews allowed her to explore her life-story and emotional memories concerning her mother. Further, this exploration appeared to unravel the twisted bonds between her memories of her mother and AW's low self esteem. The series of interviews concludes with AW indicating that she had increased levels of well-being and personhood, as is shown through her increased self confidence and expressed feelings of happiness, together with little obvious concern over her mother's whereabouts. These positive outcomes were substantiated by staff in the setting. Given the initial criticisms of this work, however, one must ask if this is the only possible explanation for these positive outcomes? Indeed, it is also possible to question the basic premise of the case-study. Was AW still frightened of her mother or is there some other explanation of her fear?

The first of the transcribed interviews with AW indicate that she freely introduced the topic of her mother:

Int. *Do you see your daughter very often?*
AW *Oh yes. It's also centred round my mother.*
Int. *Oh I see.*
AW *She holds the strings.*

This suggests that AW saw her mother as a powerful person. Further, this interview also suggests that AW did not have a happy childhood:

> **AW** *She [mother] did say to me ... well the last time we two had a conversation, she kept on saying "Oh thank goodness when these days are over, I just cannot stand them. It's about time these children grew up!"*

Thus, the suggestion that AW was in awe of her mother and that she may have had somewhat negative memories of her childhood, would appear to rest on AW's interpretation of meaning. Further, it will be recalled that her husband said her mother had been a difficult person who worried AW. The following conversation indicates AW's fear and dislike of her mother:

AW *I shouldn't get too friendly with her!*
Int. *... I should be frightened to death of her!*
AW *Oh Yes! Sss! (laughed). Where'd you put that stick yesterday?*
Int. *Was she like that?*
AW *She had a real cane, you know ...*
Int. *Did you ever feel you disliked her?*
AW *Oh yes! Ooh, there's not a lot of liking about it!*

AW said that she disliked arguments and loud voices:

> **AW** *I was! Ah it was terrible! ... And any horrible job that wanted doing either my mother or my father did it and then they used to stand up and have a row. (Row was said as if it was a nasty word.) Oh gosh what can you do with them!*
Int. *So you've never liked nasty atmospheres then, have you?*
AW *No! No.*
AW *She [mother] does shout! I must admit that!*
Int. *She's got a loud voice?*
AW *Mm. It frightens me you know!*

114

It was a relief when her mother died, although AW did not like admitting this:

> **Int.** *You must have felt quite relieved when she died really ...*
> **AW** *Well I was! I mean, well it's an awful thing to have to say isn't it, about your own mother?*

Again, the interpretations of the main themes of AW's life rest upon her own words. She frequently referred to her `worrying nature´ throughout the series of interviews. However, her worries appeared to stem from memories of her mother:

> **AW** *I do worry! It's no good to say I don't. I do! I'm always worried about her.*
> **AW** *Oh I ... Oh, yes. I managed to keep it in there. (Pointed to her chest.)*
> **Int.** *Do you think it is your mother who made you a nervous lady?*
> **AW** *I think so really! I know it's unkind to say I suppose, but I used to be able to hear her shout from one end of the house to the other.*

When AW was asked if she thought she would ever forget about her mother, she replied:

> **AW** *No ... Little things come back in my mind every now and again, you know, and it was " What are you doing up here? You'll have to go on downstairs out of the way. I can't be troubled with you!" And things like that, you know. I mean, it hurts!*
> **Int.** *Oh yes ... So all your memories of your mum they're ... they're hurtful memories are they?*
> **AW** *Yes ... Oh yes!*

The case-study gives many examples of AW's lack of self esteem. AW felt full of `badness´. She did not feel good at anything and was surprised that people in the setting liked her. She saw herself as very fearful. When asked if she ever wanted to drive, she replied that she had no courage for that. She said that she thought about her mother every day. AW felt it was her mother who had made her nervous:

> **Int.** *You carry it on your shoulder ... So a born worrier?*
> **AW** *Mm ...*
> **Int.** *Probably your mum started that off though, wasn't it?*
> **AW** *Oh yes!*

Int. *Because if you were brought up like that ...*
AW *It follows doesn't it?*

AW's final sentence suggests that she followed the conversation and agreed with the interviewer's interpretations. The evidence, so far, indicates that the significant themes of AW's life, as suggested by the interviewer, appear to be correct. This is substantiated by the words of this informant. However, during the tenth interview, AW spoke of her shame at having to disclose her feelings concerning her mother:

Int. *And we've talked about your relationship with your mother a lot.*
AW *That was awful wasn't it? ... Oh I felt awful!*
Int. *It was your mother who helped you feel like that ...*
AW *Mm ... Yes ...*
Int. *But she's gone now ...*
AW *Shame isn't it?*
Int. *Shame she's gone, or a shame that she was so horrible?*
AW *That I was ... I was ashamed to think that, you know, I had to ... sort of talk to people and ...*
Int. *About your mother?*
AW *Mm.*

The interviewer suggested that this was a significant conversation, in that AW was able to recall that she had spoken of her mother in detail and that, on some level, the disclosures had been beneficial for her. The interviewer claimed that this recall is, perhaps, challenging to existing knowledge as dementia negatively affects both short term and long term memory structures and processes, although the decline is most evident in short term memory. Further, the interviewer argued that these recalled memories of AW were comparatively recent and should, perhaps, be less readily available. Therefore, it might be possible to tentatively suggest that, in some way, the high emotional content and personal meaning of AW's story of her mother allowed her to retain and access these memories, in spite of inhibiting damage to neural structures and pathways. This finding is of some significance and should be carefully examined. Scrutiny of the actual conversation indicates that, at the beginning of the conversation, AW may have tried to say that speaking of her negative feelings concerning her mother made her feel uncomfortable:

Int. *And we've talked about your relationship with your mother a lot.*
AW *That was awful wasn't it? ... Oh I felt awful!*

116

Further, the interviewer offered AW a choice of meanings:

> **AW** *Shame isn't it?*
> **Int.** *Shame she's gone, or a shame that she was so horrible?*

AW chose neither of these interpretations:

> **AW** *That I was ... I was ashamed to think that, you know, I had to ...*
> *sort of talk to people and ...*
> **Int.** *About your mother?*
> **AW** *Mm.*

AW, therefore, gave meaning to her own words and explained her meaning to the interviewer. The conclusions which must be drawn, given the evidence, is that AW did recall recently speaking of her mother to the interviewer and, possibly, the emotions surrounding her memories of her relationship with her mother generated this recall. As the interviews progressed, AW appeared to experience increased levels of well-being. She said that she used to hide her feelings and worries:

> **AW** *No! (laughed joyously) I used to tuck them away! Written on a*
> *piece of paper! ...*
> **AW** *Oh yes! You must get rid of these feelings mustn't you, that hurt*
> *you ...*

AW reported feeling happier and having more confidence:

> **AW** *No I've ... Well I can definitely say I do feel happy now! Really*
> *happy!*
> **AW** *Well, I I sh sh sort of felt ... sort of more confident!*

The evidence for AW's increased levels of well-being would appear to be strong, supported as it is by her own words and the staff in the setting. However, the interviewer does suggest that the psychotherapeutic approach used throughout the investigation, together with the process of the interviews, allowed AW to resolve her troubled memories of her mother. This resolution aided and encouraged well-being and personhood. The interviewer argues that AW's own words, from one of the final interviews, support this thesis:

117

Int. *Do you think about the old days at all?*
AW *No!*
Int. *No ... Just about now ...*
AW *I've got no ... I've got no regrets as to where my mother is or ... has gone or, you know ... But ... you know, for a week or two I was quite upset.*

It is possible that this is not the only explanation for this finding. It could be argued that the memory loss due to the process of dementia may have been responsible for this loss of anxiety concerning her mother. AW may no longer have possessed many negative memories of her mother. However, AW did recall that she had been upset. Further, she spontaneously spoke of her mother without immediate prompting. Nevertheless, the effects of dementia are well documented and it is impossible to state, unreservedly, that AW had reached a stage of resolution due to the interventions used during the interviews. However, neither is it possible to dismiss the arguments that resolution did occur, and that this was largely due to the psychotherapeutic approach used during this investigation.

Although an examination of this particular case-study suggests that this informant was held in high regard by the interviewer, the use of the informant's own words to tell her story does minimise biased interpretations. This, of course, applies to all informants. Moreover, the data largely support the interpretations given by the interviewer/researcher. Nevertheless, it is impossible to unconditionally concur with all interpretations, due to present incomplete knowledge of this illness and its processes. However, this informant did indicate a link between cognition and emotion through the recall of her emotional memories. She also gave small parts of her life history which gradually cohered into her own personal narrative and which contained strongly emotional memories of the self. Further, AW appeared to have enjoyed the process of the interviews and her relationship with the interviewer. Finally, this informant indicated a changed personality and clear evidence of increased well-being.

Discussion

The meta analysis of these case-studies supports the argument that, to varying degrees, all informants possessed emotional memories. This suggests and supports the concept of a linked and intertwined relationship between cognition and emotion. In addition, the discussion of the narrative is of some significance. It is evident from these case-studies that all informants told their stories and these stories gradually dissolved as the effects of the dementing process increased. This is clearly indicated in the case-studies of Mr Silverthorne, Mrs Pinks, Mr Biddley and Mr Rider. The case-studies of Mrs Woodley and Mr Raft also indicated the beginnings of this process of narrative loss. This dissolution of a sense of narrative identity within dementia is of some consequence. Those interventions which seek to maintain the narrative within dementia are therefore of great importance. Maintenance of story was linked to maintenance of personhood and well-being in the informants.

Mrs Woodley's sense of a more complete narrative identity enabled her to experience greater happiness than before. Her mother had less of a negative influence upon her. The final interview with this informant and evidence from staff in the setting, supports this argument. Mr Silverthorne, too, experienced greater levels of well-being for a time. His levels of self esteem were supported by the interviewer. He enjoyed recalling meetings with his former staff and the welcome they gave him. Mr Clerkenwell gained pleasure in recalling some of his past. Although his memories of the war were brutal, they did not overshadow more happier times. Further, he enjoyed his relationship with the interviewer. Mrs Pinks experienced greater well-being for a time. Her case-study gives clear evidence that she appreciated the social aspects of this investigation and the opportunity to tell her stories. This was also true of Mr Biddley. He loved to laugh and to tell the interviewer that this made life worthwhile. Mr Coxley found the investigation to be therapeutic. He was able to explore his painful memories of his mother but also to recall happier times spent working on the farm. Mr Rider, although severely affected by this illness, appeared to have gained pleasure from most of the interviews. He, too, recalled more cheerful times and this appeared to give him happiness. The final informant, Mr Raft, clearly experienced therapeutic benefits from the investigation. He was a happier person at the conclusion of the investigation than before.

There are, therefore, both theoretical and therapeutic implications attached to these findings. All of the case-studies indicate that informants experienced increased levels of well-being through the process of the investigation. Various arguments are offered to support findings for each individual. However, it would appear that the concept of individual interviews to recall the past, with the aid of interviewer counselling skills are of benefit to some older people with dementia. These therapeutic and theoretical implications require further examination and discussion and will, therefore, be scrutinised in greater depth during the next two chapters of this work.

During the introduction to this chapter, an initial examination of the case-studies as a whole suggested two possible areas of concern. One was the possibility of bias in the interviewer's interpretation of informant's responses. The meta analysis of the individual case-studies suggests that the interpretations offered by the interviewer were largely substantiated. Although alternative explanations could be offered to explain informant's meanings, they did not disprove but rather qualified the arguments of the interviewer.

The second area of concern was the interviewer's depth of regard for all informants. The examination of individual case-studies suggests that this is made manifest in all case-studies. However, although all informants were treated with sympathy and understanding, the interviewer sought to minimise bias through the use of the actual words of all informants. The informants told their own stories. The evident regard held by the interviewer for all informants did not allow the interviewer to offer faulty interpretations during these case-studies. Thus, although positive bias was present, it did not cloud the case-studies. Is it possible to guard against such positive bias in an investigation of this nature? It is probably impossible to do so. The characteristics of this type of research suggest that it is the relationship between informant and interviewer which generate such rich data. Perhaps this type of longitudinal relationship can only be achieved when genuine liking is present. It would be difficult to do this type of research if there was indifference or actual dislike of informants. It is probable that this category of research is more often undertaken by those investigators who like older people with dementia. The interviewer, herself, is one such investigator. During the introduction to this work, it is made clear that she likes and respects older people, with or without dementia. It is, therefore, probable that positive bias will exist in research of this nature. Nevertheless, interviewers should be made aware of this personal characteristic and, where possible, seek to moderate its effects without any reduction of therapeutic benefits for those who take part in this type of inquiry.

6 Implications for therapeutic practice

Introduction

The individual and group therapeutic effects of this investigation will be discussed further during this chapter, together with the importance of the counselling skills used extensively throughout all interviews with the informants. Finally, the chapter will close with an examination of the ethical considerations in the use of this approach with vulnerable demented people.

Therapeutic considerations

Indications that the therapeutic benefits were generalised suggest that these outcomes might not be wholly influenced by individual informant personality, life chances and present state of health, but rather on the approach used during this investigation. Further, if the approach benefitted all informants without exception, then this may have additional implications in the management and care of other sufferers of dementia. All informants, without exception, showed signs of a marked increase in levels of well-being. For some, this increase in well-being continued after the conclusion of the interviews. One explanation for this occurrence is that the meanings they had attributed to some of their life experiences had altered. This may have led to positive change in the perception of self, or, as Kitwood and Bredin (1992) would suggest, a return/recreation of personhood and well-being. This reworking or rewriting of the personal narrative, is supported by McAdams (1993) who argues that the life story is not fixed or final, but is always open to change. These immediate therapeutic changes have been well documented in the literature, as is discussed in chapter one of this work. Extended individual therapeutic change however, has not received the same level of attention, although it is implicit in the work of many practitioners including that of Feil (1982, 1985, 1992), Kitwood (1990a, 1990b, 1993), Kitwood and Bredin (1992) and Sinason (1992).

Therapeutic implications for individual informants

Mr Robert Biddley

The case-study concerned with Mr Biddley indicated that he still retained many social skills. Although well known in the locality he had few close friends. As with other informants, he enjoyed the interpersonal aspects of the investigation. Talking to other people gave him pleasure:

> *Oh, I've always em, have a chat with anybody, you know.*

It is, perhaps, this facet of his personality that allowed him to take delight in some of the interviews. He very much enjoyed laughing and sharing a joke and, prior to the increase in the severity of his illness, laughter filled many of the interviews. Mr Biddley found it difficult to share his feelings, although he displayed clear grief at the loss of his cognitive abilities. He continually spoke of the importance of accepting life and others and he did not appear to have any major regrets about his life:

> *... You just do the best things you can, don't you?*
> *... I think I'm I'm just as good good as most ...*

Again, as with other informants, Mr Biddley said that he enjoyed his conversations with me:

> *You and I talking our bits ... Quite decent isn't it?*

Although Mr Biddley deteriorated rapidly during the course of the investigation, and, indeed, was admitted to the secure wing of a psychogeriatric nursing home, he was still able to enjoy much of our time together. Compared to other informants, this timespan may have been short, but it existed.

Mr Charles Clerkenwell

Mr Clerkenwell, too, gained much enjoyment from the interview process. He was a hesitant person but one who had a good social veneer which covered his feelings of inadequacy:

I have been shy in my time, yes ... Believe me!

Again, the psychotherapeutic approach benefitted this informant. This approach sustained and supported him during his recall of a traumatic past:

You ... don't be dramatic, but you came at death's door several times.

The loss of his eyesight gave him much grief:

This is the curse (pointed to his eyes).

These brief snippets of information do not do justice to the rich recall displayed by Mr Clerkenwell. He told his stories with verve and flamboyance, and the sharing of his narrative gave him much pleasure. Our relationship also seemed meaningful for him. He readily expressed his desire to continue our meetings:

And you're a very charming person, and I'd be delighted!

He loved to make me laugh:

Oh ... now ... I've cracked a funny! This is lovely! Oh, I'm not going to let you go!

He was more ready to be happy than unhappy:

What's the good of being miserable when it's so easy to be happier?

Although there is no question that Mr Clerkenwell's past experiences were frightening, the interviews allowed him to review his past life with some support. The process appeared to be therapeutic for him as he endeavoured to understand the reasoning and cruelty of his captors. He was also able to look back on his life as a whole and see that it was good. The strength of his stories was evident. Mr Clerkenwell demonstrated the meaningful relationship between life and story with great clarity. The sharing of his narrative enabled him to retain a sense of narrative identity and to indicate to others the importance of this role.

Mr Andrew Coxley

Mr Coxley was a slow speaking quiet man who initially found it difficult to share his concerns and feelings. He appeared to be the sort of person who "tucked it all away" as Mrs Woodley would say. He, too, was not given to emotional displays. However, Mr Coxley enjoyed taking part in the investigation. His memory loss was mild and he was well able to remember our conversations and to look forward to our meetings. Initially, he reminisced about his work on the farm, a time that gave him great pleasure. As the interviews progressed, he was able to speak of his troubled childhood. Gradually it became apparent that he had never fully resolved his grief and guilt over his mother. He tried very hard to believe that he had done his best for her. Even towards the end of the investigation, he spoke of his feelings at being in the same setting as his mother. He would often point out the building to me:

She was then over there. That place haunts me, over there.

It upset him to pass by the building on his way to the day hospital:

Oh, it's that bit over there. I hate coming ... round that bit.

However, Mr Coxley was able to speak of much of his past life with acceptance. He often reminisced about aspects of his life on the farm. He was aware that these days were never to return. Nevertheless, recalling them gave him pleasure. Overall, he enjoyed the process of the interviews. He felt it had been helpful talking to me:

Oh yes! Makes a difference for the say, don't it?

Again, this informant benefitted from the psychotherapeutic approach used throughout this investigation. Unlike Mrs Woodley, we were never able to fully resolve his grief and guilt over his mother, but possibly speaking about it allowed him to come to terms with much that had been worrying him. He was able to say that he had tried to do his best, although he was constantly reminded of this part of his life by his present environment. More positive aspects of his reminiscence was his ability to recall his beloved farm and his tractor. He was also able to act as a teacher/historian, and taught me to view agricultural work from a different perspective. This gave him satisfaction and contentment.

Mrs Bessie Pinks

Mrs Pinks was a lady who loved the interpersonal aspects of the investigation. She enjoyed laughing and talking with others and recounting her past achievements pleased her. She had travelled extensively in her younger days and had welcomed the opportunity to experience other cultures. Although this might suggest that Mrs Pinks had an extrovert personality, she was, in fact, quite a shy person who was not given to readily disclosing her feelings other than on a social and superficial level. She did however, speak of her feelings at leaving her home and going to work before she left school:

> *I was always looked on as a little girl, but all of a sudden I was turned into a grown woman!*

Mrs Pinks enjoyed her growing relationship with the researcher as the investigation progressed:

> *You know, it's lovely getting to know you.*

Mrs Pinks liked the pleasant things in life. She did not like being miserable or worried:

> *I don't like being miserable ... No ... Just take things as they come ...*

A review of the interviews with Mrs Pinks suggests that this lady, too, can be considered to have experienced greater levels of well-being during most of this investigation.

Mr Hugh Raft

Mr Raft initially was, perhaps, the unhappiest of all the informants. He became part of the investigation purely for therapeutic purposes and most of his case-study describes the personal therapeutic benefits of the investigation. He was a quiet man with limited insight concerning his behaviour and relationships. Further, he had a poor self image which was probably due to his emotional neglect and physical abuse in his early childhood years. Reports from his wife and other carers who had known him for some years prior to the onset of dementia, suggest that his adaptive self was not strong. The progression of his illness and life circumstances further weakened this part of his personality, allowing his very vulnerable experiential self to come under attack (Kitwood, 1988). There was great stress in his life. Initially, at the beginning of the investigation, he was a very unhappy man who wanted to die:

It is a good I think you if you can get dead somehow!

However, as the interviews progressed he gradually became happier. He possessed sufficient insight to acknowledge that the investigation had been partly responsible for this:

Especially thanks to you ...

Life began to improve for him and by the end of the investigation, he saw himself as a different person:

What a different man I became! Be truthful!

For this informant the therapeutic benefits of the investigation were very evident. There are a number of possible explanations for this. The process of the investigation allowed him to form a stable and successful relationship with the researcher. Further, he had a very good relationship with his social worker. Both of these relationships gave him respect and encouragement. They would appear to have supported him throughout a very stressful period in his life. Moreover, the exploration of his earlier life, the death of his first wife and his painful relationships in the present, allowed him to re-evaluate and thus, rewrite his narrative. In general terms, he saw his life as less bleak and himself as more worthwhile, even as his illness progressed. This might of course be attributed to the process of dementia. It might be argued that Mr Raft may have forgotten that he was ever unhappy, and that this absence of remembered unhappiness led him to believe he was happy. However, the absence of a negative feeling state does not ensure the presence of a positive feeling state. Feeling states are based on biological, psychological and social processes.

As the interviews progressed, Mr Raft slowly moved from a negative state of mind to a more positive state of mind. He implied that he felt good about himself and pleased with life. Feeling good about himself allowed him to experience and report feelings of increased well-being.

Mr Melvin Rider

Mr Rider was also an informant who liked meeting other people. His illness had severely damaged his cognitive abilities but, even so, he found many of the interviews to be pleasant. This apparent enjoyment was displayed more by his affectionate behaviour rather than his conversation. However, he also enjoyed recalling his times of past accomplishments:

> *Oh it's good good days! ... Yes, yes yes yes ... (He smiled joyously as he said this. His tone of voice sounded happy.)*

He seemed to have no major regrets that he could recall, concerning his life:

> **Int.** *You've had a good life? ...*
> **MR** *Mmm ...*
> **Int.** *Do you have any regrets?*
> **MR** *(Paused) ... No! Does it gain, no ... Good!*

However, Mr Rider did have many major concerns and anxieties which were concerned with the present. Like Mr Silverthorne, his illness had led to a state of powerlessness. There were times when he was bereft at being separated from his wife. This was never more apparent than during the interview which took place on the secure ward of the setting. Was the process of disclosure during these times good for him? This is difficult to say. I certainly felt we had shared some very painful times and this may suggest possible therapeutic implications for him. Even so, I am still not sure and perhaps this is for others to judge. Mr Rider was always delighted to see me and welcomed me with great hugs and expressions of affection. Possibly this alone might indicate that he found the process of the investigation to be beneficial for him. His recounted experience of the subjective world of the dementia sufferer could decidedly benefit other victims of this illness, through changes in the management of this disease.

Mr Ronnie Silverthorne

Mr Silverthorne was a very private person who appeared to have led a very structured existence prior to the commencement of his illness. During his working life, he had kept his work (public life) and his home life (private life) distinctly separated. Evidence from his wife and colleague supported this viewpoint. He was quite surprised when I told him that I occasionally worked at home:

> *Been at home working? (He sounded incredulous.)*

During the investigation, he was found to be a highly anxious man who found great difficulty in coping with the loss of autonomy due to his illness:

> *Well that's it's gone from glory hasn't it?*

Throughout the investigation it was difficult to encourage Mr Silverthorne to say how he felt. He appeared to be quite reticent:

> *I think I'm going to stop, because I don't know how much I've said!*

However, the approach used in the interviews allowed him to retain his senior managerial stance. He found it extremely easy to tell me what to do. Further, he still felt able to assert his authority at times:

> **Int.** *Do you feel you're made to do things? Do you think people make you do things?*
> **RS** *Like to!*

However, he knew that this authority was slowly waning:

> **Int.** *You'd rather be at home?*
> **RS** *Well you don't get it as easy as that!*

He was aware that there were things he would never be able to do again:

> *I've said I'd like like to do it again, but I don't suppose I will (he sounded sad).*

He did, however, appear to experience some enjoyment through speaking to the researcher:

Anyway, it's pleasant seeing you for a spot.

Although disclosing his stories did not allow him the same degree of ease as Mrs Woodley, he did find some pleasure in recalling the past. He spoke of his achievements in some detail and it will be remembered that he repeatedly recalled his former staff greeting him when they saw him after he had retired. This meant a great deal to him. Further, the evidence from this informant suggests that he found some therapeutic benefits from the investigation. He was able to retain a sense of autonomy and control over the interview process. His adaptive self, which was so important to him, was supported by the interviewer stance of deference and respect. His experiential and feeling self was largely hidden throughout our time together, but, again, this reserve was respected. Mr Silverthorne appeared to enjoy our conversations. He was able to be himself, or, perhaps, which ever of these selves he wanted to be (Kitwood, 1988, 1990a, 1993).

Mrs Abigail Woodley

Mrs Woodley was one of the informants who appeared to gain much from the psychotherapeutic nature of the investigation. Initially, this quiet and introspective lady found it difficult to disclose her thoughts and feelings, but eventually was able to speak of her outer and inner `burden´ of worries:

Oh yes, I carry it on my shoulder ... Oh I ... Oh, yes. I managed to keep it in there (pointed to her chest).

The main focus of her narrative was her troubled relationship with her mother. She was able to say that she was relieved when her mother died. It was not easy for her to admit this. The disclosure and acceptance of her feelings appeared to be therapeutic. She said that it was important to disclose negative and painful feelings:

Oh yes! You must get rid of these feelings mustn't you, that hurt you ...

She admitted that it was something she had not done before:

I used to tuck them away! Written on a piece of paper! ...

Staff reported that she had begun to laugh more frequently and seemed to find life more enjoyable. During the last recorded interview she was able to think of her mother with less regret:

I've got no ... I've got no regrets as to where my mother is or ... has gone or, you know.

She said she felt more confident:

Well, I I sh sh sort of felt ... sort of more confident!

She retained her feelings of well-being:

Yes! ... Crumbs, a lot happier ...

The evidence suggests that Mrs Woodley found the process of the interviews to be very therapeutic for her. Further, her reported feelings of happiness remained with her, even as her memory continued to decline. Mrs Woodley could not recall our individual meetings. Indeed, I am not sure if she remembered any of them. However, she continued to recognise me when I appeared in the setting, even after an absence of many weeks. Our last meeting was in May 1994 and she smiled with pleased surprise when she looked up and saw me walk into the dayroom. Staff in the setting commented on how happy she was to see me. It is probable, therefore, that Mrs Woodley associated me with pleasant experiences.

Therapeutic outcomes generated by most forms of psychotherapy depend on memory. Painful episodes are recalled and explored with the therapist who endeavours to help the client achieve understanding and resolution. Mrs Woodley, however, did not remember this process, but the beneficial outcomes of lessened anxieties and greater levels of happiness appeared to remain with her. It was as if a psychological healing had occurred and the essence of this event was retained somewhere in memory. There is little in the literature to explain this phenomenon, although there is some supporting evidence in the work of Feil (1985, 1992), Gardner (1993), Kitwood (1990a, 1990b), Kitwood and Bredin (1993), Hausman (1992) and Sinason (1992). There is, therefore, growing recognition of the importance of psychotherapeutic interventions for people with dementia. Coleman (1994) suggests that there exists the unrealised potential of life review counselling for older people.

Finally, not only does this brief review of the informants' words indicate that, at various stages during the interviews, they all reported feelings of well-being, it also suggests that they felt good about life during this time. A number of references have been made to this therapeutic finding, and it is now appropriate to examine this area in more detail.

Considerations of personality traits within dementia

Feelings of well-being are associated with the personality trait of extraversion, which is seen as one of the five major basic personality traits in human functioning, as identified by McCrae and Costa (1987). McAdams (1990) suggests that the `big five´, traits of neuroticism (N), extraversion/introversion (E), conscientiousness/undirectedness (C), openness to experience (O) and agreeableness/antagonism (A), are generally accepted as providing a rough but useful taxonomy in personality research. Further, it is posited by Costa and McCrae (1988) and Digman (1990) that basic personality traits in adult humans are well established and suffer little change throughout life. Recent research by Siegler et al. (1991) and Williams et al. (1995) suggest that there are personality changes which are associated with dementia. Further, Eysenck (1967) has speculated that some personality traits, such as extraversion/introversion and neuroticism, are caused by varying response times in brain function and structures. These brain structures and processes are known to become compromised in dementia (Damasio et al., 1990). However, this biological underpinning of traits is not universally accepted within trait psychology. McAdams (1990) argues that personality traits are more generally seen as a product of both nature and nurture. Nevertheless, the research into personality changes in dementia has highlighted changes in the personality traits of extraversion, neuroticism and conscientiousness, with sufferers of dementia becoming less conscientious and extravert, but more neurotic. The study by Siegler et al. (1991) also found informants to be slightly less open but with little difference in the trait of agreeableness. Williams et al. (1995) found little mean difference in these two traits. These studies relied on carers completing personality inventories on those in their care. Thus, all reported personality changes relied on carer's interpretations.

The dimensions of personality traits encompass many aspects of human behaviour. McAdams (1990), among others, suggests that extraverts are seen as outgoing, sociable and impulsive people. Conscientious people are typified as being more conscientious, careful, reliable, well-organised, self-disciplined and persevering. People who might be labelled as neurotic will experience chronic anxiety, depression, emotional lability, nervousness, moodiness, hostility, vulnerability, self consciousness and hypochondriasis. Eysenck (1973) perceives low E and high N in terms of the classical concept of a melancholic personality, which incorporates such behaviours as chronic sadness, anxiousness, pessimism and moodiness. Thus, studies suggest that sufferers of dementia are more likely to become melancholic personalities with more undirectedness, which will be manifest in such behaviours as carelessness, disorganisation, undependability and negligence.

Although this present investigation was not concerned with informants' personalities but rather their emotional memories, a review of informants' conversations suggests that they were, on occasion, subject to aspects of the melancholic personality, combined with obvious undirectedness. However, on other occasions they were not. Some personality traits changed quite dramatically. Mrs Woodley moved from a state of sadness to a state of happiness, as did Mr Raft. Other informants moved in and out of these sad/happy states more readily.

The informants, therefore, did not display increasing N and lowered E and C as the investigation progressed. However, some of the informants who were in or entering the terminal stages of the illness, did display such traits. Further, the primary carers of the informants may have reported such changes, had they been asked. All that can be said is that informants did not consistently display these identified changes in personality traits to the researcher during the interviews. This may have been due to the psychotherapeutic approach used throughout the investigation.

However, if this approach did mitigate negative changes in personality, it is possible to suggest that changing personality traits in dementia may be influenced, in part, by the social and psychological management of the illness. Managing dementia is, of course, very stressful, especially if the carer is a relative whose care-giving may last for many years. Carers, too, may be adversely affected by the malignant social psychology which surrounds this illness (Woods, 1997). This may have some implications for research into personality changes in dementia, when personality inventories are completed by carers. However, most aspects of work with dementia sufferers involves stress for all dementia care workers. This investigation was no exception.

Therapeutic implications and researcher stress

Although the overall approach was beneficial to informants and to the investigation, it was not without some difficulties for the researcher. It was not always easy to listen at this level. It was found to be tiring and draining. The emotions displayed by informants themselves were often negative, powerful and intense. Occasionally these feelings transferred themselves to the researcher, who during these times felt helpless, vulnerable and forlorn. This is a finding that has also been reported by Froggatt (1988), Gibson (1994) and Mills and Coleman (1994), among others.

Therapeutic implications and the main setting used in the investigation

Throughout the investigation, there were regular meetings between the researcher and staff in the day hospital. All staff were very interested in the process and outcomes of the interviews. As the investigation slowly concluded, reminiscence group work began to take place on a regular basis. This group was run by the deputy of the unit who had an interest in counselling. The group proved to be popular with the clients in the setting and the senior charge nurse said there was never any problem in attendance. "They queue up to get in there" he said. He was asked if he felt that the investigation had had anything to do with the formation of the reminiscence group. The senior charge nurse said that it had always been an area of interest but that they had never organised a formal group for this activity. He felt that the investigation had highlighted the therapeutic benefits of reminiscence, it had "drawn their attention" to its importance. At the time of writing the reminiscence group continues to run most successfully.

Therapeutic implications of the study

Although the overall therapeutic aspects of the investigation were found to be beneficial, the intensity of disclosure varied amongst informants. This was probably due to the personality of the informants, together with the extent of cognitive impairment caused by their illness. However, there are also cultural and social implications associated with disclosure. According to Rogers (1961)

133

most individuals need to feel emotionally safe and in a trusting relationship before speaking of emotional problems, or the deep emotions associated with past experiences.

This group of informants belong to a older generation for whom this rule was especially strong. Equally, one must look to the skills of the researcher. Perhaps another researcher with more developed skills might have enabled all informants to disclose more deeply. The most likely conclusion is that the amount of disclosure generated from informants depended on all of these considerations. Coleman (1986b) argues that not all older people will want to reminisce and Scrutton (1989) suggests that it is very likely that not all older people will want to discuss/disclose their emotional past. Other investigations concerned with this area of research may also experience similar findings. However, whatever the level of disclosure, all informants experienced some benefits from being part of the investigation.

Another area of possible interest is the informants' personalities, prior to the onset of this illness. Hillgard et al. (1979, p.601) defines personality as "the individual characteristics and ways of behaving that, in their organisation of patterning, account for the individual's unique adjustments to his or her environment". Thus, the informants' ability to cope with the changes wrought by their illness would, in part, depend on their individual personalities. Further, according to Kitwood (1988, 1997), dementia will disrupt the patterns of personality by severely weakening the cognitively structured, adaptive social self and leaving the experiential self vulnerable and unable to cope.

Kitwood (1990a) further suggests that this self is vulnerable in all of us and it is often the locus of hidden pain. To be aware of and to understand this part of our being is psychologically healthy. Most counsellors are required to have a course of personal therapy, prior to counselling others, in order to gain knowledge of their own vulnerabilities and defences. Defences defend, but they can also distance individuals from each other within close interpersonal interactions. Awareness of one's own areas of vulnerability and the defences employed to protect them, allows the experiential self to become known and understood. It allows this part of the self to grow and to mature. It is possible to suggest that it is the strength of the hidden self which determines the degree of loss which might be tolerated. A vulnerable and immature experiential self would probably be unable to tolerate extreme loss without external support and/or internal denial.

The maturation process for this part of any person is life long and ends only with death. It is also a highly individualised process with little reference to biological ageing. An older person may have an immature experiential self which is unable to cope with the losses of the ageing process. Kitwood (1988) tentatively suggests that many sufferers of dementia might have highly vulnerable experiential selves, which compound the effects of the illness or even predispose the elderly person towards that state of cognitive loss. Neuropathic changes found in elderly demented brains during post mortem are present, to some degree, in many non demented elderly brains (Kitwood, 1988, p.126). Further, Kitwood points to the fact that some elderly people become demented with little accompanying neuropathology. The narratives of most informants who took part in this study suggest that they were wounded people who frequently felt lost and vulnerable. Background information from their relatives, friends and colleagues implied that most informants did experience major trauma and loss which had great effect on their personalities. These reports, combined with the actual words of the informants, suggest that the informants may indeed have had insecure experiential selves prior to the onset of dementia. This is often the result of disturbing earlier experiences.

Mr Biddley seemed to have grown up with a fear of poverty. He worked very long hours and did not believe in wasting money. He led a structured existence. Further, he had a long history of depression, prior to the commencement of Alzheimer's disease. Coleman et al. (1993) suggest that low mention of others outside the family circle appear to be related to low levels of self esteem in the elderly which, in turn, is associated with depressive disorders. Mr Biddley mainly spoke of his relatives during the interviews. He found it difficult to form close relationships and had never married.

Mr Clerkenwell had a troubled childhood. His memories of his father seemed tinged with some anger and bitterness. The loss of his eyesight caused him anguish and his reported experiences as a POW in the second world war were very traumatic. Mr Coxley's memories of his childhood were full of pain and confusion due to his mother's illness. His own poor health caused him to leave the agricultural work which meant so much to him. He was constantly reminded of his mother's illness whenever he visited the setting. Mrs Pinks, too, had experienced loss at a young age. Her father died and she went out to work before she had left school, due to family poverty. She had also lost her only child.

Mr Raft, seemingly, had the most difficult childhood of all. His memories of this period of his life were very painful. His childhood vulnerability had appeared to remain with him and coloured all aspects of his existence. He was a very unhappy, lonely and threatened person at the commencement of the investigation. Mr Rider, like Mr Biddley, had a history of depression prior to the diagnosis of Alzheimer's disease. His wife regarded him as something of a perfectionist. Mr Rider himself said that he wanted everything he did "to be good". Mrs Rider further felt that his mother had constantly pushed him to achieve when he was young.

Mr Silverthorne compartmentalised his life. Work and home were kept very separate. He, too, led a very structured existence, which appeared to have swiftly crumbled as cognitive supports were removed. The final informant, Mrs Woodley had a very troubled childhood which left her with little self confidence and a desire to keep the peace at all times.

However, it is not possible to state, without reservation, that these experiences predisposed any informants to the state of dementia. Nonetheless, their life experiences could be said to have wounded them in many ways. Their experiential selves may have been hidden and immature and unable to withstand the onslaught of cognitive loss. The only evidence that would support this theory is the fact that all informants experienced therapeutic benefits from this investigation. Again, using Kitwood's arguments, this may have been due to the psychotherapeutic approach used throughout the interviews, in which informants' feelings or vulnerable experiential selves, were supported and validated (Kitwood 1988, 1990a, 1990b). It is, of course, difficult to say if interventions would have helped at earlier stages of informant's illnesses. However, many of my own residents have some form of dementing illness and a similar psychotherapeutic approach is used with them. Some of these residents have been with us for a considerable number of years, and it is noticeable that their rate of cognitive decline tends to proceed more slowly when compared to the cognitive rate of decline in residents admitted more recently (Mills, 1997a).

There are, of course, a number of other factors which would help to account for this slow decline of cognitive abilities. Some of these factors might be incorporated in the provision of an enriched environment which allows residents to develop greater autonomy. Studies by Annerstedt et al. (1987) and Karlsson et al. (1987) suggest that it is the lessening of staff restrictions on autonomy which contributed to positive changes in levels of functioning. Nonetheless, these developmental theories of personality are of great interest to those of us who are involved in any way with dementia care. They highlight the acute vulnerability of dementia sufferers and the imperative need for them to have understanding and support from all carers and managers in this area of work. The brief discussion of theories of personality in this chapter suggests that this is a topic worthy of further exploration.

Other considerations of the therapeutic implications for informants of this study were the long term relational aspects of the investigation. Dementia care traditionally involves change, both for the clients and carer. Many aspects of these changes are perceived as unwarranted and threatening by older people with dementia. During this study I was the only interviewer and I became a familiar and remembered visitor to the setting. This provision of constancy appeared to form part of the therapeutic benefits of the investigation.

Considerations of the counselling skills used during the study

The therapeutic outcomes of this study indicate the importance of interviewer counselling skills. All too often, counselling is seen as a relatively low level skill that can be managed by most health care professionals. This is not the case. It is unfortunate that counselling has a wide generic meaning which can be applied to a variety of situations from phone-in agencies to psychoanalytic encounters. Counselling is more than the possession of high level interpersonal skills. At a psychotherapeutic level, it involves intense contact between the client and the counsellor in a series of planned interviews. It is a discipline that has its own forms of training and recognised levels of expertise. These forms of training are allied to the various psychotherapeutic disciplines, all of which cluster under the umbrella of counselling. During this study, the most common counselling strategy used was based on Rogerian principles. This might be understood as a simple form of counselling in which the interviewer reflects and shares the world of the client. Some extracts from conversations between the informants and the interviewer illustrate the principles of reflection:

    AW *No! No, I got no courage for that!*
    Int. *No courage for that?*
    AW *Oh the burns were horrible!*
    Int. *They were horrible?*
    CC *Well ... What have I achieved? ... One asks ...*
    Int. *What do you think you've achieved?*

137

CC *He mostly ran away, I think!*

Int. *He ran away?*

The reflection of content allows the clients to feel that their message has been heard and acknowledged. It has not been rejected, overlooked or dismissed. Further, this acceptance of the message leads to understanding and empathy. The use of primary level empathy, in which the client's expressed feelings are acknowledged within the counselling relationship, encourages disclosure:

Int. *And you've been married a long time ... It's good!*

AC *Mm! And we d don't go far. We w de go ... like e e each other.*

Int. *So you never knew ... you used to come home from school and you wouldn't know what she was going like?*

AC *No, no ... Didn't ... Never had no tea ready or anything, you know ...*

Int. *Mmm ... You feel helpless, don't you?*

AC *Yes! You feel you want to go somewhere and get some help. Don't help, but you can't! ... But when she was alright, you know, she were alright. You couldn't wish for anybody better, but it didn't last long see ...*

AC *She died in there, You see ... I went in there one afternoon and she was gone.*

Int. *Did you feel it was a blessed release really?*

AC *Yes, I did!*

Int. *Mmm.*

AC *I sort of come out, went to get me bike ... I ... I didn't sort of realise it that she were gone, but I sort of thought, well that's er a lovely release.*

The use of primary level empathy led to advanced accurate empathy, which is an interpretative response. The feelings and emotions experienced by the client, which are implicit in their words, are gently made explicit by the counsellor. The use of advanced accurate empathy by the interviewer allowed informants to disclose at a deeper level. This is indicated by the following excerpt from an interview with Mrs Pinks. She had said that she went to work before she left school. I felt that she was trying to say that she lost her freedom at a young age. She was working when perhaps she still felt like playing with her friends:

BP *Oh yes! I missed playing outside and ...*

Int. *You became grownup before wanted to?*

BP *I ... I did! Actually I did! Yes. Because I was always looked on as a little girl, but all of a sudden I was turned into a grown woman!*

Int. *Yes ...*

BP *Just like that!*

An acknowledgement of Mr Biddley's desire to see his story as yet uncompleted, led him to admit failure but to still see himself as worthwhile:

Int. *So you think you've had a good life do you?*

RB *Well I'm not ready to give up the ghost yet! (He laughed.)*

Int. *Oh no ... Well lets say, `So far'. So far, has it been ok?*

RB *I've ... I've enjoyed it! I've made mis mistakes, we all do. There's no one can tell me they've made no mistakes and things like that, but I **know**, I think I'm I'm just as good good as most ...*

The use of advanced accurate empathy also allowed Mr Clerkenwell to discuss his great sadness over his failing eyesight:

CC *A blow comes with this thing. It's when ... specialist says "I'm ... I'm sorry it will never better", you know. Oh thank you very much!*

Int. *That must have been a terrible blow ...*

CC *What dear?*

Int. *That must have been a terrible blow ...*

CC *Yes, it is you think, well it'll be all right one day, you know ... And then this chap in his very ... e ... r what can I say his um ... thorough examination after several ... well several months! ... And then I said, "Surely there must be some improvement!" But, "I'm afraid not ... Not in your case! ... Just not showing any improvement! And after a long examination I'm sure there will not be one!"*

Int. *I feel sad that that should happen to you ...*

CC *Yes, you go along thinking there's hope you know. There's always hope, and then you find er he's only doing his job anyway, and you find there is no hope! (CC gave a wry chuckle) ... Except by some magic ...*

The identification of the feelings experienced by Mr Rider during his stay in the secure unit, allowed him to express himself with painful fluency:

> **Int.** *And you feel angry?*
> **MR** *I do! Very ! Very!*
> **Int.** *Very angry ... yes ... Do you feel people are making you do things?*
> **MR** *What!*
> **Int.** *Do you feel people are telling you what to do?*
> **MR** *N No!*
> **Int.** *No ...*
> **MR** *N N N N I can't can't can't do d told. I I I not not not said! I've never seen la seen er ... and anything else! And that's what's on on on my my my bad head!*
> **Int.** *That's what on your mind? ... All the time?*
> **MR** *Yes! Yes!*
> **Int.** *And you're very upset ...*
> **MR** *I I am!*
> **Int.** *I'm upset for you. I feel sad that you're upset ... I don't like ... I feel sad for you ...*

Mr Coxley was also able to discuss his feelings concerning his mother through the use of advanced accurate empathy. Interviewer sympathy and understanding of his need to hear that he had done his best allowed him to accept that this was indeed so:

> **Int.** *No ... Sometimes you just can't win whatever you do ...*
> **AC** *No! I used to come in here and I don't know what she's going to be like today, and then she'd have one of her moods on, you know, and I couldn't get nowhere with her ...*

Additional methods, other than Rogerian strategies, were also explored. One such method is to seek for repeated patterns of behaviour. These behaviours are often learned in early childhood and establish the basis for most adult behaviours. Occasionally, it was possible to enable informants to understand the effects of their early experiences. Mrs Woodley was able to understand that her mother's influence had allowed her to feel unworthy and unloved. As a child she probably felt that it was her fault that she was unlovable. These feelings of unworthiness as a child seemed to have created anxieties which were always with her. Mrs Woodley admitted that she had always been a worrier:

Int. *You carry it on your shoulder ... So a born worrier?*
AW *Mm ...*
Int. *Probably your mum started that off though, wasn't it?*
AW *Oh yes!*
Int. *Because if you were brought up like that ...*
AW *It follows doesn't it?*

She expressed surprise that she was liked in the setting and indicated that she felt unworthy of this. However, she was again able to see her mother's influence in this view of herself:

Int. *Everyone likes you here.*
AW *I can't understand that at all.*
Int. *You can't understand that?*
AW *No. All the badness running through.*
Int. *All the badness running through you?*
AW *Yes.*
Int. *That's your mother talking Abigail!*
AW *Yes!*

Mr Raft was another informant who was able to make conscious connections between his poor upbringing and his poor self image:

HR *Yes ... Yes ... I had a self ... bad image of meself, cause of me parents.*
Int. *Yes ... Yes ...*
HR *Used to get some bloody good hidings, mind. I'm not ashamed to admit it. Cor! I used to get whacked!*

He, too, seemed to feel unworthy and unloved. However, he questioned why he was not loved and helped by others. He felt it was unfair. He felt he deserved better:

HR *I'm silly like that ... I I help anybody, but the little buggers don't seem to want to help me!*

Often, apparent repeated behaviours due to past life experiences were not recognised by the informants but were still able to be addressed during the interviews. Mr Silverthorne experienced intense frustration over his inability to control managerial aspects of the setting. This was most obviously expressed over transport arrangements:

RS *What's the time?*
Int. *The time's er just quarter past two. The car won't come just yet.*
RS *Yes, but it doesn't take long to set em up and gets 'em. Because some of the girls don't wasn't to mmm ... get away.*
Int. *So do you worry that you will miss the bus?*
RS *I do of course! Cause I've been a long time on it.*
Int. *Do you feel you've been here a long time?*
RS *I know I've been here a long time, yes!*

Mr Clerkenwell occasionally experienced the setting as a prison. He was contained in the present as he was, so many years ago, by the Japanese:

CC *The trouble is, I'm chained in here you see. I can't just get up and walk out.*
Int. *Do you get fed up with coming here?*
CC *Only in the sense I like ... seeing people and so ... No I like coming here but what I object to is the doors clang behind me, and there's ... I have a feeling I've just walked in into Pentonville, or some similar prison.*

His perception of the setting as a prison, appeared to stimulate memories of his time as a POW. Many of these stories were new to me. This seeking of repeated patterns of behaviour, as with other psychoanalytic schools of thought, forms part of the psychodynamic approach to counselling. Hausman (1992) suggests that psychodynamic counselling can be effectively used with clients who have some form of dementia.

The psychodynamic approach

The psychodynamic approach is part of the psychoanalytic school of thought in that, within the counselling relationship, areas of client concern are illuminated and explored. Past concerns can produce multi-layered anxieties, all of which must be defended in order to minimise psychological pain. Defence mechanisms themselves can be many and varied. The psychodynamic counsellor must, therefore, be aware of defence mechanisms which mask anxieties. Exploration of these two phenomena should lead to the source of conflict. Thus, psychodynamic counselling is interactive and interpretative. The use of the psychodynamic approach during this investigation allowed a greater understanding of all informants by the interviewer. This understanding of clients' concerns was not always equal. The nature of their illness frequently inhibited this process of understanding. However, the ability of some informants to share in a new understanding of themselves is a measure of the strength of the interpretative relationship.

It was possible to understand Mrs Woodley's negative view of herself through the exploration of her relationship with her mother. Further, Mrs Woodley herself gained understanding which was retained on some level, after completion of the interviews. Mr Silverthorne's frustration and unhappiness over his loss of autonomy was easier to understand when one considered his ordered life and the many years he had `managed´ others. Mr Clerkenwell, too, could be understood more clearly when seen in the context of his whole life. He had been abandoned by his father for whom he appeared to feel much contempt. This probably overlaid his deeper feelings of rejection and unworthiness. His time in Changi prison was painful for him and he found it hard to accept and understand the cruelty of his captors. Again, his present life contained much that reminded him of his POW days. The loss of his eyesight seemed to underpin much of his present grief and unhappiness. This comparatively new grief appeared to trigger off many old and possibly unresolved griefs. He, himself, was able to have insight into the effects of his many losses on his levels of well-being.

The fifth informant, Mrs Pinks, had experienced severe grief in her life, but much of this had been repressed and/or forgotten. The death of her son must have been painful for her. Other experiences which were told to me by her husband and not disclosed by herself, were reported as being very hurtful for her. Mrs Pinks always wished to recall only the pleasant and happy things of her life. This would suggest that she might have defended herself against unhappy memories prior to her illness. The psychodynamic approach allows understanding of her use of this defence. Denial might have been necessary in the past in order to allow her to cope with life traumas. It certainly appeared to protect her in the present. It allowed her to be a happy lady who seemed to be remarkably free from anxieties.

Mr Coxley, too, could be more easily understood through the use of this approach. His tumultuous childhood appeared to have left him with the need to seek stability and solace through his work on the land. His grief over his mother remained largely unresolved and he was constantly reminded of this phase in his life by his own presence in the setting. Mr Coxley was able to explore some of his grief during the interviews at his own pace. The interpretative approach requires great sensitivity in staying with the client yet tentatively exploring the topic under discussion. The counsellor must listen intently to ensure that the client is ready and able to confront/discuss the topic at a deeper level. The counsellor too, must be aware of his or her own personal prejudices which may hinder this process. I was conscious that Mr Coxley, at times, was speaking of topics which were deeply meaningful for him and which he did not discuss with his wife.

Yet another of the informants, Mr Rider, was understood on a psychodynamic level. He had achieved academically and was justifiably proud of his successes. His illness stripped away his memories of his competencies and left him bereft. He was always trying to centre or locate himself in the present. He wanted to be with his wife because he knew her and loved her. He became angry and violent when he was prevented from returning to her, or to known and familiar locations such as his home. The sharing of his anguish permitted great understanding of this man. Kitwood (1990b) suggests that those of us who work in the field of dementia care need to 'hold' and support the shattered personality of the elderly person with dementia. I endeavoured to return to Mr Rider a sense of well-being and personhood even in the midst of his devastating illness. Occasionally I felt that I succeeded, but there were many occasions when I felt that I had failed. However, I understood how he was feeling and how he perceived his present world.

Finally, Mr Raft benefitted from the use of the psychodynamic approach. Through his stories I was able to understand much of his behaviour. He himself was able to make use of this knowledge by displaying greater understanding of the effects of his traumatic childhood on his life. Much of this understanding was implicit rather than explicit, in that he was able to take a more objective stance when speaking of his painful past. At the beginning of the investigation he assumed the role of victim with great ease. This was not so obvious at the conclusion of the investigation.

Discussion

A review of the counselling strategies used during this investigation suggests that they played a significant role in the therapeutic benefits experienced by all informants. Further, it suggests that the degree of interviewer counselling skills necessary for this work needed to be of a certain informed standard. The content and length of training courses in counselling techniques is very varied. The British Association of Counselling is endeavouring to instil a sense of unity into the many counselling courses which are run by various organisations throughout the country. However, a full time diploma course in counselling is normally of one to two years duration, with the completion of some hundreds of supervised counselling hours necessary for accreditation. These awards are not given lightly and require time and commitment on the part of the student. Moreover, Zarit and Knight (1996b, p.11) stress the intersect between psychological and medical problems. Specialised training would appear necessary for those workers who wish to engage in life review counselling with older people, with or without dementia. The importance of adequate training for professional/formal carers of the elderly has only achieved full prominence in recent years. Prior to this time, the picture was very different. It would be a retrograde step to assume that carers of elderly people need only a short basic eight week course in counselling to qualify them to undertake in-depth work of this nature. However, Fleming et al. (1986) and Roybal (1988) during the discussion of psychotherapeutic interventions for the elderly in chapter one of this work, suggest that this is an area which is under resourced. This is especially true for those older people with dementia. Gardner (1993), Goldsmith (1997) and Hausman (1992) argue that the concept of providing a professionally recognised service for this client group is exciting and innovatory. It might well become one of the major strategies for use in the developing paradigm of dementia care.

Ethical justification for this study

It is at this point that one can ask if it is ethical to ask older people with dementia about their memories of the past. What if these memories are likely to be painful? Should we leave well alone? What right have we to intrude into their private griefs and fears? These questions must and should be answered. Firstly, one must ask if it is right not to ask older people with dementia of their concerns? Humanitarian principles alone would suggest that it is wrong not to address these concerns. The locus of the inherent conflict surrounding this issue centres on the depth of exploration. The intensive discussion on the use of counselling principles, adhered to throughout this study, argues that this is an area that should not be undertaken by under qualified workers. Therefore, it is assumed that all workers who help older people to explore painful experiences, will themselves have the expertise to handle delicate, painful and sensitive material, together with the relational aspects of this work.

The issue of whether older people with dementia are able to cope with this type of exploration is linked to the expertise of the worker, but also to their own ability to handle grief and loss. Coleman (1994, p.18), together with Zarit and Knight (1996) suggest that it is important to bear in mind that loss and griefwork are essential parts of the experience of ageing. Guttman (1980), too, suggests that older people in general are well equipped to handle grief. Most older people with dementia will have experienced the many losses that accompany the ageing process before the onset of their illness. This illness will, itself, have generated more substantial loss which some sufferers may wish to share with others. Again, there will be some who will not, but they should all be offered the opportunity. This investigation suggests that there were some informants who welcomed the opportunity for disclosure more than others. This would probably be the case with other older people with dementia. The choice must be theirs. However, it will be recalled that no informant refused to disclose/discuss painful experiences with the interviewer, and all informants, without exception, benefitted from the experience. Ethical justification for this study would appear to rest on the degree of skills offered by the researcher/interviewer and, again, highlights the importance of professional training for this type of intervention.

To those highly private individuals, who would themselves dislike the intrusive aspect of this therapeutic relationship and perceive all older people with dementia as having similar feelings, one must answer that these informants, like the critic, have the right to refuse to take part. It is, however, morally wrong to refuse these vulnerable older people, who are often unhappy and confused, the opportunity to share their loneliness, pain and fear with a caring, supportive and knowledgeable `other´. Perhaps the final words on the ethical justification for this study should be left to Robert Davis, who, in his account of his own journey into dementia, says, "Be gentle with your loved ones. Listen to them. Hear their whispered pain" (Davis, 1989, p.18).

This discussion on the ethical justification for this study forms part of the psychotherapeutic implications found amongst the informants who took part in the investigation. This chapter suggests that these interventions might have highly significant implications for other er people with dementia. This, however, is one aspect of the investigation. Theoretical considerations of the findings from this study have yet to be discussed.

7 A theoretical discussion

Introduction

The theoretical considerations of this study and the implications for future practice are of importance. Life review and life review counselling will form part of the ensuing discussion, as informants were often inclined to evaluate individual experiences and to comment on their lives as a whole. Further, the emotional repertoire of older people with dementia is deemed to be a central feature of this work and certainly has significance within the new culture of dementia care (Kitwood, 1997a). It is proposed to examine this finding in the context of the literature and informants' narratives. The main discussion of this chapter, however, is focused on the loss of the life story or personal narrative in dementia leading to the eventual loss of narrative identity. As has been shown, all informants suffered some loss of personal narrative throughout the process of this investigation. Loss of narrative would, therefore, seem an integral part of the dementing process. Moreover, this finding will be supported by observations of other patients in the setting, together with personal experience of residents within my own residential unit. Finally, the chapter will conclude with an examination of the major findings of this study and a brief review of the work as a whole.

The emotional memories of informants

All informants had emotional memories available for recall. These memories were autobiographical in nature, and concerned events which happened many years ago. The findings support Conway (1990) who suggests that these memories are vivid, resilient and strongly accessible for recall. Further, following Brewer's (1986) arguments, they were all concerned with self experiences. Although often fragmented, these self stories formed part of their narrative or life story. The neuronal damage associated with dementia typically compromises functions of memory (Van Hoesen and Damasio, 1987). However, as discussed in chapter two, Moscovitch and Umiltà (1990) suggest a non hippocampal route to memory involved in the storing and retrieval of old but frequently recalled memories. The repetitious nature of many of the informants' stories tend to support this hypothesis.

The argument that emotional autobiographical memories carry personally relevant meaning (Salaman, 1982), is also applicable. For some of the informants, these meanings may have developed, allowing a certain strength to be added to these memories. Not all of the strongly emotional memories of informants were without conflicting meanings. However, as Salaman argues, resolution is possible and for some informants, such as Mrs Woodley, Mr Coxley and Mr Raft, a certain sense of resolution did seem to occur following a period of life review.

The link between emotions and cognition

Through the recall of their personal past, all informants indicated theoretical links between cognition and emotion. Chapter two contains strong arguments for a relationship between memory and emotion within the cognitive school of thought. The findings from this investigation would suggest that the links between memory and emotion are, indeed, quite powerful. The case-studies of informants appear to offer some support for these theoretical suggestions. Mrs Woodley made the connection between her lack of confidence and her mother's treatment of her as a child:

> **Int.** *Because if you were brought up like that ...*
> **AW** *It follows doesn't it?*

And Mr Raft:

> *Yes ... Yes ... I had a self ... bad image of meself, cause of me parents.*

Informants displayed a wide range of emotions throughout the series of interviews. Many of them displayed such emotions as interest, joy, surprise, anger, fear, shame, sadness and guilt, which are defined by Izard (1991) as belonging to the group of fundamental emotions, which are basic to human nature. However, informants gave less evidence of disgust and contempt when compared to the emotions of interest and enjoyment. Fear, too, was less obvious but may have occasionally generated the emotion of anger which was displayed by some informants at times.

The emotions of sadness, guilt and shame were associated with most informants' recollections, except for those of Mrs Pinks who preferred to dwell on the pleasant things of life. She did not display undue sadness over the death of her son, for instance, although it could be argued that she had lost many memories of his life and death. Further, Mr Silverthorne showed little evidence of guilt in his narrative. Throughout many of his interviews he made it clear that he still thought of others and he had lived his life according to certain standards. Mr Raft, too, denied feeling guilty. He felt that he had been a good person who did his best in all circumstances, regardless of how he was treated by others. It might be argued that it is possible that he did feel this emotion and that he was in a state of denial. This is, however, speculative. Nonetheless, the findings indicate that most of the fundamental emotions were still part of informants' memories to a greater and lesser extent, even in the midst of dementia.

From a scientific stance, emotions may be perceived as an untidy bundle of variables that are probably impossible to isolate and to quantify. Izard (1991) and Leventhal (1984) indicate that they are, however, variables that permeate all aspects of life. It is the relational aspect of these phenomena which is the focus of this work, for emotions, according to the literature, are with us from the moment of birth until death. Izard (1991), Leventhal (1984) and Tomkins (1981, 1987) suggest that they attach themselves to our behaviours, to our experiences and to our memories. They have a crucial part to play in states of well-being or ill-being and, as such, occupied a central role in this study of memory within dementia.

The importance of emotions within dementia

The importance of the role of emotions for human beings has been discussed in previous chapters. Their strongly expressed existence within and throughout the state of dementia suggests that they are associated with brain structures that, according to Verwoerdt (1981), remain relatively unaffected throughout long periods of this illness. However, it is unwise to perceive the emotions as being a function of particular locations in the brain due to the interconnected nature of the nervous system (Buck, 1988). Nonetheless, following the emotional expression of informants appeared to encourage further recall. Cheston (1996), Hausman (1992) and Sinason (1992), together with the pilot study (Mills, 1991), also suggest that acknowledging the emotional content of informants' conversations may allow the recall of further memories. The work of Damasio et al. (1990), Moscovitch and Umiltà (1990) indicate that these memories may have remained accessible, despite damage to neural structures and pathways. Moreover, emotions, in evolutionary terms, emerged prior to increased cognition. Certainly Tomkins (1981) argues that the newborn are extremely emotional beings with immature cognitive processes, suggesting that cognitive abilities within dementia may diminish prior to the fading of emotional structures. Teasdale and Barnard's (1993) complex theory of information processing, or interacting cognitive subsystems (ICS) approach, offer some support for this argument. Their model offers a substantial explanation of the strength of adult "affect laden records". Within this study, even the most cognitively impaired informants expressed strongly emotional memories, albeit with limited content. At times, their emotional recall was in sharp contrast to their factual memories of the world. This tentative hypothesis tends to be implicit, rather than explicit, in the works of other theorists. However, the findings from this investigation support the argument that emotional processes within dementia would appear to have considerably more durability than cognitive processes. This finding has significance for the therapeutic interventions used in dementia care work, together with the maintenance of well-being for all dementia sufferers.

Tobin (1991) suggests that preservation of self is one of the adaptive challenges of ageing. It is this aspect of self survival which is so threatened in dementia, for this disease attacks our psychological existence. Although dementia is a progressive illness, most strategies are concerned with this affliction endeavour to slow down/mitigate its effects. They are concerned, therefore, with the preservation of the psychological life of the sufferer. A `good´ psychological existence implies that individuals are aware of their own reality and identity, an identity which Tobin (1991) suggests is strengthened by society's acknowledgement of this existence. Nevertheless, within the final stages of the dementing process, and, as personal awareness fades, most of the requirements for a good psychological existence are almost entirely met by the `society´ surrounding and supporting the dementia sufferer (Kitwood, 1993; Kitwood and Bredin, 1992). Nonetheless, the personal narrative, in part, gives a sense of identity to individuals before this point is reached. Moreover, the narrative contains the type of stories which, as Mr Clerkenwell reminds us, "live long in the memory of a mind".

The importance of a personal narrative within dementia

These theoretical considerations, therefore, suggest the importance of encouraging the maintenance of the narrative in dementia. Enabling sufferers of dementia to retain their life story suggests that this enhances the existence of psychological survival of the self which, according to Bender (1994) and Tobin (1991), leads to increased levels of well-being and a return of personhood. However, it must be recognised that the recall/maintenance of a personal narrative through reminiscence work with older people who have dementia is only possible during certain stages of the dementing process. Reminiscence work within the final stage of dementia is not practicable. Nonetheless, earlier reminiscence/life review work that has been undertaken with this client group does allow carers to have some knowledge and understanding of those in their care even when communication, on the part of the sufferer, is reduced to non verbal methods only. For older people with dementia who are able to reminisce, carers with knowledge of the practical implications of reminiscence work can utilise these skills during group work and in one to one interactions. Further, knowledge of theory and practice aids communication between the carer and the person who is in receipt of care. The encouragement of all methods of communication within this work is an inherent part of the new culture of dementia care.

Various methods, which encourage the maintenance/repair of identity in dementia, are concerned with aspects of reminiscence. Coleman (1994, p.8) argues that within all reminiscence is a life story or an autobiography, unique to each person. The discussion of reminiscence within chapter one of this work, indicates that this is a multifaceted phenomenon, which has therapeutic implications for demented older people. Gibson (1997) and Coleman (1994) suggest that the use of reminiscence with the aged requires sensitivity in the meeting of individual needs. Coleman stresses the importance of reinforcing positive memories for some older people. This was a strategy employed during this investigation. Other older people, he suggests, need to grieve. Again, this was a finding from this study.

Most informants had unresolved griefs associated in some cases with very old memories. Further, Coleman perceives the use of life review counselling to be beneficial for some older people. As Knight (1986b) argues, in some sense, all psychotherapy involves some elements of life review.

Reflecting on informants' life review

Much of the literature concerned with reminiscing interventions used with older people, suggests that this therapeutic work is often used as a group activity which will focus on a discussion about the past. Although an enjoyable activity, this type of reminiscence is not life review. Coleman (1986b), Haight (1991) and Wong and Watt (1991), all argue that life review cannot be equated with general reminiscence. Reminiscence and life review have different goals although they both use past memories. Haight and Dias (1992) suggest that the main goal of simple reminiscence, which takes place within a group, is to socialise. Coleman (1974) agrees that simple reminiscence is beneficial to older people, but suggests that life review is of more significant benefit. One of the goals of life review is to enable older people to reach a state of integrity through an evaluation of their past. Haight's (1988, 1989a, 1989b) three studies of individual structured life review indicates that all three groups found positive benefits from this process. Haight and Dias (1992) suggest that the most therapeutic way to reminisce is through a structured, evaluative life review performed on an individual basis. The three variables, therefore, which contribute to successful reminiscence are individuality, evaluation and structure which incorporates the whole life span. It is the life review modality which is best suited to individual needs in certain situations, such as grief, exploration, evaluation and the need to move towards a state of integrity. However, the pain that can often accompany the physical aspects of ageing has been shown to influence life review. Walker et al. (1990) suggest that older people who have long term painful illnesses tend to recall negative past experiences.

Murphy (1982), in common with a number of other studies, found that physical health problems were linked to depression in the elderly. This has some links with the work of Williams et al. (1988, p.168) who suggest that depressed, but not generally anxious subjects may selectively remember negative material. During this investigation, informants who were experiencing painful health problems were found to be lower in mood. Occasionally they felt so ill that they discontinued the interviews or were disinclined to speak. The role of acute pain within the ageing process is, therefore, of great importance for practitioners and investigators of reminiscence and life review. Elderly people with painful illnesses may benefit from psychotherapeutic interventions which may enable them to reinterpret their past more positively. Butler and Lewis (1982) suggested that life review might be used as a therapy. They described life review as an ongoing self analysis, enhanced by the intervention of a therapist to make the life review more conscious, deliberate and efficient. Gradually, theorists and practitioners, such as Coleman (1994) and Garland (1994) have begun to advocate the use of life review therapy for older people. However, there is little in the literature of the use of such techniques with older people who have dementia. Nonetheless, the works of such practitioners as Feil (1985, 1986, 1992, 1993), indicate that she uses many of the goals of life review in her efforts to validate and resolve the feelings and behaviour of such clients.

All informants appeared to review aspects of their life at times. This was more obvious in the case-studies of Mr Clerkenwell, Mr Coxley and Mr Raft. However, these three informants were the least cognitively impaired of the group. Mrs Woodley, too, appeared to evaluate certain life events, although these were principally concerned with her relationship with her mother. Nevertheless, evaluation could have occurred earlier in informants' lives, prior to the onslaught of dementia and these evaluated events may still have been retained in memory. Therefore, the question of whether all informants actually engaged in life review is speculative. Their words suggest that they evaluated some life experiences and this sense of listening to a life review was stronger in the interviews with less cognitively impaired informants. This finding is supported by Woods et al. (1992). Their study indicates that life reviews can be conducted with older people who have mild to moderate levels of cognitive impairment. However, the data suggests that the life reviews of informants were similar to Gibson's (1994) use of life history work with dementia sufferers.

Within this study, the variables associated with successful life review was applicable to all informants. They engaged in structured life review in that they were encouraged to speak of any aspect of their lives that they wished and that they could remember. In addition, all informants were seen individually and finally, they appeared to evaluate some of their personal past. Haight and Dias (1992) suggest that this is a very important part of the therapeutic process. Further, they, too, suggest that this intervention of evaluation must be handled with care because of the implication of therapy. Moreover, they regard paraprofessionals as able to undertake this task. However, their discussion of key variables in reminiscence does not include work with confused elderly people who have a greater vulnerability.

Types of reminiscence found in the investigation

During this study, all informants engaged in various types of reminiscence throughout their interviews. No one interview ever contained just one type of reminiscence, neither was it possible to anticipate what type of reminiscence would emerge during these times. Although this study was not concerned solely with occurrences/types of reminiscence, it is of interest to note that informants' conversations reflected many of the characteristics of the six types of reminiscence associated with Wong and Watt (1991). That is, they gave examples of integrative reminiscence which is concerned with a sense of meaning and coherence to the life story. It is also concerned with life review. Thus, this form of reminiscence is evaluative. Yet another type, that of instrumental reminiscence, is involved with managing difficult situations and experiences in life. All informants recounted stories of challenging experiences and the manner in which they coped with them. Equally, all spoke of experiences which they found traumatic and which remained unresolved. Further, the category of transmissive reminiscence, which is concerned with the passing on of wisdom and knowledge, was applicable to all informants' stories of the past. It is acknowledged, however, that it was Mr Clerkenwell and Mr Coxley who more readily engaged in this facet of reminiscence. Another two categories, that of escapist and obsessive reminiscence is appropriate to describe some informants' recollections, although not unduly. No informant expressed a wish to `escape´ back to earlier times. Nonetheless, it is possible that some informants' recalled memories were unresolved griefs and concerns and thus might be labelled as obsessive.

Nevertheless, it is the category of narrative reminiscence which is applicable to all informants. All informants told stories and did so during each and every interview. Their stories were often fragmented and difficult to understand, but they gave informants and myself great pleasure. Possibly, some of their stories which could be labelled repetitive or obsessive, might not be regarded as narrative reminiscence but these stories still formed part of the whole of informants' life experiences. Non dementing people of varying ages will also reminisce in a repetitive or obsessive manner, especially during periods of life crises and stressful events. Thus, considerations of the reminiscences of informants suggest that narrative reminiscence was the most significant category for all informants. Watt and Wong perceive instrumental and integrative reminiscence as being most beneficial to older people, with obsessive reminiscence as being the least beneficial. A review of the findings does suggest that while most informants engaged in types of obsessive reminiscence, they were more frequently concerned with stories of a meaningful and significant past, with themes of survived and surmounted difficulties, interspersed with more simple reminiscences.

Interviews which were largely filled with simple reminiscence were enjoyed by all informants. They appreciated the social aspects of our relationship and found much pleasure in laughter. These interviews were experienced by the interviewer, too, as social and enjoyable. I found these types of interviews to feel `warm and cosy´, as opposed to life review type interviews which were full of strong emotion. I found I had to listen with greater intensity during the times informants appeared to review their lives, in order to understand what was being said. These accounts were often painful and had to be handled with great care. Even so, it appeared to be therapeutic for informants to have their feelings and memories validated by another individual.

Studies of life review, however, require some expansion. The findings from this investigation would suggest that there are differing uses of life review, in that some informants engaged in life review type reminiscence more extensively and more frequently than others. This did not appear to be solely related to the degree of cognitive impairment of informants but rather to the need to tell their story and/or their personalities. Further, the concept of life review, as defined by Butler (1963, p.66) who argues that it is a "naturally occurring, universal mental process characterised by the progressive return to consciousness of past experience ... prompted by the realisation of approaching dissolution and death, and the inability to maintain one's sense of personal invulnerability", would not appear totally applicable to the informant's evaluative recollections of a personal past. Moreover, Molinari and Reichlin (1985, p.83) suggest that not only does life review require an evaluative component, it should also contain conflict in order to allow resolution to occur. Again, it might be argued that it is possible to evaluate one's life without reaching a state of resolution or perhaps achieving only partial resolution.

Although, as a modality, life review would appear to have a number of variables which would prove worthy of further investigation, it is suggested that a more careful conceptualisation of life review is necessary. Investigations into what makes a good life review are, of course, hedged with difficulties and this study suggests that types of life review are beneficial. However, this may not be the case for all older people, nor for all older people who have dementia. More stringent guide lines for the use of life review and life review therapy are required, although Haight (1988, 1989b), Haight et al. (1995) offer important research in this area. The theories of reminiscence give some understanding of the importance of the life story or personal narrative of the informants. Respondents in Goldsmith's (1996) study, most of whom were practitioners, found knowledge of a client's past to be a prerequisite for good dementia care.

Considerations of the personal narratives of the informants

For the researcher, understanding of the importance of story came through listening to and studying the text of informants' stories. When each set of interviews began, it was very much a journey into the unknown. I was unsure if any informants would be able to recall emotional memories or if they would want to speak about them, even if such memories came to mind. I always felt rather nervous at the beginning, wondering if they would like me. I also wondered if they would be able to sustain a long relationship, and if I possessed sufficient of the skills, as identified by Bromley (1990), Haight and Dias (1992) to enable them to do so. These fears subsided as the investigation progressed and our relationships developed into one of mutual liking and strength. The informants became very important to me and I became concerned for their welfare. This offering of Roger's (1961) concept of unconditional positive regard, which is so necessary for trust and disclosure to develop, allowed all informants to speak about their more private selves and the life experiences that had formed their personalities. It is interesting to note that all informants, even the most cognitively impaired, needed time to become used to me before they spoke of their deeper feelings.

Initially, I was expecting to find that any emotional memories from this investigation would relate to similar themes found in the pilot investigation. But as I began to analyse the data, I realised that informants were telling me self stories and through the literature, I began to gain some understanding of their life stories in the form of a personal narrative. A review of the hermeneutic approach to the narrative, enabled their life story to be understood as one that is narrated yet also lived. Widdershoven (1993) suggests that we live our lives in such a way that enables us to tell stories of our experiences and actions. Further, in telling these stories we change the meanings of our experiences and actions (Wetherell and Maybin, 1996). Life, therefore, is expressed, articulated and modified in stories. Moreover, stories are interpretations of life in which the meaning of life is spelled out in much the same way as the meaning of a text is spelled out in a literary translation. Further, Widdershoven (1993) argues that the intertwining of experience and story lies at the core of individual life and psychological understanding. The personal narratives of informants, therefore, indicate a certain commonality with that of others. The characteristics of the narrative appeared to be shared by all human beings.

As these theoretical concepts developed, considerations of the importance of the narrative in dementia gained in clarity. If the concept of narrative was common to other members of society, then any enabling of narrative retention allowed demented older people to occupy a more stable position in their environment. It gave identity and a sense of being for a time, even though the progressive ravages of this illness led to a lessening of this form of identity and to an eventual parting of our ways. However, Gibson (1994) suggests that it is possible to put off this parting, this ending, by the use of therapeutic strategies. These strategies suggest a variety of methods which include reminiscence, life review and life review counselling. The importance of a personal narrative in dementia cannot, therefore, be overestimated. During this investigation, I perceived the retention of a personal narrative as the retention of psychological life for these people. However, as their narratives faded from memory, I did not feel as if their psychological lives had ended. It was as if my knowledge of their story, in part, enabled this life to continue. Their narrative had gone, but the understanding remained. In some sense, this retention of understanding appeared to offer support for the continuing psychological existence of informants.

There is a steady increase in the therapeutic use of life recording methods for older people with or without dementia (Murphy and Moyes, 1997). However, most case notes of older people have a paucity of information on their social history, a comment that has been made elsewhere (Gibson, 1994; Johnson, 1976; Mills and Chapman, 1992). Research by Bornat (1994), together with Bornat and

158

Adams (1992), indicate that the obtaining of a life-history of clients during assessments gives a more accurate understanding of present needs and wishes, both in the community and in long stay settings. Any recording of the narrative at an early stage of the illness would enable carers to have some knowledge of their client's meaningful past. Gibson (1994) suggests that carers in turn can use clients' life-histories to make sense of seemingly confused messages, and to remind/return this personal narrative to those in their care. This was an often successful strategy used during this investigation. I was frequently amazed when withdrawn and isolated informants suddenly recalled complex memories of the past after cues and prompts. Mr Clerkenwell did this during our final interview, as did Mr Silverthorne, Mrs Pinks and Mr Biddley at other times.

However, the most important strategy was that of addressing the emotional message given by the informants. This strategy did not always involve verbally identifying the emotions that were expressed. It was often just enough to listen and accept these emotional messages. This form of acceptance appeared to 'hold' and support most informants in their efforts to recall and disclose very deep concerns. The findings suggest that I was able to encourage informants to tell their stories and also hold and support them as they began to lose the ability to remember their story.

The dissolution of the narrative in dementia

At the commencement of the interviews, all informants were able to recall pieces of their personal past. However, the content of these recalled memories were not uniform for all informants who were in different stages of the dementing process and had differing levels of mental ability. See Figure 7.1. Not all test scores fitted neatly on this scale. Mr Clerkenwell's MMSE scores were given as 11/27. This can be read as scoring fractionally over the mid way point. However, it is still well below the cut off point of twenty-three. Further, Mr Rider's hospital notes do not give actual test results but state that he was able to answer most questions correctly. It was decided to give him an approximate score of 8/10. Not all informants were cognitively tested at this time using the MTS, MMSE or MSQ as in the case of Mr Biddley. However, his CT scan had revealed fairly substantial changes and a definitive diagnosis of primary degenerative dementia had been given.

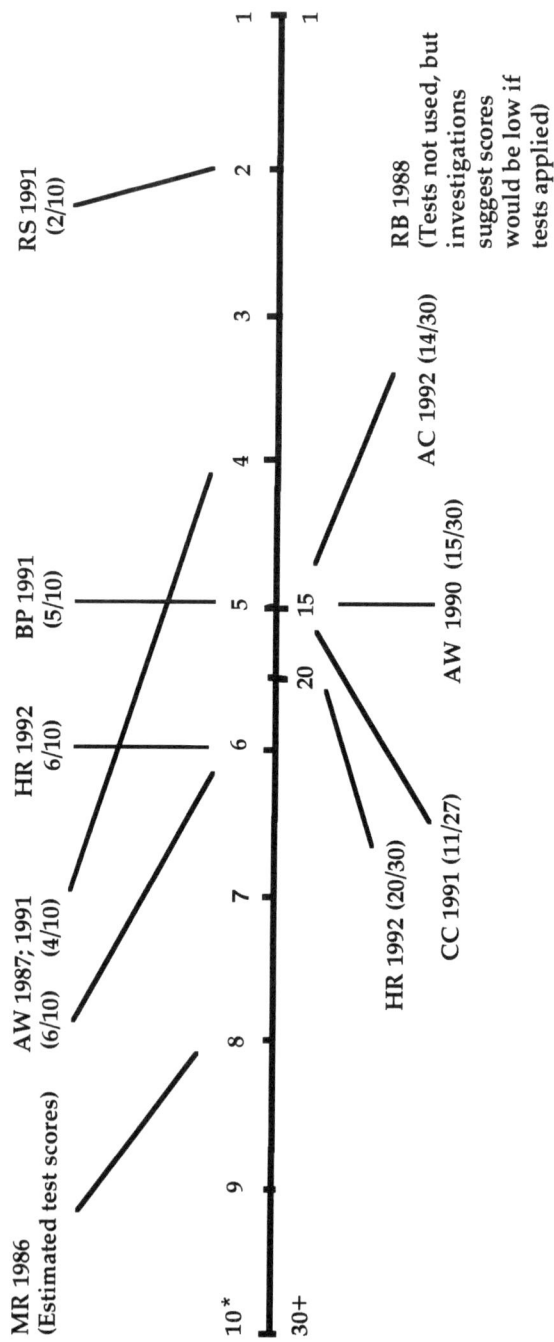

Figure 7.1 Informants' cognitive test scores prior to commencement of interviews

MR 1986
(Estimated test scores)

AW 1987; 1991
(6/10)   (4/10)

HR 1992
6/10

BP 1991
(5/10)

RS 1991
(2/10)

HR 1992 (20/30)

CC 1991 (11/27)

AW 1990 (15/30)

AC 1992 (14/30)

RB 1988
(Tests not used, but
investigations
suggest scores
would be low if
tests applied)

*   MSQ/MENTAL TEST SCORE

+   MMSE

The cognitive powers of informants continued to show evidence of decline throughout the life of the investigation. The evidence for decline was supported, in part, by additional cognitive testing which took place some time after initial diagnosis. See Figure 7.2. However, not all informants were tested, neither did one MTS show this decline. Mrs Pinks' MTS did not change during the series of interviews, even though her diminishing recall of past events, prior to this final testing, indicated evidence of a greater cognitive impairment. There was also additional difficulty in interpreting the MTS of Mrs Woodley who was tested in 1993. She was able to answer one question, in that she could recall her Christian name and surname, but all other information appeared to have gone. However, her hospital notes indicated that the clinician abandoned the test after four questions, due to her difficult mood. In response to one query, Mrs Woodley said, "That's a silly question". It was decided, therefore, to place her score on the lower end of the scale, as shown in Figure 7.2 slightly above point one. Although there were no test scores available for Mr Coxley, Mr Rider, and Mr Raft, their case-studies, too, indicated evidence of further cognitive decline. For some informants this decline ended in death. Both Mr Silverthorne and Mr Clerkenwell died during the study. During 1994, Mr Rider and Mr Coxley also died. Of the remaining informants, Mrs Woodley, Mrs Pinks, Mr Biddley and Mr Raft had much reduced mental functioning. In 1995, Mrs Woodley died. However, at the close of 1997, Mr Biddley, Mrs Pinks and Mr Raft were still living in their nursing home.

The findings from this investigation indicate that the narrative of some informants ended prior to biological death. This was most clearly shown in the case-studies of Mr Silverthorne, Mr Biddley and Mr Rider. The final interview with Mrs Pinks showed that she retained little memory of the past. It was only with great difficulty that she managed to recall the name of her former employer. Further, the case-studies of Mrs Woodley and Hugh Raft indicate that the content of their memories was diminishing. Mr Clerkenwell, too, although able to surprise the interviewer with his account of further deprivations and atrocities experienced as a POW only a few months before his death, still indicated a loss of narrative and a partial loss of narrative identity. Finally, Mr Coxley, although able to recall many of his former stories, had also begun to lose previously expressed detail and depth to these accounts. These findings are in marked contrast to the commencement of the study when all informants were able to recall their narrative and thus possessed a sense of narrative identity. See Figure 7.3.

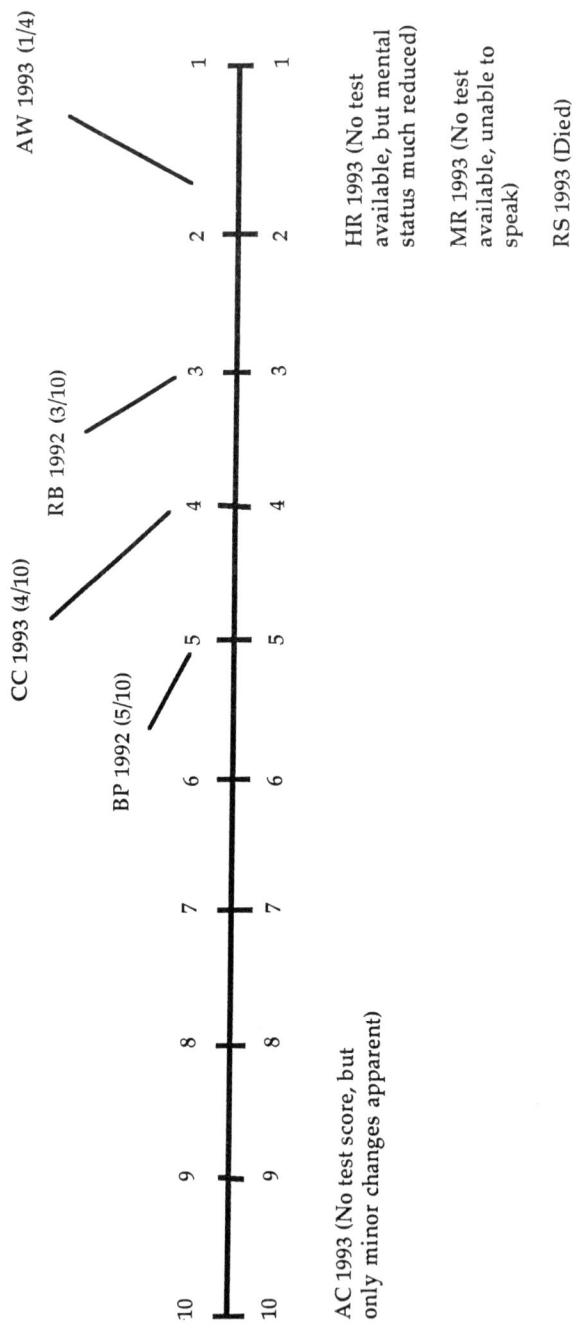

AW 1993 (1/4)

RB 1992 (3/10)

CC 1993 (4/10)

BP 1992 (5/10)

AC 1993 (No test score, but only minor changes apparent)

HR 1993 (No test available, but mental status much reduced)

MR 1993 (No test available, unable to speak)

RS 1993 (Died)

Figure 7.2 Informants' cognitive test scores in latter stages of the investigation

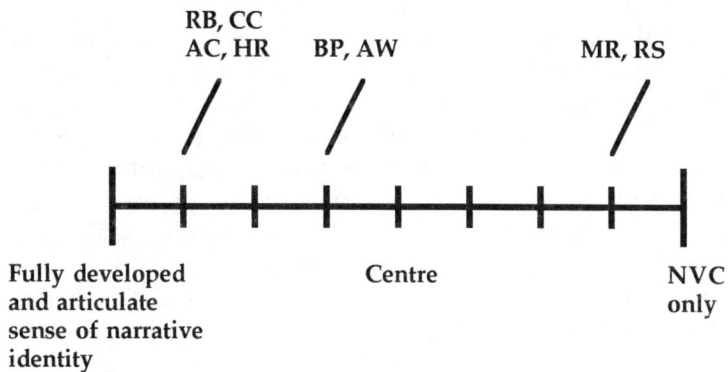

RB, CC
AC, HR   BP, AW   MR, RS

Fully developed   Centre   NVC
and articulate   only
sense of narrative
identity

Figure 7.3 Integrity of narrative identity in informants at
            commencement of interviews

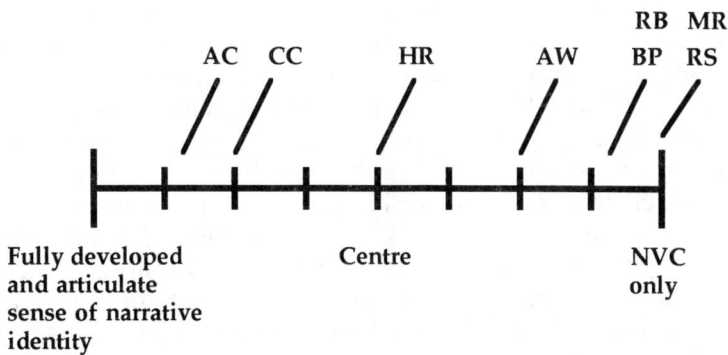

                                          RB MR
        AC   CC   HR   AW   BP RS

Fully developed   Centre   NVC
and articulate   only
sense of narrative
identity

Figure 7.4 The extent of dissolution of narrative identity at
            conclusion of interviews

With the decline of cognitive abilities came the dissolution of the narrative, although the latter appeared to decline more slowly. Figure 7.4 indicates that all informants experienced a reduction in their memories of past experiences and narrative identity. Figures 7.3 and 7.4 indicate the integrity of the narrative from two perspectives. On the left of the diagram is the fully developed and articulate narrative identity, on the right is the state of non verbal communication only. It is this inability to communicate, other than through largely non verbal methods, which is seen to be experienced by many sufferers of this disease in its more severe form. The criteria for placing informants on one of the equidistant points of this scale were the intactness of their narrative identities at the beginning of the series of interviews and again on conclusion. The mid point is deemed to divide these two states of being. The placing of informants' names one over the other on this scale is not meant to suggest that one narrative is considered to be more intact than another, but rather follows the order of the presentation of the informants through this work.

Figure 7.3 suggests that at the commencement of the interviews, Mr Biddley, Mr Clerkenwell, Mr Coxley and Mr Raft were considered to have a fully developed and articulate narrative identity. This is not to suggest that their narratives were fully intact and indeed there are obvious omissions in these accounts, but rather that their words and stories point to a less diminished concept of selfhood. Mr Biddley retained a strong sense of narrative identity for the early part of the investigation although this was quickly overcome by the onslaught of his rapidly progressive disease. However, it is considered that he had a strong sense of selfhood. Mr Biddley struggled to keep this intact through his ability to enjoy social interactions, especially the interactions within the interviews themselves. Mr Clerkenwell was not only able to relate many of his past experiences, he was also able to relate them to the present. Thus, he saw himself as influenced by past and present events. It is true that some earlier experiences seemed to be lost from memory and it is probable that the cognitive impairment associated with his dementia was largely responsible for this. However, some of these `forgotten´ times were painful events. His first wife had committed suicide and he had no recollection of her at all, yet he was able to remember other painful memories, both past and present. Mr Coxley, too, had a more complete narrative and thus a more intact sense of narrative identity at this stage. He was able to speak of his past and present experiences and to have a sense of accomplishment over some of his achievements. Much of his earlier life, especially the grief occasioned by his mother's illness remained unresolved. However, he was able to speak of these times and to hold them in memory although the pain at times was great. Mr Raft, the final member of the group, told his story with some clarity when viewed from his own perspective. He saw himself as a victim, as being misunderstood and as feeling very unhappy. He was able to relate his fundamental emotions to these past experiences and to those of the present.

A review of the narratives of these four informants suggests that they held a strong sense of narrative identity. All four were able to speak of various topics associated with the past and in their own way, relate them to the present. When they told their stories, one had the impression that they were acting as an observer, which is a feature of memory reconstruction, and as a participant - the re-experiencing of the event under discussion. These facets of their narratives gave a certain strength and depth to their accounts. It did not seem as if they were recalling all of these memories by rote. Many of their stories appeared to be spontaneously recalled and freshly examined.

The decision to place the narratives of Mrs Woodley and Mrs Pinks slightly beyond the mid way point between the centre of the scale and the state of having a more intact and developed narrative identity is, of course, open to criticism, as are all comments made throughout this particular section. These two informants both had stories to tell and, indeed, the interviews with Mrs Woodley suggest that the central core of her narrative consisted of the intact memories of her unhappy relationship with her mother. They were intact in the sense that the emotions associated with this relationship were strong, powerful and readily available for recall. However, both Mrs Woodley and Mrs Pinks had a less fluid narrative than the previous four informants. Many of their memories were more fragmented and overlearned. Mrs Pinks could recall her days at the vicarage and driving her Trojan car, but the repetitious and perhaps obsessive nature of these accounts did suggest that these memories were `fixed´ and well established. However, as she recounted more of these times more pieces of her story gradually emerged.

Both Mr Silverthorne and Mr Rider are placed at a point slightly over mid way between the centre of the scale and the furthest point, which indicates that informants were capable of non verbal communication only. Even at commencement of the interviews, the data suggest that these two informants found it difficult to retain a sense of narrative identity. Both were frequently overwhelmed by feelings of loss and abandonment in the setting, suggesting that the integrity of their respective narrative identities was in a fairly advanced state of dissolution.

Possible effects of change on informants' narrative identity

This discussion of the integrity of the narrative identity of informants at the commencement of the interviews does indicate that some informants had a less intact personal narrative than others. There are many variables that play their part in this finding. All informants were affected in different ways by the dementing process. Further, as is indicated in the discussion of dementia in chapter two of this work, dementia presents differently in different individuals. All that can be said of this illness relating to memory is that the dissolution of memory is a feature of this disease. Individual decline in memory, however, is variable. Other considerations that have great bearing on the recall of the narrative are the changes that occurred in the lives of some of the informants. Some informants did experience change quite early on in the investigation. Mr Biddley had experienced a recent change in residence just prior to the commencement of the study. He had moved to long term residential care. Mr Raft, too, had experienced change. He had only recently joined the setting. Yet another informant, Mr Rider, was experiencing change continually as he became unable to locate himself in the present and desperately longed for the familiar and loved face of his wife and their home. Another major consideration in a discussion of the memories of informants was the drugs regime which was part of their lives. As is mentioned in chapter four of this work, all informants were on some type of medication which was frequently changed throughout the life of the investigation. Although it was decided not to dwell too heavily on this aspect of patient care, which is applicable to most sufferers of dementia, it was acknowledged that the psychotropic drugs used in dementia care effect mood and recall. It is a tribute to the strength and durability of the narrative of informants, that none of these considerations completely overshadowed their ability to recall their emotional stories and experiences.

The extent of dissolution of narrative identity at the conclusion of the interviews

At the conclusion of the interviews, Figure 7.4 gives some indication of the changes that had taken place in the ability of informants to recall their story. As memory further declined, the ability to recall the past faded. For some informants, such as Mr Silverthorne and Mr Rider, it had gone completely. For Mr Biddley and Mrs Pinks, their narratives remained as shadows of former substance. Their final interviews show this with some clarity. Mrs Pinks was seen between April 1992 and August 1993. Early interviews indicated that she was able to recall the vicarage where she first worked, the vicar and his wife, the car she drove for them and some details of her immediate kin. This was not the case in August 1993 when we met for our final interview together. Prior to asking her about topics from her past, I explained that I had been to see her many times before but I had not seen her for a long time. I told her she used to talk to me of her past life and it was very interesting. She smiled. I gently led her into a discussion of major themes that had emerged during the investigation.

Int. *Do you remember much about when you were younger?*
BP *Not much really ...*
Int. *Not much? A bit of a blur is it?*
BP *Mm?*
Int. *A bit of a blur?*
BP *Yes.*
Int. *What about when you were at the rectory? Do remember that?*
BP *Oh yes ... That's wrong. It ... ong time ...*
Int. *Mm! You worked there a long time ...*
BP *Mm ... Yes I did ...*
Int. *Do you remember the name of the vicar?*
BP *Yes!*
Int. *What was his name?*
BP *... Dear ... Don't remember...*
Int. *You drove their car didn't you?*
BP *Er, William ...*
Int. *William?*
BP *William Rom ... Ney ...*
Int. *William Romney ... Yes ...*
BP *Yes ...*
Int. *And you drove their car ...*
BP *Yes.*
Int. *What sort of car was that?*
BP *... Now ...*
Int. *You were very proud you drove the car, weren't you?*
BP *Mm ...*
Int. *Do you remember what colour it was?*
BP *Singer ... A Singer ...*

Int. *I thought it was a Trojan ... A Trojan car ... you drove for them ...*
BP *We had a Trojan ...*
Int. *Yes. The Romneys had a Trojan car ... A blue one ...*
BP *Yes ...*
Int. *And you drove it ... You told me it had got very hard wheels ... Solid tyres.*
BP *Solid tyres!*
Int. *Yes. A bit of a devil when it was frosty and icy.*
BP *Yes ... Yes ...*
Int. *You've done everything haven't you?*
BP *(Gave a little laugh.) Yes ...*
Int. *Driven the car ... And you worked ... You got friendly with a maid, didn't you, at the ... Rectory ...*
BP *Yes.*
Int. *What was her name?*
BP *... Can't remember ...*
Int. *Is it Mabel?*
BP *... Can't remember what name was ...*
Int. *You worked at the rectory before you left school didn't you?*
BP *Mm?*
Int. *Worked hard ...*
BP *Yes, indeed ...*
Int. *Did a bit of everything.*
BP *Mm ...*
Int. *Including driving the car ...*
BP *Mm ... Yes indeed ... I stepped in a few jobs.*
Int. *You stepped into that before you left school didn't you? (Pause to allow BP time to answer.) Because your mum was widow wasn't she? ... (Pause.) Was it two brothers you had? (Pause.)*
BP *Mm?*
Int. *Was it two brothers you had?*
BP *... No I don't think so ...*
Int. *You don't ... But you remember the rectory?*
BP *Yes.*
Int. *A big place ...*
BP *Yes.*

Mrs Pinks dropped off to sleep or perhaps pretended to do so. Her voice was very faint and quavery throughout this interview. The above conversation gives some indication of the extent of the dissolution of her narrative. It was only with great difficulty that she recalled the Trojan car, the name of the vicar and the rectory. She did not recall that she had two brothers, neither did she remember the name of the maid who had been so influential in her early life. She did, however, recall that it was a long time ago. Further, information from the setting suggests that these memories were not stimulated through simple reminiscence. It is possible that the use of this intervention may have helped to encourage recall for a longer period.

Mr Biddley, too, showed a marked dissolution of his personal narrative. His dementia had rapidly progressed and he seemed more cognitively impaired than Mrs Pinks. Indeed, Figure 7.2 gives some support for this argument. As discussed in chapter five, I went to see him for a final interview to see if any fragments of his past stories remained in memory. This visit was very short. He was fast asleep when I arrived at the setting. He looked very frail and much older, although the sister in charge said he was now much better than he was. However, his behaviour was much as before. He said very little and when awake was `continually on the move´. The final interview with him suggests only a faint trace of his original stories. He appeared to have a faint recollection of his mother and, possibly, British Rail. However, this is speculative and his replies may have been influenced by the questions asked. What is apparent, however, is that this final interview shows the extent of the dissolution of his personal narrative and his sense of narrative identity. The data from other informants, too, suggest a loss of narrative identity. Mrs Woodley's final recorded interview, although indicating a certain sense of resolution and calm, did not contain the content or the depth of earlier meetings. This was also applicable to Mr Raft. Although the final meeting with this informant was unrecorded, ethnographic observation and notes suggest that he, too, possessed this measure of calm and tranquillity although many of his former memories were no longer available for recall.

Mr Clerkenwell was, perhaps, the most surprising member of the sample. The final recorded interview with this informant unleashed a flood of past memories. These memories, however, were all concerned with loss, grief, abandonment and cruelty. There is a recognised link between memory and mood in mood congruent memories (Baddeley, 1990; Blaney, 1986; Bower, 1981) and some evidence of the link between memory and mood in dementia (Mills and Walker, 1994). Mr Clerkenwell gave evidence to support this theory in the recall of his POW memories and, to a lesser extent, of his father `running away´. His life at this time may have encouraged the fundamental emotions of sadness, anger, disgust and fear and thus encouraged the recall of past experiences which were associated with similar emotions. The final interview with Mr Coxley was, again, unrecorded, but it is noted in his case-study that his recall of a personal past, although largely unchanged, had diminished in content and depth. His narrative, too, showed evidence of the beginning of dissolution.

Discussion

Consideration of the final interviews and observations of all informants indicate that all informants suffered a loss of their personal narrative to a greater or lesser extent. That this loss was linked to their failing memories is undeniable, however influenced by changes in personal circumstances and general ill health. Moreover, other people in the setting displayed this characteristic. It will be recalled that the pilot study for this investigation took place in the long stay ward of the hospital. I was also a frequent visitor to this ward during the times that informants stayed there for respite care and, therefore, had the opportunity to observe other patients. Some of these patients had been there for several years. They had also attended the day hospital.

During my visits to the ward I would frequently speak to these `non informants' and notice their interactions with others. Mrs Hopper was one such person. She was a tall slim lady with a commanding presence, given to wearing colourful tracksuits. At the beginning of the investigation I would quite often see her walking purposefully around each of the settings, talking to staff and visitors alike. She would also try to talk to other patients. I spoke to her on a number of occasions. She was a very sad tearful woman who wanted to go home to her family. She would talk about them in a fragmented but obviously recalled manner. I saw Mrs Hopper again in the early part of 1994. She was sitting in an armchair in the main lounge of the ward, looking vacantly into space. I spoke to her but she did not reply. However, she was not showing signs of her previous anxiety and unhappiness. It may be argued that this was due to the process of dementia and/or possibly the medication she was taking. It is probable that her loss of unhappiness and anxiety was a combination of all such variables.

Yet another visitor to both settings, Mr Axwell, did not display unhappiness. Indeed, rather the reverse. He showed signs of great happiness and contentment. When I last saw him in 1995 during a visit to the day hospital he was standing in the corridor with his trousers rolled up below his knees. He smiled at me sweetly as I approached. I had forgotten his first name and he could not remember it. I asked one of the staff who was passing by and he told me that Mr Axwell's first name was Archie. Mr Axwell again smiled and said with great unconcern, "That's right". I told him he looked happy and asked if he felt happy. He said he did. These observations, together with evidence from the staff in the setting would appear to support his feelings of well-being. This evidence of loss of anxiety/personal unhappiness is also evident in the findings from this study. Not all informants showed signs of grief as their narrative approached dissolution. Mr Silverthorne was one such person. Some of the final meetings with this informant suggest that he was content and free from his previous anxieties. Neither did Mrs Pinks or Mr Biddley show signs of great unhappiness, rather it is the unhappiness experienced by the interviewer which is evident in the final interviews with these two informants.

On a more personal level, within my own residential unit there are residents who have experienced the loss of their personal narrative. Two such residents are in the latter stages of the dementing process and have experienced a total loss. One cannot speak and the other has very few moments when her speech is comprehensible. They are in need of total care. Yet these residents give every indication of experiencing states of well-being. Mrs Lodge, the lesser impaired of the two, will tell carers that she loves them and hugs her soft cuddly toy given to her by her daughter. If she is noisy, she becomes calmer when staff speak to her and gently stroke her face, or hold her hand. She appears to listen when they are speaking. The sound of gentle voices appear to give her pleasure. Mrs Lodge has been living with us for five years.

The other of these two residents, Mrs Corner, has been a resident in the Home for nine years. She is a tiny lady who sits in her chair, constantly moving her head and arms whilst chuckling and laughing to herself. She enjoys the experience of touch and will stroke silky smooth material or furry fabric, with signs of pleasure. However, it must be said that these two ladies are greatly loved by the staff who supervise all aspects of their care. It is rare that any aspect of their care is found to be less than excellent. Moreover, many of the staff have been there for many years. The deputy has been in position for thirteen years, the cook and another senior carer for twelve years. The total number of years of service for twenty two staff add up to over a hundred. Thus most carers have had a long relationship with these two residents. Perhaps most importantly, staff knew them when they were less incapacitated and they are aware of their previous history and preferences. In this sense, the personal narrative of each of these residents has been retained and held by those who care for them.

A further nine residents who are in a state of narrative dissolution due to the dementing process, also exhibit signs of well-being, albeit to varying degrees. Again, many have been with us for some years and their personal narratives are retained by those who care for them. I am able, therefore, to recall parts of their narratives as I write these words without recourse to their personal records. I know that one of the nine kept a corner shop for seventy-three years, where she sold her highly popular home made faggots. She always had a soft spot for `our boys´ who were on leave during the second world war. She would give them little treats from her stock of sweets and cigarettes. She also assiduously collected items for Red Cross parcels. Another lady aged ninety-five years of age, cared for her blind husband with great devotion. They had no children, which was a source of great anguish for them both. Yet another lady was a professional actress and I know the London theatres where she appeared and the parts she played. I also know of the Guernsey tea shop which she and her husband kept after retirement and the many hundreds of scones she made each day for visitors to the island. She remembers to this day how much she disliked doing this. This particular resident has also allowed me to have a glimpse of what helps the dementia sufferer to achieve well-being in dementia. "Things don't matter." she said. "People matter, and good kindness."

As with other practitioners, it is probable that I could give quite a full account of these residents' personal narrative from memory alone. This is due to the many times that we have discussed their past lives and emotional experiences. Further, I am able to feed parts of their stories back to them to encourage recall. They are frequently amazed at the strength of my memory! If these people live long enough it is probable that they will experience a total dissolution of narrative and the corresponding loss of narrative identity, prior to death. The retention of their narrative by others enables the final stages of the dementing process to be endured. It gives carers respect and understanding of the needs, emotions and behaviours of dementia sufferers, which is so necessary in dementia care work (Mills, 1997a, 1997b). This understanding enables the maintenance of personhood which is, essentially, the relationships that all human beings have with others (Kitwood, 1997a; Kitwood and Bredin, 1992).

The new culture of dementia care is devoted to the preservation of personhood in dementia, whereby the sufferer's uniqueness of being is validated, respected and treated with `good kindness´ until the end.

Through the maintenance of personhood, it is possible to achieve well-being. The loss of the ego does not automatically bring devastation and despair. Good carers are able to preserve personhood in others by their remarkable knowledge and skills which are such a fundamental part of dementia care work. The loss of the personal narrative and loss of narrative identity might not be the tragedy that we who are non dementing might suppose. This is not to say that carers should not seek to maintain the personal narratives for dementia sufferers for as long as is practicably possible but to recognise that dementia has its own agenda, which will involve further cognitive decline. Whatever the therapies, whatever the interventions and no matter how skilful carers may be, narrative identity in dementia will eventually disappear. It is at this point that the ongoing and underlying work of the maintenance of personhood assumes a clarity of purpose and a recognition of its importance in dementia care.

Reflections on the role of the interviewer

Throughout the series of interviews with each of the informants it is possible to describe the role of the interviewer as that of a friend. Certainly, many informants saw me in that light. Occasionally some seemed to think that I had authority and that I was attached to the medical/social work team in the hospital. Mr Biddley indicated that he saw me as having knowledge of the decision making process in the setting. Mr Rider felt that I had the authority to release him from the confines of the secure ward and Mr Raft thought I was something to do with the `Welfare´. Nonetheless, overall I was seen as more of a friend than an interviewer, researcher or counsellor. However, the informants' case-studies indicate that my role was therapeutic in that all informants experienced increased levels of well-being. Further, I knew most of the informants well and our relationship lasted for a long period of time. My role, therefore, might be perceived as that of a companion and therapist in the exploration of their narratives. However, for some informants I was also a companion and therapist as they moved into the final stage of dementia. This incorporated a facilitating role of `holding´ and sustaining the personhood of informants as they sustained further losses associated with the dementing process.

The role of the `other´ in dementia care work is crucial to the well-being of demented elderly people (Mills, 1997b). Much of the literature on this topic has focused on the practicalities of this work.

Moreover, most theoretical inquiries concerned with in-depth study of well-being in older people with dementia have, perforce, used small samples. This investigation was no different. The sample under discussion was small, but the extensive data collected over an extended timespan gives support for the theoretical arguments concerned with the importance of a facilitating other, in all aspects of dementia care work.

Conclusion

As the many threads of this investigation are finally woven into a more complete whole, it is possible to see with some clarity the intertwining of the complex phenomena of emotion and memory in dementia. Theoretical considerations give some understanding of the immense strength of the emotions and their role as underpinning variables in all aspects of human behaviour. Although there is a paucity of literature concerning the relationship between emotion, memory and dementia, other disciplines have recognised the individual importance of these phenomena. This study has sought to develop this relationship by positing an interdependency between memory and emotion.

Although present knowledge of brain structures and processes are incomplete, the emotions also appear to have a profound effect on memory in dementia.

Further, it is suggested that there is a strength and durability in informants' emotional autobiographical memories that was not apparent in other aspects of memory. It has been argued that life histories (Thompson, 1988), some types of reminiscence (Bender, 1994; Butler, 1963; Coleman, 1994) and psychotherapeutic interviews (Garland, 1994; Knight, 1986b) are also concerned with emotional memories of the self. Other theorists and practitioners have also made this claim within dementia. Thus, Gibson (1994) finds emotions displayed in the recall of life histories, together with reminiscence work. Further, Hausman (1992), Sinason (1992) and Sutton (1995) write convincingly of the emotional agenda present in psychotherapeutic work with this client group. It is argued, therefore, that the phenomena of dementia, memory and emotion have a common meeting place, both theoretically and therapeutically, within the recall of the personal narrative for sufferers of dementia. It is the concept of narrative that links the theoretical and therapeutic aspects of this study. A major finding of this work is that informants, all of whom were at various stages of the dementing process, were still able to recall their narrative. Funkenstein (1993) suggests that memory and narrative are inextricably linked. The disappearance of the narrative is the disappearance of narrative identity. However, the narrative is dependent on existing memory structures and processes. This suggests a second major finding of this work. As memory structures and processes weaken, through the progressive nature of dementia, the narrative dissolves and fades into oblivion. Narrative identity is lost.

This, it is argued, is not the final ending of the psychological life of sufferers of dementia. Their biological and psychological life continues. A natural and logical consequence to the loss of the narrative identity is that future work with older people who have dementia must then be concerned with the maintenance and preservation of personhood. It is this continuing psychological task which is at the heart of dementia care. However, the various strategies which facilitate this work would benefit from a knowledge of the personal narrative of sufferers of dementia. It is argued that the sharing of such a narrative within dementia care, reinforces carer attitudes of respect, understanding and acceptance. In this sense, therefore, the personal narrative of dementia sufferers is never lost. It continues its existence in the form of a treasure which is bestowed on others to use how they will. It is hoped that the discovery of the presence of the narrative in dementia, made possible by the generosity of the informants, will be instrumental in enriching the lives of other sufferers of dementia. This would be a reward and a source of joy to all informants who took part in this investigation.

8 A final word

Introduction

The importance of the narrative or life story in dementia has been a major theme in this work and is an area of interest to other theorists and practitioners. This has led to a general consensus that knowledge of a client's past enables greater communication between client and dementia care worker (Coleman and Mills, 1997; Gibson, 1997; Goldsmith, 1996; Mills and Chapman, 1992; Sutton and Cheston, 1997). In this brief closing chapter it is proposed to broaden this argument by suggesting that this viewpoint may have too narrow a focus. The narrative enables greater communication within dementia care work than might first be supposed. Recent research at the University of Southampton offers some support for this perspective (Coleman et al., 1997).

The personal narrative can be seen as a public, semi public or private account of a life which can take place in reminiscence groups (Bender, 1994; Gibson, 1997), recorded in autobiographies, personal diaries or life story books (Short, 1993) and within the life review or counselling interview (Knight, 1986b). The life story can, of course, encompass all three modes. Certainly, the psychological case-study embraces all aspects. It is gathered through conversation/discourse, it is a written record and it uses psychotherapeutic processes to collect/interpret information and to protect client anonymity. Finally, the resultant record is scrutinised and judged (Bromley, 1986).

However, it will be recalled from chapter three that Bromley (1990) asserts that this type of case-study is more concerned with a single slice/episode in the life course. He maintains that a longer term approach should be seen as the life-history method. Nevertheless, it will be argued that it is not impossible to combine life history and

176

psychological case-study methods to tell a `psychological´ life story that meets the biological, psychological and social needs of the individual.

The case-study: an effective form of learning?

This discussion commences with an account of a one year investigation whose aims were to develop and test a training course for dementia care staff in residential homes for older adults and to design a research instrument to measure the impact of the course on patterns of residential care (Coleman et al., 1997). The course, itself, was heavily influenced by Bowlby's lifespan theory of attachment which seeks to explain the quality of the internalised mother-child relationship (Bowlby, 1969). It is this attachment which is thought to form the foundation for patterns of subsequent relationships. Bowlby's thinking has been developed over the last four decades (Holmes, 1997) and elaborated by `post-Bowlbian´ theorists and practitioners. One such is Bère Miesen (1992, 1993, 1997), a Dutch psychogerontologist who has compared the seemingly emotionally disorganised behaviours of dementia sufferers to early attachment behaviours, where the older person will seek to be safe, to be `held´ and to be understood. In addition, Kitwood (1997a) and Miesen (1997) argue that the attachment histories of dementia carers themselves are of great importance within dementia care work. In effect, this was a course designed to encourage greater awareness and understanding of the interconnected nature of relationships across the life span and their influence on client well-being. This underpinned all theoretical and practical sessions, from communication to lifting and handling.

The course consisted of eighteen three hour weekly sessions and was delivered in two residential homes, over the course of nine months, by two experienced trainers and researchers. The range of course topics and number of sessions were: attachment experiences over the life course (3); study skills (1); understanding dementia (2); depression and dementia (2); communication with the person with dementia (3); upsetting behaviours (2); communication about the person with dementia (1); moving and handling people with mobility difficulties (1); death and dying (1); caring for people who are different (1); medication (1); meaningful activities in dementia (1).

Group one contained six females aged between twenty-eight and fifty-two years of age. Group two contained eight females and two males aged between twenty-seven and fifty-four years of age. One person in group one possessed a professional qualification with another in the process of gaining a National Vocational Qualification (NVQ) level 2 in direct care. Group two contained no one with a professional qualification although some were considering undertaking NVQ training. An offshoot of the project was to design a cost effective dementia care course which would lend itself to the training needs of the care sector. The eighteen week course was then reduced to eight weeks and piloted in a residential home which specialised in dementia care. The course topics were chosen by the manager of the unit and research project members. These were: understanding dementia (2); communicating with people with dementia (2); disturbing behaviours (2); communicating about people with dementia (1); caring for people who are different (1). 'Communication with people with dementia' contained aspects of attachment theory, together with in-depth discussion on lifespan relationships. This group consisted of six females and two males aged between eighteen and fifty-five years. Again, none of the participants possessed a professional qualification but three had just completed NVQ 3 in direct care, with a further two just beginning this level of training, having completed NVQ level 2.

Although there were several written assignments for all three groups, the major evaluated work was a research based, in-depth case-study. This, in many ways, proved to be the most effective form of learning. Groups one and two were given the choice of completing the task either individually or in small groups, with both homes choosing the last option. They were given firm guidelines on ethical considerations and, through group discussion, how to go about collecting information. In the end, clients, families, friends and other carers were approached. As the set time given for completion was over an eight to ten week period, both groups had sufficient time to complete the project. The case-studies were produced to a good standard in group one and to an excellent standard in group two. However, the project team's evaluation of the first set of case-studies led to more comprehensive directions for the second group. The results were extremely positive, with some changes in the care practices of both homes, possibly influenced by the case-study exercise. These included changes to the environment and greater sensitivity in meeting needs. Principally, carers said they felt they had greater understanding of clients and were able to suggest alternative strategies to improve well-being. They also felt that relatives were pleased to be involved in the case-study exercise and they now enjoyed a greater rapport with them.

However, because the third group were together for a much shorter period of time, they were asked to select one of their key clients for the case-study exercise. Again, ethical considerations and the need to gain permissions were discussed. Feedback from groups one and two had suggested that the guidelines needed to be more specific. Group three, therefore, were given a two page handout which included a list of headings for the factual content of page one. These included name, age, date of birth etc., together with educational, occupational, social and medical history. Further, each case-study had to be marked `confidential`. Group three were then asked to write a story about their client that might show ways of improving well-being and/or validate existing practices.

The following quotes are from the handout: "Case-studies can often identify unrecognised needs, or suggest alternative care strategies. Equally, they may validate existing practices which can then be used in other situations. The more personal information that can be gathered about a person the better. This essentially allows information to be cross-checked and perhaps to recognise that there may be no single explanation but rather several different interpretations of life events and experiences. The second part of the case-study is about your relationship with your client. This is the story of a life. What kind of person are they? Describe their personality, their likes and dislikes: anything you think might help to offer more person centred care to the person."

Again, all case-studies were presented to a high standard and contained information from the client, except in two instances where the severity of the illness made this impossible. However, both participants interviewed family members and friends. Moreover, these and other relatives provided written accounts for carers. They also sought the assistance of senior members of staff who had known these clients for some years. Clients who were able, read and approved the final account. Relatives, too, who provided information read and approved the finished case-study before it was handed in for assessment. The case-studies were marked by the tutor. Her comments, together with the case-studies themselves, were evaluated by the research project co-ordinator.

One case-study began:

I am going to write about my key client and friend, Miss A. The first impression of this lady is of a shy and withdrawn person who does not want to draw attention to herself. However, when she gets to know people and to feel safe with them, she begins to come out of her shell and will chat and answer questions.

Using information obtained from the client, the author continued with an account of the client's childhood, some of which was new to the Home: "Her best friends at school were Elsie, Anne, Jessie and Joe. Her favourite subjects at school were needlework and music ... she still enjoys these activities today."

A recurrent theme in this story was the client's history of epilepsy which led to her first major brain surgery at the age of twenty-six years. Miss X lived at home with her parents until they finally found her illness and behaviour too difficult to manage. She was then admitted to a local psychiatric hospital, aged forty-one years. She was to stay in the hospital for a further fifteen years, the last five of which were spent in a psychogeriatric ward. The author was indignant at the management of her client's illness and cites evidence from hospital notes to support her argument:

In 1988 the last letter from the EEG department asks, "Why is this lady still in this hospital?".

She continues:

Miss X spent five years in a geriatric ward and presents as much older than she is. She came to our Home for the Elderly in 1989 and we needed special permission from Social Services as she was only 56 years old ... Miss X has not had much of a life but we encourage her to make as many choices as possible. She has been to the first dance of her life ... She likes to do jigsaws and we have just started to do cross stitch together and she is enjoying it. I also now hope to take her out once a week ... She is a lovable lady who you have to meet in person to get the full benefit of her warmth and charm.

Shortly before completion of the case-studies, an interview with the manager of the home, who was herself a course participant, elicited the fact that care practices had indeed changed with regard to this client and with four other residents who also featured in the case-studies. These changes ranged from increased social activities and improved relationship with the keyworker, as is shown in the above example. Further, care staff were able to perceive some behaviours as originating from past experiences:

> R loves icecream, this is because he was not allowed to have it when young, due to the possibility of TB in the family ... Because of his grandfather's attitude, R grew up with low self esteem and a fear of being ill ... This fear of illness is still with him ...

> Miss Y was very academic and did well in all her school exams. She wasn't allowed to go to University as her brother's education was considered more important, even though he was less clever. However, she was learning Greek at the age of 79 years and passed a lay readers course when she was 81 years old with flying colours.

There were also individual changes in practical care routines, such as different times and settings for meals, bathing arrangements and a greater encouragement of client choice in personal care arrangements. Interestingly, participants had also offered suggestions for the improved care of other residents who did not feature in the case-studies. Thus there was evidence of positive change in meeting clients' personal care needs, together with positive change in meeting clients' psychological and social needs. Further, staff were open in their comments about their clients.

> Mrs X makes me want to come to work, she makes me feel my job is worthwhile.

And others:

> This is an account of a very special person who I will always remember. In conclusion, this is a true account of Miss Y. She is a kindly, gentle person who has had little chance in life. My aim is to make sure the rest of her life is different.

One participant wrote that her client was quite difficult and always spoke her mind. This was what she liked best about her! Further, participants remarked how helpful relatives were. They also said that the exercise had been very useful. Echoing the work of Goldsmith (1996) they suggested that every resident should have a case-study of this nature and it should be part of their files. This would make it possible for all staff to have a greater understanding of residents. It would give care staff topics for conversation and allow them to assess and meet needs more easily. They also felt that copies of the residents' case-studies should form part of their notes in other settings, such as hospitals and day centres.

This evidence suggests that this type of case-study might have a useful part to play in dementia care training, although its characteristics are possibly more complex than are first imagined. The interactive nature of narrative construction, the interpretation of text and the bias that is inherent in compiling a narrative is discussed in some detail in chapter three. Thus, it can be suggested that the above examples quoted from the last set of case-studies contain the intertwined stories of two people - client and carer. Their stories form a single created text, an account of an enhanced and emotionally resonating relationship.

This is an example of secondary intersubjectivity, an elaboration of primary intersubjectivity which is the first empathic bond connecting the baby and care-giver, thus enabling needs to be sensitively met (Trevarthen, 1984). The characteristics of secondary intersubjectivity contain trust, a valuing and being valued, positive and non judgmental regard, an acknowledgment that the other is a unique experiencing being who has an identity or life story (Kitwood, 1997a; Mills, 1997b). Many of these attributes were clearly present in the attitudes of the writers of the case-studies and in their key clients' behaviour towards them. Further, the tutor visited the Home after the completion of the course. During this visit a resident who featured in one of the case-studies pointed to his keyworker and said, "This ... this is the pièce de résistance here." They then smiled at each other. Secondary intersubjectivity was also evident in those who contributed to the case-study content and/or read the finished story. Again, as is shown in chapter five, unconditional positive regard was clearly evident, although negative behaviours did not go undiscussed. The Home plans to use its case-studies to make other involved agencies see clients as "people with a past, a present and a future". They envisage the future to contain good relationships, person centred care and increased client well-being, although well aware that the process of dementia will inexorably continue.

182

Tom Kitwood has written:

> If personhood is to be maintained, it is essential that each individual be appreciated in his or her uniqueness. Where there is empathy without personal knowledge, care will be aimless and unfocused. Where there is personal knowledge without empathy, care will be detached and cold. But when empathy and personal knowledge are brought together, miracles can happen. (Kitwood, 1997b, p.39)

Apart from finding cures for this condition, the idea of linking miracles and dementia is probably beyond most expectations and experiences. However, there is a unique wonder in the recent cultural transformations that have taken place in dementia care. Further, it is hoped that this final chapter underpins and extends the value of the case-study within dementia care work and training. In turn, this bringing together of empathy and personal knowledge through case-study methods must add to our understanding of the experiential world of dementia and a more positive approach in our treatment of older people with this disease.

Bibliography

Adams, J. (1984), 'Reminiscence in the Geriatric Ward: an undervalued resource', *Oral History Journal*, vol.12, pp.54-59.

Adams, J. (1986), 'Anamnesis in Dementia: restoring a personal history', *Geriatric Nursing*, Sep/Oct, 1986, pp.25-27.

Adams, J. (1994), 'A Fair Hearing: Life review in a hospital setting', in J. Bornat (ed.), *Reminiscence Reviewed: perspectives, evaluations, achievements*, The Open University Press: Buckingham, Philadelphia.

Agar, M. & Hobb, J.R. (1982), 'Interpreting Discourse: coherence and the analysis of ethnographic interviews', *Discourse Processes*, vol.5, pp.1-32.

Allport, G.W. (1937), *Personality: a psychological interpretation*, Holt, Rinehart and Wilson: New York.

Annerstedt, A., Alfredson, B. & Risberg, G. (1987), 'Effects of an Alternative Mode of Care for Demented Elderly', Paper presented at the 111rd Congress of the International Psychogeriatric Association, Chicago.

Averill, J.R. (1986), 'Acquisition of Emotions during Adulthood', in R. Harre (ed.), *The Social Construction of Emotions*, Basil Blackwell: New York, Oxford.

Baddeley, A. (1990), *Human Memory: Theory and Practice*, Lawrence Erlbaum Associates: Hillsdale, NJ.

Baddeley, A. (1992), 'Is Working Memory Working?', The Fifteenth Bartlett Lecture, *The Quarterly Journal of Experimental Psychology*, vol.44, no.1, pp.1-31.

Banister, P., Burman, E., Parker, I., Taylor, M. and Tindall, C. (1995), *Qualitative Methods in Psychology: A Research Guide*, The Open University Press: Buckingham.

Barkham, M. (1996), 'Quantative Research on Psychotherapeutic Interventions: methodological research issues and substantive findings across three research generations', in R. Woolfe and W. Dryden (eds), *Handbook of Counselling Psychology*, Sage: London.

Bartlett, F.C. (1932), 'Remembering', Cambridge University Press: Cambridge.

Bayles, K.A. (1991), 'Alzheimer's Disease Symptoms: prevalence and order of appearance', *Journal of Applied Gerontology*, vol.10, no.4, pp.419-430.

Bayles, K.A. & Kaszniak, A.W. (1987), *Communication and Cognition in Normal Ageing and Dementia*, Little & Brown: Boston.

Behar, R. (1993), *Translated Women: crossing the border with Esperanza's story*, Beacon: Boston.

Bender, M.P. (1994), 'An Interesting Confusion: what can we do with reminiscence groupwork?', in J. Bornat (ed.), *Reminiscence Reviewed: perspectives, evaluations, achievements*, Open University Press: Philadelphia, Buckingham.

Berg, B.L. (1989), *Qualitative Research Methods for the Social Sciences*, Alyn and Bacon: Boston.

Billings, A.G. & Moos, R.H. (1981), 'The Role of Coping Responses and Social Resources in Attenuating the Stress of Life Events', *Journal of Behavioural Medicine*, vol.4, pp.139-157.

Bingham, W.V.D. & Moore, B.V. (1959), *How to Interview*, 4th edition, Harper and Row: New York.

Blaney, P.H. (1986), 'Affect and Memory: a review', *Psychological Bulletin*, vol.99, pp.229-246.

Bond, J., Briggs, R. & Coleman, P.G. (1990), 'The Study of Ageing', in J. Bond & P.Coleman (eds), *Ageing and Society: an introduction to social gerontology*, Sage Publications: London, Newbury Park, New Delhi.

Bornat, J. (1985), 'Exploring Living Memory: The Uses of Reminiscence', *Ageing and Society*, vol.5, pp.333-337.

Bornat, J. (1994), 'Introduction', in J. Bornat (ed.), *Reminiscence Reviewed: perspectives, evaluations achievements*, Open University Press: Buckingham, Philadelphia.

Bornat, J. & Adams, J. (1992), 'Models of Biography and Reminiscence in the Nursing Care of Frail Elderly People', in J.M. Via & Portella (eds), *Proceedings of the 4th International Conference on Systems Science in Health-Social Services for the Elderly and Disabled*, vol.11, A. Camps: Barcelona.

Bower, G.H. (1981), 'On Mood and Memory', *American Psychologist*, vol.36, pp.129-148.

Bower, G.H., Gilligan, S.G. & Monteiro, K.P. (1981), 'Selectivity of Learning Caused by Affective States', *Journal of Experimental Psychology [Gen]*, vol.110, pp.451-473.

Bower, G.H. & Cohen, P.R. (1982), 'Emotional Influences in Memory and Thinking: data and theory', in M.S. Clark & S.T. Fiske (eds), *Affect and Cognition*, Lawrence Erlbaum Associates: Hillsdale, NJ.

Bowlby, J. (1969), *Attachment and Loss: Volume 1, Attachment*, The Hogarth Press: London.

Brewer, W.F. (1986), 'What is Autobiographical Memory?', in D.C. Rubin (ed.), *Autobiographical Memory*, Cambridge University Press: Cambridge.

Bromley, D.B. (1966), *The Psychology of Human Ageing*, Penguin, Harmondsworth: New York, Victoria, Ontario.

Bromley, D.B. (1986), *The Case-Study Method in Psychology and Related Disciplines*, John Wiley & Sons: Chichester.

Bromley, D.B. (1990), *Behavioural Gerontology: Central Issues in the Psychology of Ageing*, John Wiley & Sons: Chichester.

Bruner, E.M. (1986), 'Experience and its Expressions', in V.W. Turner & E.M. Bruner (eds), *The Anthropology of Experience Urbana*, University of Illinois Press: Illinois.

Buck, R. (1988), *Human Motivation and Emotion (2nd edition)*, John Wiley and Sons: New York.

Busfield, J. (1986), *Managing Madness: Changing Ideas and Practice*.

Butler, R.N. (1963), 'The Life Review: An Interpretation of Reminiscence in the Aged', *Psychiatry*, vol.26, pp.65-76.

Butler, R.N. & Lewis, M.I. (1982), *Ageing and Mental Health: positive psychosocial and biomedical approaches*, Mosby: St.Louis.

Campbell, D.T. (1975), 'Degrees of Freedom and the Case-Study Comparative', *Political Studies*, vol.8, pp.178-193.

Cannon, W.B. (1927), 'The James-Lange Theory of Emotion: a critical examination and an alternative theory', *American Journal of Psychology*, vol.1, pp.106-124.

Carlson, C.M. (1984), 'Reminiscing: toward achieving ego integrity in old age', *Social Casework: The Journal of Contemporary Social Work*, Feb.1984, pp.81-89.

Castelnuovo-Tedesco, P. (1978), 'The Mind as a Stage: Some Comments on Reminiscence and Internal Objects', *International Journal of Psychoanalysis*, vol.59, pp.19-25.

Chernitz, W.C. (1986), 'The Informal Interview', in W.C. Chernitz & J.M. Swanson (eds), *From Practice to Grounded Theory: Qualitative Research in Nursing*, Addison Wesley: Menlo Park, CA.

Chertkow, H. & Bub, D. (1990), 'Semantic Memory Loss in Dementia of the Alzheimer's Type: what do various measures measure?', *Brain*, vol.113, pp.397-417.

Cheston, R. (1996), 'Stories and Metaphors: talking about the past in a psychotherapy group for people with dementia', *Ageing and Society*, vol.16, pp.579-602.

Cohen, F. (1984), 'Coping' in J.D. Matarazzo, M.Sh. Weiss, J.A. Herd, N.E. Miller, M.St. Weiss (eds), *Behavioural Health: a handbook of health enhancement and disease prevention*, John Wiley: New York.

Coleman, P.G. (1974), 'Measuring Reminiscence Characteristics from Conversation as an Adaptive Feature of Old Age', *International Journal of Aging and Human Development*, vol.5, no.3, pp.281-294.

Coleman, P.G. (1986b), *Ageing and Reminiscence Processes Social and Clinical Implications*, John Wiley and Sons: Chichester, New York.

Coleman, P.G. (1994), 'Reminiscence Within the Study of Ageing' in J. Bornat (ed.), *Reminiscence Reviewed: perspectives, evaluations, achievements*, Open University Press: Buckingham, Philadelphia.

Coleman, P.G., Aubin, A., Robinson, M., Ivani-Chalian, C. & Briggs, R. (1993), 'Predictors of Depressive Symptoms and Low Self Esteem in a Follow-Up Study of Elderly People Over 10 Years', *International Journal of Geriatric Psychiatry*, vol.8, pp.343-389.

Coleman, P.G. and Mills, M.A. (1997), 'Listening to War Memories in Late Life Depression and Dementia' in L. Hunt, M. Marshall and C. Rowlands (eds), *Past Trauma in Late Life: European Perspectives on Therapeutic Work with Older People*, Jessica Kingsley: London.

Coleman, P., Conroy, C., Jerrome, D., Meade, R. and Mills, M.A. (1997), 'Changing Patterns of Dementia Care Through Staff Training: the effects of a course which draws on attachment theory'. Paper presented at Elder Power in the 21st Century, Annual Conference of the British Society of Gerontology.

Conway, M. (1990), *Autobiographical Memory: an introduction*. Open University Press: Milton Keynes, Philadelphia.

Cook, J.B. (1984), 'Reminiscing: how it can help confused nursing home residents', *Social Casework: The Journal of Contemporary Social Work*. Feb.1984, pp.90-93.

Costa, P.T. & McCrae, R.R. (1988), 'Personality in Adulthood: a six year longitudinal study of self reports and spouse ratings on the NEO personality inventory', *Journal of Personality and Social Psychology*, vol.54, no.5, pp.853-863.

Cummings, E. & Henry, W. (1961), *Growing Old: The Process of Disengagement*, Basic Books: New York.

Damasio, A.R., Van Hoesen, G.W. & Hyman, B.T. (1990), 'Reflections on the Selectivity of Neuropathological Changes in Alzheimer's Disease' in M.F. Schwartz (ed.), *Modular Deficits in Alzheimer-Type Dementia*, The MIT Press: Cambridge, Massachusetts, London.

Darwin, C. (1872), *The Expression of the Emotions in Man and Animals*, Philosophical Library: London, New York.

Davies, M. (1993), 'Counselling: a statistical analysis within the primary health care team', *The Journal of Counselling in Medical Settings*, vol.37, pp.5-10.

Davis, R. (1989), *My Journey into Alzheimer's Disease*, Scripture Press.

Denzin, N.K. (1989a), *Interpretive Interactionism*, Sage Publishers: Newbury Park, CA, London.

Denzin, N.K. (1989b), *Interpretive Biography*, Sage Publishers: Newbury Park, CA, London, New Delhi.

Digman, J.M. (1990), 'Personality Structure: emergence of the five factor model. Annual review', *Psychology*, vol.41, pp.417-440.

Dobrof, R. (1984), 'Introduction: a time for reclaiming the past' in M. Kaminsky (ed.), *The Uses of Reminiscence: new ways of working with older adults*, The Economist, Haworth Press: New York.

Economist, The (1990), *Vital World Statistics: a complete guide to the world in figures*, The Economist Books, Hutchinson: London.

Egan, G. (1975), *The Skilled Helper: model, skills, and methods for effective helping*, Brookes/Cole: Monterey, CA.

Ekman, P. (1984), 'Expression and the Nature of Emotion', in K. Scherer & P. Ekman (eds), *Approaches to Emotion*, Lawrence Erlbaum Associates: Hillsdale, NJ.

Ekman, P., Friesen, W.V. & Ellsworth, P. (1972), *Emotion in the Human Face*, Pergammon Press: Elmsford, New York.

Erikson, E.H. (1963), *Childhood and Society (2nd edition)*, Norton: New York.

Eysenck, M.W. (1967), *The Biological Basis of Personality*, Thomas: Springfield, Illinois.

Eysenck, M.W. & Keane, M.T. (1990), *Cognitive Psychology: a students handbook*, Lawrence Erlbaum Associates: London, Hillsdale, NJ.

Eysenk, H.J. (1973), *Eysenk on Extraversion*, John Wiley: New York.

Falkingham, J. (1989), 'Dependency and Ageing in Britain: a re-examination of the evidence', *Journal of Social Policy*, vol.18, no.2, pp.211-213.

Farran, C.J. & Keane-Hagerty, E. (1989), 'Communicating Effectively with Dementia Patients', *Journal of Psychosocial Nursing*, vol.27, no.5, pp.13-17.

Feil, N. (1982), *V/F Validation: the Feil method*, Edward Feil Productions: Cleveland, Ohio.

Feil, N. (1985), 'Resolution: the final life task', *Journal of Humanistic Psychology*, vol.25, no.2, pp.91-105.

187

Feil, N. (1992), 'Validation Therapy with Late-Onset Dementia Populations', in Jones G.M.M. and Miesen B.M.L. (eds), *Care-giving in Dementia: Research and Applications*, Tavistock/Routledge: vol.1: London.

Feil, N. (1993), *The Validation Breakthrough: simple techniques for communicating with people with Alzheimer's type dementia*, Health Professions Press Inc: Baltimore.

Flemming, A.S., Rickards, L.D., Santos, J.F. & West, P.R. (1986), 'Report on a Survey of Community Mental Health Centres', Washington D.C: Action Committee to Implement the Mental Health Recommendations of the 1981 White House Conference on Ageing.

Folkman, S., Lazarus, R.S., Gruen, R. & Delongis, A. (1986), 'Appraisal, Coping, Health Status and Psychological Symptom', *Journal of Personality and Social Psychology*, vol.50, pp.571-579.

Freeman, M. (1993), *Rewriting The Self: history, memory, narrative*, Routledge: London, New York.

Freud, S. (1920/1955), 'Beyond the Pleasure Principle', vol.18 of the Standard Edition, Hogarth: London.

Froggatt, A. (1988), 'Self-awareness in Early Dementia' in B. Gearing, M. Johnson & T. Heller (eds), *Mental Health Problems in Old Age*, John Wiley, in association with The Open University: New York, Chichester.

Funkenstein, A. (1993), 'The Incomprehensible Catastrophe: memory and narrative' in R. Josselson & A. Lieblich (eds), *The Narrative Study of Lives*, Sage: London.

Gardner, I. (1993), 'Psychotherapeutic Intervention' in A. Chapman and M. Marshall (eds), *Dementia: new skills for social workers. Case Studies for Practice 5*, Jessica Kingsley: London.

Garland, J. (1994), 'What Splendour, It all Coheres: life-review therapy with older people', in J. Bornat (ed.), *Reminiscence Reviewed: perspectives, evaluations, achievements*, Open University Press: Buckingham, Philadelphia.

Gibson, F. (1994), 'What Can Reminiscence Contribute to People with Dementia?', in J. Bornat (ed.), *Reminiscence Reviewed: perspectives, evaluations, achievements*, Open University Press: Buckingham, Philadelphia.

Gibson, F. (1997), 'Owning the Past in Dementia Care: creative engagement with others in the present', in M. Marshall (ed.), *State of the Art in Dementia Care*, CPA: London.

Gilligan, S.G. & Bower, G.H. (1984), 'Cognitive Consequences of Emotional Arousal', in C.E. Izard, J. Kagan, R.B. Zajonc (eds), *Emotions, Cognition and Behaviour*, Cambridge University Press.

Glaser, B. & Strauss, A. (1967), *The Discovery of Grounded Theory: Strategies for Qualitative Research*, Aldine: Chicago.

Goffman, E. (1959), *The Presentation of Self in Everyday Life*, Doubleday: New York.

Goldsmith, M. (1996), 'Hearing the Voice of People with Dementia', in M. Marshall (ed.), *State of the Art in Dementia Care*, CPA: London.

Goldwasser, A., Auerbach, S.M. & Harkins, S.W. (1987), 'Cognitive, Affective, and Behavioural Effects of Reminiscence Group Therapy on Demented Elderly', *International Journal of Ageing and Human Development*, vol.25, no.3, pp.209-222.

Goudie, F. & Stokes, G. (1989), 'Understanding Confusion', *Nursing Times*, Sep 27, vol.85, p.39.

Guttman, D.L. (1980), 'Psychoanalysis and Aging: a developmental view', in S.I. Greenspan & G.H. Pollock (eds), *The Course of Life: psychoanalytic contributions towards understanding personality development. Vol.III: Adulthood and the Aging Process*, US Department of Health and Human Services: Washington, D.C.

Hagberg, B. (1995), 'Life History as a Formative Experience', in B.K. Haight and J.D. Webster (eds), *The Art and Science of reminiscing: Theory, Research, Methods, and Applications*, Taylor and Francis: Washington, London.

Hagberg, B. (1997), 'The Individual's Life History as a Formative Experience in Aging', in G.M. Jones and B.M. Miesen (eds), *Care-Giving in Dementia: research and applications*, vol.2, Routledge: London.

Haight, B.K. (1988), 'The Therapeutic Role of a Structured Life Review Process in Homebound Elderly Subjects', *Journal of Gerontology*, vol.43, pp.40-44.

Haight, B.K. (1989a), 'Life-review: a method for pastoral counselling: Part 1', *Journal of Religion and Aging*, vol.5, no.3, pp.17-29.

Haight, B.K. (1989b), 'Life-review: a report of the effectiveness of a structured life-review process: Part II', *Journal of Religion and Aging*, vol.5, no.3, pp.31-41.

Haight, B.K. (1991), 'Reminiscing: the state of the art as a basis for practice', *International Journal of Ageing and Human Development*, vol.33, no.1, pp.1-32.

Haight, B.K. & Dias, J.K. (1992), 'Examining Key Variables in Selected Reminiscing Modalities', *International Psychogeriatrics*, vol.4, no.2, pp.279-289.

Haight, B.M. & Hendrix, S. (1995), 'An integrated Review of Reminiscence', in B.M. Haight and J.D. Webster (eds), *The Art and Science of reminiscing: Theory, Research, Methods, and Applications*, Taylor and Franci: Washington, London.

Haight, B.M., Coleman, P.G., Lord, K. (1995), 'The Structured Life Review', in B.M. Haight and J.D. Webster (eds), *The Art and Science of reminiscing: Theory, Research, Methods, and Applications*, Taylor and Francis: Washington, London.

Hammersley, M. & Atkinson, P. (1983), *Ethnography: principles in practice*, Tavistock Publications: London, New York.

Hanley, I. & Hodge, J. (1984), *Psychological Approaches to the Care of the Elderly*, Croom Helm: London, Sydney, Methuen, New York.

Hargie, O., Saunders, C. & Dickson, D. (1981), *Social Skills in Interpersonal Communication*, Croom Helm: London, Sydney.

Harre, R. (1986), 'The Social Constructionist Viewpoint', in R. Harre (ed.), *The Social Construction of Emotions*, Basil Blackwell: New York, Oxford.

Hasher, L., Rose, K.C., Zacks, R.T., Sanft, H. & Doren, B. (1985), 'Mood, Recall and Selectivity Effects in Normal College Students', *Journal of Experimental Psychology [Gen]*, vol.114, pp.104-118.

Hausman, C. (1992), 'Dynamic Psychotherapy with Elderly Demented Patients', in G.M. Jones and B.M. Miesen (eds), *Care Giving in Dementia: research and applications*, vol.1, Routledge: London.

Hawker, R. (1982), 'The Interaction between Nurses and Patients Relatives', unpublished thesis, University of Exeter.

Helling, I.K. (1988), 'The Life History Method: a survey and discussion with Norman K. Denzin', *Studies in Symbolic Interaction*, vol.9, pp.211-243.

Highlen, P.S. & Hill, C.E. (1984), 'Factors Affecting Client Change in Individual Counselling: current status and theoretical speculations', in S.D. Brown & R.W. Lent (eds), *Handbook of Counselling Psychology*, John Wiley: Chichester, New York, Brisbane.

Hillgard, E.R., Atkinson, R.L. & Atkinson, R.C. (1979), *Introduction to Psychology, (7th edition)*, Harcourt Brace Jovanovitch: London, New York, Tokyo.

Holden, U. (1995), *Ageing, Neuropsychology and the 'New' Dementias: definitions, explanations and practical approaches*, Chapman and Hall: London, New York.

Holland, J.L. (1973), *Making Vocational Choices: a theory of careers*, Prentice-Hall: Englewood Cliffs, NJ.

Holland, L. (1987), 'Life Review and Communication Therapy for Dementia Patients', *Clinical Gerontologist*, vol.6, pp.62-65.

Holmes, J. (1997), 'Attachment, Autonomy, Intimacy: some clinical implications of attachment theory', *British Journal of Medical Psychology*, vol.70, no.3, pp.231-248.

Hutchinson, S. (1986), 'Grounded theory: the method', in P.L. Munhall & C.J. Oiler (eds), *Nursing Research: a qualitative perspective*, Appleton-Century-Croft: Norwalk, Conn.

Ineichen, B. (1987), 'Measuring the Rising Tide: how many dementia cases will there be by 2001?', *British Journal of Psychiatry*, vol.150, pp.193-200.

Isen, A.M., Clark, T.E. & Carp, L. (1978), 'Affect, Accessibility of Material in Memory and Behaviour; A Cognitive Loop', *Journal of Personal Social Psychology*, vol.36, no.1, pp.1-12.

Isohanni, M. (1990), 'Coping with Institutional Life at the Old People's Therapeutic Community', *Psychiatry*, vol.53, pp.148-157.

Izard, C.E. (1971), *The Face of Emotion*, Apple-Century-Crofts: New York.

Izard, C.E. (1984), 'The Facets and Interfaces of Emotions', in R. Bell, J.L. Green, & J.H. Harvey (eds), *Interfaces in Psychology*, Texas Tech Press: Lubbock, TX.

Izard, C.E. (1991), *The Psychology of Emotions*, Plenum Press: New York, London.

James, W. (1894), 'The Physiological Basis of Emotion', *Psychology Review*, vol.1, pp.516-529.

Johnson, M.K. (1983), 'A Multiple Entry, Modular Memory System', in G. Bower (ed.), *The Psychology of Learning and Motivation: advances in research theory*, vol.7, pp.81-123, Academic Press: New York.

Johnson, M.K. (1985), 'The Origins of Memory', in P.C. Kendall (ed.), *Advances in Cognitive Behavioural Research and Therapy*, vol.4, pp.1-27, Academic Press: New York.

Johnson, M.L. (1976), 'That Was Your Life: a biological approach to later life', in J.M.A. Munnichs & W.J.A. van den Heuvel (eds), *Dependency and Independency in Old Age*, Martinus Nijhoff: The Hague.

Jones, G. & Burns, A. (1992), 'Reminiscing Disorientation Theory', in G.M. Jones and B.M. Miesen (eds), *Care-Giving in Dementia*, Research and applications, vol.1, Routledge: London.

Kaminsky, M. (1984), 'Transfiguring Life: images of continuity hidden among the fragments', in M. Kaminsky (ed.), *The Uses of Reminiscence: new ways of working with older adults*, Haworth Press: New York.

Karlsson, I., Brane, G., Ekman, R., Kihlgren, M., Norberg, A. & Widerlof, E. (1987), 'Biochemical and Psychological Effects of Integrity Promoting Care', Paper presented at the 3rd. Congress of the International Psychogeriatric Association, Chicago.

Kazdin, A.E. (1980), *Research Designs in Clinical Psychology*, Harper & Row: New York.

190

Kiernat, J.M. (1979), 'The Use of Life Review Activity with Confused Nursing Home Residents', *American Journal of Occupational Therapy*, vol.33, pp.306-310.

Kitwood, T. (1988), 'The Contribution of Psychology to the Understanding of Senile Dementia', in Gearing B., Johnson M., Heller T., (eds), *Mental Health Problems in Old Age*, John Wiley and Sons in association with The Open University: Chichester, London.

Kitwood, T. (1989), 'Brain, Mind, and Dementia: with particular reference to Alzheimer's disease', *Ageing and Society*, vol.9, no.1, pp.1-15.

Kitwood, T. (1990a), 'Psychotherapy and Dementia', *Psychotherapy Section Newsletter*, vol.8, pp.40-56.

Kitwood, T. (1990b), 'The Dialectics of Dementia: With Particular Reference to Alzheimer's Disease', *Ageing and Society*, vol.10, pp.177-196, Cambridge University Press.

Kitwood, T. (1993), 'Towards a Theory of Dementia Care: The Interpersonal Process', *Ageing and Society*, vol.13, no.1 (March), pp.51-67, Cambridge University Press.

Kitwood, T. (1997a), *Dementia Reconsidered: the person comes first*, Open University Press: Buckingham, Philadelphia.

Kitwood, T. (1997b), 'The Uniqueness of Persons in Dementia', in M. Marshall (ed.), *State of the Art in Dementia Care*, CPA: London.

Kitwood, T., Bredin, K. (1992), 'Towards a Theory of Dementia Care: Personhood and Well-Being', *Ageing and Society*, vol.12, no.3, pp.269-287, Cambridge University Press.

Knight, B. (1986a), 'Management Variables as Predictors of Service Utilisation by the Elderly in Mental Health', *International Journal of Ageing and Human Development*, vol.23, pp.141-147.

Knight, B. (1986b), *Psychotherapy with Older Adults*, Sage: Beverley Hills, CA.

Kramer, M., Taube, C.A. & Redick, R.W. (1975), 'Patterns of Use of Psychiatric Facilities: past, present and future', in C. Eisdorfer & M.P. Lawton (eds), *The Psychology of Adult Development and Ageing*, American Psychological Association: Washington, DC.

Kratochwill, T.R. (1978), *Single Subject Research*, Academic Press: New York.

Laing, R.D. (1967), *The Politics of Experience and The Bird of Paradise*, Penguin, Harmondsworth: New York, Victoria, Ontario.

Lange, C.G. (1895), 'Om Sindsbevaegerser. et Psyko', Fysiolog Studie, Keonar: Copenhagen. Source: J.G. Thompson (1988), *The Psychobiology of Emotions*, Plenum Press: New York, London.

Lazarus, R.S. (1982), 'Thoughts on the Selection between Emotion and Cognition', *American Psychologist*, vol.37, pp.1019-1024.

Lazarus, R.S. (1984a), 'On the Primacy of Cognition', *American Psychologist*, vol.39, pp.124-129.

Lazarus, R.S. (1984b), 'Thoughts on the Relationship between Emotion and Cognition', in K.R. Scherer & P. Ekman (eds), *Approaches to Emotion*, Lawrence Erlbaum Associates: Hillsdale, NJ.

Lazarus, R.S. (1991), *Emotion and Adaptation*, Oxford University Press: Oxford, New York.

Lazarus, R.S. & Folkman, S. (1984), *Stress, Appraisal and Coping*, Springer: New York.

Leventhal, H. (1984), 'A Perceptual-Motor Theory of Emotion', in L. Berkowitz (ed.), *Advances in Experimental Social Psychology 17*, Academic Press: New York.

Lewis, M.I. & Butler, R.N. (1974), 'Life Review Therapy: putting memories to work in individual and group psychotherapy', *Geriatrics*, vol.29, pp.165-173.

Lieberman, M.A. & Tobin, S.S. (1983), *The Experience of Old Age, Stress, Coping and Survival*, Basic Books: New York.

Liebert, R.M. & Spiegler, M.D. (1978), *Personality: strategies and issues Holmwood, 111*, Dorsey Press: Aspen.

Linton, M. (1982), 'Transformations of Memory in Everyday Life', in U.Neisser (ed.), *Memory Observed: remembering in natural contexts*, Freeman: San Francisco.

Lishman, W.A. (1978), *Organic Psychiatry*, Blackwell: London.

Lofland, J. & Lofland, L.H. (1984), *Analysing Social Settings (2nd ed)*, Wadsworth Publishing: Belmont, CA.

Lo Gerfo, M. (1980), 'Three ways of Reminiscence in Theory and Practice', *International Journal of Ageing and Human Development*, vol.12, no.1, pp.39-48.

Luria, A.R. (1973), *The Working Brain: an introduction to Neurophysiology*, Penguin: Middlesex, Baltimore, Victoria.

Lyons, W. (1982), 'Coping with Cognitive Impairment: some family dynamics and helping roles', *Journal of Gerontological Social Work*, vol.4, pp.3-21.

Maclean, P.D. (1990), *The Triune Brain in Evolution*, Plenum Press: New York.

Magee, B. (1985), *Popper*, Fontana: London.

Mandler, G. (1987), 'Emotion', in R.L. Gregory (ed.), *The Oxford Companion to the Mind*, Oxford University Press: Oxford, New York.

Mayes, A. (1992), 'Brain Damage and Memory Disorders', in M. Gruneberg & P. Morris (eds), *Aspects of Memory. vol. 1 the practical aspects (2nd ed)*, Routledge: London, New York.

McAdams, D.P. (1990), *The Person. An Introduction to Personality Psychology*, Harcourt Brace Jovanovich, Publishers: London, New York, Tokyo.

McAdams, D.P. (1993), *Stories We Live By: personal myths and the making of the self*, William Morrow: New York.

McCrae, R.R. & Costa, P.T. (1987), 'Validation of the Five Factor Model of Personality Across Instruments and Observers', *Journal of Personality and Social Psychology*, vol.52, pp.81-90.

McKeith, I., Fairbairn, A., Perry, R., Thompson, P., Perry, E. (1992), 'Neuroleptic Sensitivity in Patients with Senile Dementia of Lewy Body Type', *British Medical Journal*, vol.305, pp.673-678.

McMahon, A.W. & Rhudick, P.J. (1964), 'Reminiscing: adaptional significance in the aged', *Archives of General Psychiatry*, vol.10, pp.292-298.

Mead, G.H. (1934), *Mind, Self, and Society*, University of Chicago Press.

Merleau-Ponty, M. (1964), *Signs*, Northwestern University Press: Evanston, ILL.

Merriam, A.E., Aronson, M.K., Gaston, P., Wey, S.L. & Katz, I. (1988), 'The Psychiatric Symptoms of Alzheimer's Disease', *Journal of the American Geriatric Society*, vol.36, pp.7-12.

Miesen, B.M. (1990), *How Demented Elderly Persons Experience their Parents*, Versluys: Almere.

Miesen, B.M. (1992), 'Attachment Theory and Dementia', in G.M. Jones and B.M. Miesen (eds), *Care Giving in Dementia: research and applications*, vol.1, Routledge: London.

192

Miesen, B.L. (1993), 'Alzheimer's Disease, the Phenomenon of Parent Fixation and Bowlby's Attachment Theory', *International Journal of geriatric Psychiatry*, vol.8, pp.147-153.

Miesen, B.L. (1997), 'Psychic Pain Re-Surfacing in Dementia: from new to past trauma?', in L. Hunt, M. Marshall, C. Rowlands (eds), *Past Trauma in Late Life: European Perspectives on Therapeutic Work with Older People*, Jessica Kingsley: London.

Mills, M.A. (1991), *Making the Invisible Visible: a qualitive study in the use of reminiscence therapy and counselling skills with dementing elderly people*, Thesis, University of Bournemouth.

Mills, M.A. (1993), 'Hidden Wealth Within Dementia', in K. Tout (ed.), *Elderly Care: a world perspective*, Chapman & Hall: London, New York.

Mills, M.A. (1995), *Narrative Identity and Dementia: narrative and emotion in older people with dementia*, Volume two, PhD Thesis, The University of Southampton.

Mills, M.A. (1997a), 'Residential Care, Well-Being and Dementia; some longitudinal evidence', Unpublished manuscript, University of Southampton.

Mills, M.A. (1997b), 'Person Centred Care Series 12, The gift of her friendship', *Journal of Dementia Care*, vol.5, no.5, pp.24-25.

Mills, M.A. & Chapman, I.M.H. (1992), 'Understanding the Story', *Nursing the Elderly*, vol.4, no.6, pp.27-30.

Mills, M.A. & Coleman, P.G. (1994), 'Nostalgic Memories in Dementia: a case study', *International Journal of Aging and Human Development*, vol.8, no.3, pp.203-219.

Mills. M.A. & Walker, J. (1994), 'Memory, Mood and Dementia: a case study', *Journal of Aging Studies*, vol.8, no.1, pp.17-27.

Mishler, E.G. (1986), 'The Analysis of Interview Narratives', in T.R. Sarbin (ed.), *Narrative Psychology: the storied nature of human conduct*, Praeger: New York.

Molinari, V. & Reichlin, R.E. (1985), 'Life Review Reminiscence in the Elderly: a review of the literature', *International Journal of Ageing and Human Development*, vol.20, no.2, pp.81-92.

Moscovitch, M. & Umiltà, C. (1990), 'Modularity and Neuropsychology: modules and central processes in attention and memory', in M.F. Schwartz (ed.), *Modular Deficits in Alzheimer-Type Dementia*, The MIT Press: Cambridge, Massachusetts, London.

Murphy, C. & Moyes, M. (1997), 'Life Story Work', in M. Marshall (ed.), *State of The Art in Dementia Care*, CPA: London.

Murphy, E. (1982), 'Social Origins of Depression in Old Age', *British Journal of Psychiatry*, vol.141, pp.135-142.

Myers, J.E. (1990), 'Ageing: an overview for mental health counsellors', *Journal of Mental Health Counselling*, vol.12, no.3, pp.245-259.

Myers, J.E. & Blake, R. (1984), 'Employment of Gerontological Counselling Graduates: a follow-up study', *Personnel and Guidance Journal*, vol.62, no.6, pp.333-335.

Nathan, P. (1988), *The Nervous System*, Oxford University Press: London, Oxford.

Neisser, U. (1981), 'John Dean's Memory: a Case Study', *Cognition*, vol.9, pp.1-22.

Nelson-Jones, R. (1993), *Practical Counselling and Helping Skills: how to use the lifeskills helping model*, Cassell: London, New York.

193

Noerager Stern, P. (1980), *Grounded Theory Methodology: its uses and processes*, Image, vol.X11, no.1, pp.20-23.

Odenheimer, G.L. (1989), 'Acquired Cognitive Disorders of the Elderly', in B.S. Bender & G.J. Caranosos (eds), *The Medical Clinics of North America*, vol.73, no.6, pp.383-1411.

Office of Population, Censuses and Surveys (1982), 'General Household Survey', 1980, HMSO: London.

Orbach, A. (1996), 'Not too late', *Psychotherapy and Ageing*, Jessica Kingsley: London, Pennsylvania.

Paget, M.A. (1983), 'Experience and Knowledge', *Human Studies*, vol.6, no.2, pp.67-90.

Parkin, A. (1987), *Memory and Amnesia: an introduction*, Blackwell Ltd: Oxford.

Parkin, A.J. (1993), *Memory: phenomena, experiment and theory*, Basil Blackwell: Cambridge, Massachusetts, Oxford.

Parloff, M.B., Waskow, I.E. & Wolfe, B.E. (1978), 'Research on Therapist Variables in Relation to Process and Outcome', in S.L. Garfield & A.E. Bergin (eds), *Handbook of Psychotherapy and Behaviour Change: an empirical analysis*, John Wiley: New York.

Perry, E.K., Marshall, E., Kerwin, J. et al. (1990b), 'Evidence of Monoaminergic-cholinergic Imbalance Related to Visual Hallucinations' in *Lewy Body Dementia*, Journal of Neurochemistry, vol.55, pp.1454-1456.

Perry, E.K., McKeith, I.,Thompson, P. et al. (1991), 'Topography, Extent and Clinical relevance of Neurochemical Deficits in Dementia of the Lewy Body Type, Parkinson's Disease and Alzheimer's Disease', *Annals of the New York Academy of Sciences, vol.640: Aging and Alzheimer's Disease*.

Perry, R.H., Irving, D., Blessed, G. et al. (1989), *Senile Dementia of the Lewy Body type and Spectrum of Lewy Body Disease*, Lancet, i, 1088.

Perry, R.H., Irving, D., Blessed, G. et al. (1990a), 'Senile Dementia of the Lewy Body Type. A clinically and neuropathologically distinct form of Lewy Body dementia in the elderly', *Journal Neurological Science*, vol.95, pp.119-139.

Plutchik, R. (1980), 'A General Psychoevolutionary Theory of Emotion', in R. Plutchik & H. Kellerman (eds), *Emotion Theory, Research, and Experience*, Academic Press: New York, London.

Popper, K. (1980), *The Logic of Scientific Discovery (10th ed)*, Hutchinson: London.

Reisberg, B. (1983), 'An Overview of Current Concepts of Alzheimer's Disease, Senile Dementia and Age Associated Cognitive decline', in B. Reisberg (ed.), *Alzheimer's Disease*, The Free Press: New York.

Reiser, D.E. & Rosen, D.H. (1984), *Medicine as a Human Experience*, University Park Press: Baltimore.

Rennie, D.L. (1992), 'The Unfolding of Reflexivity', in S.G. Toukmanian & D.L. Rennie (eds), *Psychotherapy Process Research: paradigmatic and narrative approaches*, Sage: Newbury Park CA., London, New Delhi.

Rennie, D.L. & Brewer, L. (1987), 'A Grounded Theory of Thesis Blocking', *Teaching of Psychology*, vol.14, pp.10-16.

Rennie, D.L., Philips, J.R. & Quartaro, G.K. (1988), 'Grounded Theory: a promising approach to conceptualisation in psychology?', *Canadian Psychology*, vol.29, pp.139-150.

Riessman, C.K. (1993), *Narrative Analysis Qualitative Research Methods*, vol.30, Sage: Newbury Park CA, London, New Delhi.

Robinson, J.A. (1992), 'Autobiographical Memory', in M. Gruneberg & P. Morris (eds), *Aspects of Memory*, vol.1: the practical aspects, (2nd ed), Routledge: New York, London.

Rodin, J., Timko, C. & Harris, S. (1985), 'The Construct of Control: biological and psychological correlates', in M.P. Lawson & G.L. Maddox (eds), *Annual Review of Gerontology and Geriatrics*, Springer: New York.

Rogers C.R. (1961), *Client Centred Therapy*, Houghton-Mifflen: Boston.

Rogers C.R. (1975), 'Empathic: an unappreciated way of being', *The Counselling Psychologist*, vol.5, pp.2-10.

Rose, S.P.R. (1987), 'Memory: biological basis', in R. Gregory (ed.), *The Oxford Companion to the Mind*, Oxford University Press: New York, Oxford.

Rosenthal, G. (1993), 'Reconstruction of Life Stories: principles of selection in generating stories for narrative biographical interviews', in R. Josselson & A. Lieblich (eds), *The Narrative Study of Lives*, Sage: Newbury Park, CA, London, New Delhi.

Rosenthal, R. (1966), *Experimenter Effects in Behaviour Research*, Appleton-Century-Crofts: New York.

Roybal, E.R. (1988), 'Mental Health and Ageing: the need for an expanded federal response', *American Psychologist*, vol.43, no.3, pp.89-194.

Runyan, W.M. (1982), *Life Histories and Psychobiography: explorations in theory and method*, Oxford University Press: New York, Oxford.

Salaman, E. (1970), *A Collection of Moments: a study of involuntary memories*, Longman: London.

Salaman, E. (1982), 'A Collection of Moments', in U. Neisser (ed.), *Memory Observed: remembering in natural contexts*, W.H. Freeman and Co: New York.

Schachter, S. & Singer, J.E. (1962), 'Cognitive, Social and Physiological Determinants of Emotional State', *Psychological Review*, vol.69, pp.379-399.

Schafer, R. (1981), 'Narration in the Psychoanalytic Dialogue', in W.J.J. Mitchell (ed.), *On Narrative*, University of Chicago Press, Chicago.

Schulz, R. (1976), 'Effects of Control and Predictability on the Physical and Psychological Well-being of the Institutionalised Aged', *Journal of Personality and Social Psychology*, vol.33, pp.563-573.

Schwartz, M.F. (1990), 'Introduction', in M.F. Schwartz (ed.), *Modular Deficits in Alzheimer's Type Dementia*, MIT Press: Cambridge, Massachusetts, London.

Schwartz, M.F. and Stark, J.A. (1990), 'Clinicopathological Models of Alzheimer's Disease and Senile Dementia: unravelling the contradictions, in M.F. Schwartz (ed.), *Modular deficits in Alzheimer's Type Dementia*, MIT Press: Cambridge, Massachusetts, London.

Scott, S., Caird, F.I. & Williams, B.O. (1985), *Communication in Parkinson's Disease*, Croom Helm: London, Sydney.

Scott Hinkle, J. (1990), 'An Overview of Dementia in Older Persons: identification, diagnosis, assessment and treatment', *Journal of Mental Health Counselling*, vol.12, no.3, pp.368-383.

Scrutton, A. (1989), *Counselling for Older People*, Edward Arnold: London.

Shapiro, E. & Tate, R.B. (1991), 'The Impact of a Mental Status Score and a Dementia Diagnosis on Mortality and Institutionalisation', *Journal of Aging and Health*, vol.3, no.1, pp.28-46.

Sherman, E. (1985), 'A Phenomenological Approach to Reminiscence and Life Review', *The Clinical Gerontologist*, vol.3, pp.3-16.

Short, P. (1993), *My Life Story*, Springfield Technical Publishing: Wroxall.

Siegler, I.C., Welsh, K.A., Dawson, D.V., Fillenbaum, G.G., Earl, N.L., Kaplan, E.B. & Clark, C.M. (1991), 'Ratings for Personality Change in Patients Being Evaluated for Memory Disorders', *Alzheimer's Disease and Associated Disorders*, vol.5, no.4, pp.240-250.

Siminov, P.V. (1986), *The Emotional Brain: Physiology, Neuroanatomy, Psychology, and Emotion*, Plenum Press: New York, London.

Sinason, V. (1992), *Mental Handicap and the Human Condition: new approaches from the Tavistock*, Free Association Books: London.

Singer, J.L. (1973), *The Childs World of Make-Believe: Experimental Studies of Imaginative Play*, Academic Press: New York.

Singer, J.L. (1974), *Imagery and Daydream Methods in Psychotherapy and Behaviour Modification*, Academic Press: New York.

Slivinske, l.R. & Fitch, V.L. (1987), 'The Effect of Control Enhancing Interventions on the Well-being of Elderly Individuals Living in Retirement Communities', *The Gerontologist*, vol.27, pp.176-181.

Spence, D.P. (1982), *Narrative Truth and Historical Truth: meaning and interpretation in psychoanalysis*, Norton: New York.

Squire, L. (1992), Memory and the Hippocampus: a synthesis from findings with rats, monkeys and humans, *Psychological Review*, vol.99, no.2, pp.195-231.

Stivers, C. (1993), 'Reflections on the Role of Personal Narrative in Social Science. Signs', *Journal of Women in Culture and Society*, vol.18, no.2, pp.408-425.

Strauss, A. (1987), *Qualitative Analysis for Social Scientists*, Cambridge University Press: New York.

Strauss, A. & Corbin, J. (1990), *Basics of Qualitative Research: grounded theory procedures and techniques*, Sage: Newbury Park, CA, London, New Delhi.

Stuart-Hamilton, I. (1991), *The Psychology of Ageing: an introduction*, Jessica Kingsley, London.

Sutton, L.J. (1995), *Whose Memory Is It Anyway?: a discursive critique of memory, depression and dementia in psychology*, PhD Thesis, University of Southampton.

Sutton, L. (1997), 'Out of the Silence: when people can't talk about it', in L. Hunt, M. Marshall and C. Rowlands (eds), *Past Trauma in Late Life: European Perspectives on Therapeutic Work with Older People*, Jessica Kingsley, London.

Sutton, L.J. & Cheston, R. (1997), 'Rewriting the Story of Dementia: a narrative approach to psychotherapy with people with dementia', in M. Marshall (ed.), *State of the Art in Dementia Care*, CPA: London.

Teasdale, J.D. & Russell, M.L. (1983), 'Diffential Effects of Induced Mood on the Recall of Positive, Negative, and Neutral Words', *British Journal of Clinical Psychology*, vol.22, pp.163-172.

Teasdale, J.D. & Barnard, P.J. (1993), *Affect, Cognition and Change: remodelling depressive thoughts*, Lawrence Erlbaum Associates: Hove, East Sussex.

Tesch, R. (1991), 'Software for Qualitative Researchers: analysis needs and program capabilities', in N.G. Fielding & R.M. Lee (eds), *Using Computers in Qualitative Research*, Sage: Newbury Park CA, London, New Delhi.

Thal, L.J. (1988), 'Dementia Update: diagnosis and neuropsychiatric aspects', *Journal of Clinical Psychiatry*, vol.49, pp.5-7.

Thompson, J.G. (1988), *The Psychobiology of Emotions*, Plenum Press: New York, London.

Thompson, P. (1988), *The Voice of the Past*, Oxford University Press: New York, Oxford.

Toates, F. (1996), 'The embodied self: a biological perspective', in Stevens, R. (ed.), *Understanding the Self*, Sage, in association with the Open University: London.

Tobin, S.S. (1991), *Personhood in Advanced Old Age: implications for practice*, Springer: New York.

Tomkins, S.S. (1962), *Affect, Imagery, Consciousness: vol.1, the positive affects*, Springer, New York.

Tomkins, S.S. (1963), *Affect, Imagery, Consciousness: vol.2, the negative affects*, Springer: New York.

Tomkins, S.S. (1981), 'The Quest for the Primary Motives: biography and autobiography of an Idea', *Journal of Personality and Social Psychology*, vol.41, pp.306-329.

Tomkins, S.S. (1984), 'Affect Theory', in K. Scherer & P. Ekman (eds), *Approaches to Emotion*, Lawrence Erlbaum Associates: Hillsdale, New Jersey.

Tomkins, S.S. (1987), 'Script Theory', in J. Aronoff, A.I. Rabin, & R.A. Zucker (eds), *The Emergence of Personality*, Springer: New York.

Trevarthen, C. (1984), 'Emotions in Infancy: regulators of contacts and relationships with persons', in J. Scherer & P. Elkman (eds), *Approaches to Emotion*, Erlbaum: Hillsdale NJ.

Tulving, E. (1983), *Elements of Episodic Memory*, Oxford University Press: London, Oxford.

Twining, C. (1996), 'Psychological Counselling with Older Adults', in R.Woolfe and W. Dryden (eds), *Handbook of Counselling Psychology*, Sage: London.

Van Hoesen, G.W. & Damasio, A.R. (1987), 'Neural Correlates of Cognitive Impairment in Alzheimer's Disease', in V. Mountcastle & F. Plum (eds), *Higher Functions of the Nervous System. Handbook of Physiology*, American Physiological Society: Bethesda, MD.

Verwoerdt, A. (1981), 'Individual Psychotherapy in Senile Dementia', in N. Miller & G. Cohen (eds), *Clinical Aspects of Alzheimer's Disease and Senile Dementia*, Raven Press: New York.

Walker, J.M., Akinsanya, J.A., Davis, B.D. & Marcer, D. (1990), 'The Nursing Management of Elderly Patients with Pain in the Community; study and recommendations', *Journal of Advanced Nursing*, vol.15, no.10, pp.211-220.

Waters, E.B. (1990), 'The Life Review: strategies for working with individuals and groups', *Journal of Mental Health Counselling*, vol.12, no.3, pp.270-278.

Watson, J.B. & Morgan, J.J. (1917), 'Emotional Reactions and Psychological Experimentation', *American Journal of Psychology*, vol.28, pp.163-164. Source: J.G. Thompson (1988), *The Psychobiology of Emotions*, Plenum Press: London, New York.

Webster, J.D. & Haight, B.K. (1995), 'Memory Lane Milestones: Progress in Reminiscence Definition and Classification', in B.K. Haight and J.D. Webster (eds), *The Art and Science of reminiscing: Theory, Research, Methods, and Applications*, Taylor and Francis: Washington, London.

Webster, J.D. & Young, R.D. (1988), 'Process Variables of the Life Review: counselling implications', *International Journal Of Ageing and Human Development*, vol.26, no.4, pp.315-323.

Wetherell, D. & Maybin, J. (1996), 'The Distributed Self: a social constructionist perspective', in Stevens, R. (ed.), *Understanding the Self*, Sage, in association with the Open University: London.

White, H. (1973), *Metahistory*, John Hopkins University Press: Baltimore, MD.

Widdershoven, G.A.M. (1993), 'The Story of Life: hermeneutic perspectives on the relationship between narrative and life history', in R. Josselson & A. Lieblich (eds), *The Narrative Study of Lives*, Sage: Newbury Park, CA, London, New Delhi.

Williams, J.M., Watts, F.N., Macleod, C. & Mathews, A. (1988), *Cognitive Psychology and Emotional Disorders*, John Wiley & Sons: Chichester, New York.

Williams, J.M. (1992), 'Autobiographical Memories and Emotional Disorders', in S. Christianson (ed.), *The Handbook of Emotion and Memory: research and theory*, Lawrence Erlbaum Associates: Hillsdale, NJ, London.

Williams, M. (1987), 'Dementia', in R.L. Gregory (ed.), *The Oxford Companion to the Mind*, Oxford University Press: Oxford, New York.

Williams, R. (1989), *The Trusting Heart*, The Free Press: New York.

Williams, R., Coleman, P.G. & Briggs, R. (1995), 'Senile Dementia', *International Journal of Geriatric Psychiatry*, vol.10, pp.231-236.

Winnicott, D.M. (1971), *Playing and Reality*, Taverstock Publications: London.

Wong, P.T.P. (1995), 'The Adaptive Processes of Reminiscence', in B.M. Haight and J.D. Webster (eds), *The Art and Science of reminiscing: Theory, Research, Methods, and Applications*, Taylor and Francis: Washington, London.

Wong, P.T. & Watt, L.M. (1991), 'What Types of Reminiscence are Associated with Successful Aging?', *Journal of Psychology and Ageing*, vol.6, no.2, pp.272-279.

Woods, R.T. (1989), *Alzheimer's Disease: coping with a living death*, Souvenir Press: London.

Woods, R.T. (1997), *Taking Care: psychological issues in dementia care*, Second Annual Clinical Psychology Lecture: University of Southampton.

Woods, R.T., Portnoy S., Head D., Jones G. (1992), 'Reminiscence and Life Review with Persons with Dementia: Which Way Forward?', in Jones G.M.M. and Miesen B.M.L. (eds), *Care-giving in Dementia: Research and Applications*, Tavistock/Routledge, vol.1: London.

Woods, R.T. & McKiernan, F. (1995), 'Reminiscence and Dementia', in B.M. Haight and J.D. Webster (eds), *The Art and Science of reminiscing: Theory, Research, Methods, and Applications*, Taylor and Francis: Washington, London.

World Population Prospects, (1986), United Nations.

Yin, R.K. (1989), *Case-Study Research: design and methods, Applied Social Research Methods Series, 5, Revised edition*, Sage: Newbury Park, CA, London, New Delhi.

Zajonc, R.B. (1980), 'Feeling and Thinking: preferences need no inferences', *American Psychologist*, vol.35, no.2, pp.151-175.

Zajonc, R.B. (1984a), 'The Interaction of Affect and Cognition', in K. Scherer & P. Ekman (eds), *Approaches to Emotion*, Lawrence Erlbaum Associates: Hillsdale, NJ.

Zajonc, R.B. (1984b), 'The Primacy of Affect' in K. Scherer & P Ekman (eds), *Approaches to Emotion*, Lawrence Erlbaum Associates: Hillsdale NJ.

Zarit, S.H. & Knight, B.G. (1996), 'Psychotherapy and Aging: Multiple strategies, Positive Outcomes', in S.H. Zarit & B.G. Knight (eds), *A Guide to Psychotherapy and Aging: effective clinical interventions in a life-stage context.*

Zola-Morgan, S. & Squire, L.R. (1990), 'Identification of the Memory System Damaged in Medial Temporal Lobe Amnesia', in L.R. Squire & E. Lindenlaub (eds), *The Biology of Memory*, VerlagF: K. Schattauer Stuttgart, Germany.